AF757307

STABILIZATION AND PRIVATIZATION IN POLAND

International Studies in Economics and Econometrics

VOLUME 29

Stabilization and Privatization in Poland

An Economic Evaluation of the Shock Therapy Program

Edited by
Kazimierz Z. Poznanski

*The Henry M. Jackson School of International Studies
University of Washington*

SPRINGER SCIENCE+BUSINESS MEDIA, LLC

Library of Congress Cataloging-in-Publication Data

Stabilization and privatization in Poland : an economic evaluation of the shock therapy program / edited by Kazimierz Z. Poznanski.
p. cm. -- (International studies in economics and econometrics ; v. 29)
Includes bibliographical references.
ISBN 978-0-7923-9341-2 ISBN 978-94-011-2206-1 (eBook)
DOI 10.1007/978-94-011-2206-1
1. Poland--Economic policy--1981- 2. Economic stabilization--Poland. 3. Privatization--Poland. I. Poznanski, Kazimierz. II. Series.
HC340.3.S738 1993
338.9438--dc20 93-885
CIP

Copyright © 1993 Springer Science+Business Media New York
Originally published by Kluwer Academic Publishers in 1993
All rights reserved. No part of this publication may be reproduced, stored in a retrieval system or transmitted in any form or by any means, mechanical, photo-copying, recording, or otherwise, without the prior written permission of the publisher, Springer Science+Business Media, LLC.

Printed on acid-free paper.

Contents

Acknowledgments

This volume is a byproduct of the U.S.-Polish Economic Roundtable, which is jointly organized on an annual basis by the Henry Jackson School of International Studies at the University of Washington and the Economics Department of Warsaw University. Funding for these meetings has been generously provided by the IREX (International Research and Exchange Board) and by the University of Washington's Provost Office. "Seed" funding by Mr. and Mrs. Dekaban, alumni of the University of Washington, is greatly appreciated. The roundtable meetings have been coordinated by Prof. Kazimierz Poznanski and Prof. Judith Thornton of the University of Washington.

Introduction

Kazimierz Z. Poznanski

Among the East European countries Poland was the first in mid-1989 to break the political monopoly of the communist party, and when its post-communist leadership announced a radical—"shock therapy"—plan for transition to capitalism in 1990, Poland was again ahead of the rest of the region. From the very beginning, economists have wondered whether it was rational for the newly formed political leadership to invest its future in such a radical program. The question has also been raised of the practicality—and economic cost—of such an approach as compared to a more evolutionary type of reform. Moreover, debate has emerged on the more technical aspects of this transition (e.g., choice of instruments, sequencing of reforms, etc.).

When the radical program of 1990 was put into action, the government, led by Mazowiecki, predicted a brief, half-year, period of modest decline in production and increase in unemployment. The program assumed that to arrest high inflation and remove imbalances (i.e., chronic shortages) inherited from the post-communist regime of Rakowski, deflationary measures were needed, and that these would surely bring on a recession. The policymakers, expected that the inevitable recession would be shallow because deflations in other highly inflationary developing countries, fashioned on similar programs, had typically produced such results.

The outcome of Poland's shock therapy has proved to be much worse than anticipated, as the country has slid into a very deep and extended—already three years old—recession. At the end of 1992, the gross national product was more than 20 percent below the 1989 level, and way above the 5 percent target spelled out in the government's 1990 program (while industrial output fell approximately 30 percent below its 1989 level). Rather than incur a 4–5 percent rate of unemployment, for which the government was originally prepared, the country registered 12.5 percent at the end of 1992 (with some regions exceeding 25 percent).

The decline in economic activity during 1990–1992 has been serious enough for economists observing Poland's transition to capitalism to determine whether certain policy errors have been made. This question is addressed by Sachs (1992), who dismisses any such suggestion that shock therapy has been misguided on the grounds that most of the collapse in 1990 was due to the decline in demand for inventories. Inventory stocks at the outset of shock therapy were far above rational levels, reflecting chronic hoarding, which was encouraged both by low-cost credit and disorganization of the production process under previous communist regimes. However, it could be that the actual decline in inventories—undeniably sharp—removed not only the excess stock but cut deeper (so that inventory rationalization was combined with recessionary panic sell-out needed to improve cash flow (see Berg and Sachs, 1992).

The 1991 output reduction was in turn due, as Berg and Sachs claim, to another demand-shock, one stemming from the disintegration of the CMEA. No doubt, the demand-shock related to the breakup of the CMEA regime in 1991 had some negative effect on production, particularly in the machinery , drug, and textile industries, once heavily oriented toward the vast Soviet market. However, at a time when demand for Poland's exports was declining sharply, one could expect the economy to be recovering from the earlier demand-shock, i.e., the utilization of unnecessary inventories. Also, one wonders why the national product declined in 1992, even though at this stage trade with the former CMEA was not continuing to fall but in fact showed signs of recovery (and exports to hard currency market were surging).

Another argument raised in defense of shock therapy is, as Milanovic argues in this volume, that the radicalism of the steps taken in 1990 was largely dictated, or predetermined, by the failures of Rakowski's policies. In particular, his regime's price operation for farm products combined with removal of agricultural subsidies brought about near-hyperinflation in mid-1989, making harsh deflationary measures unavoidable. In fact, what Mazowiecki's regime did in 1990 was to continue to fight the inflation produced by former communist leaders, though under more favorable political conditions, i.e., with greater willingness on the part of the workers to accept the costs of disinflation.

At the time Rakowski's government was making decisions on food prices and farm subsidies, voices were raised that the moves were politically motivated, that is, that the outgoing communist elite wanted its opponents to be left with as difficult an economic situation as possible. However, the food shortages were so severe that even opposition economists argued for price adjustment upward. In addition, actions taken by the opposition did not make economic conditions any better, but had the opposite effect. By winning almost full wage indexation (and fixed cross-sector wage parities for workers, farmers, and office staff) during the early 1989 roundtable negotiations, the opposition contributed to price acceleration as well.

Although the post-communist government of Mazowiecki inherited an economy that demanded immediate care, critics claim that none of the problems left over from Rakowski's days were unsolvable without resorting to shock therapy. Kolodko (1991) has argued that inflation in 1989, while high, lacked the characteristics of a hyper-spiral, since its numerical values did not fall in the critical range nor was there any mechanism in place capable of causing such uncontrolled, escalating price increases (i.e., expectations of further price increases built into contracts). If anything, at the very end of 1989, the rate of inflation was falling—due to the diminishing impact of farm price hikes, but also because of early budgetary restrictions introduced by Mazowiecki.

That inflation rates accelerated again in early 1990, resulting in almost doubling of the price index for the whole year, had little to do with the Rakowski regime but rather was caused by the decision by Mazowiecki's cabinet to quickly eliminate the remaining subsidies. This was an attempt to cure the economy through hyperinflation, though hyperinflation should hardly have been considered an instrument for anything. Importantly, faced with self-imposed price escalation, the government then felt compelled to apply measures far harsher than those undertaken with such success before the adoption of shock therapy.

Crane does not find the "corrective inflation" of 1990 problematic, but argues in this volume that the reason why initial monetary contraction—composed of reduction in real wages, imposition of low credit ceilings, and removal of subsidies—produced a drastic output decline was the government's indecisiveness. The demand-shock instituted by Mazowiecki in early 1990 was not only needed but also well-measured, and its positive effects were mostly lost due to the premature mid-1990 relaxation of restrictive monetary policy. Moreover, this has been followed by a cycle of tightening and softening caused by policy miscalculation and political pressure from frustrated workers.

In contrast, Brada and King find Poland's disinflation program generally excessive, even with the temporary relaxations mentioned by Crane. They blame the radicalism of Mazowiecki's approach for the output collapse of 1990 and add that another demand-shock, i.e., the reduction in Soviet imports, caused damage as well. By using an econometric estimate of an aggregate demand model, they conclude that indeed these two shocks explain almost the entire decline in output. Not only has Poland become the victim of a largely man-made recession, but so have two other economies in transition included in the test, Czechoslovakia and Hungary, both of which experienced a too drastic decline in total demand (in part related to corrective inflation, which had a negative wealth effect on consumers).

On the basis of their estimate, the two authors argue that, as output losses were due to policy errors, it does not follow that transition from state planning to market capitalism—institutional change itself—must necessarily be costly. This refutes the argument of the proponents of the shock-therapy approach that apparently no economy in transition between two opposite systems can escape large-scale initial losses (see the concept of J-curve), and that a piecemeal, sequential approach to reform, if successful at all, is certain to result in higher cumulative costs.

While Brada and King (like Crane) stress the role of demand factors, a number of economists argue that Poland's recession is mostly a supply-side phenomenon, or that it is less related to macroeconomics of monetary and fiscal variables than to microeconomics, i.e., state enterprises' ability to respond to "hardening" of budget constraints (see: Svejnar, 1991). Poznanski searches for factors responsible for excessive recession on the supply-side, claiming that the economy went into a deep slide not so much because demand contraction was excessive but rather because it was executed on an economy institutionally unprepared for shock. Of particular significance is the fact that the country's primitive banking has been unable to convert household savings into investment funds, and has failed to allocate the latter to healthy enterprises.

Not only have banks been reluctant to lend, but state enterprises have been unwilling to borrow money for restructuralization. This lack of interest by enterprises in restructuring might be surprising given that monetary contraction created, for the first time, a demand barrier, while removal of state subsidies "hardened" financial conditions. It appears, however, that, as Poznanski stresses, the post-1990 reforms have failed to resolve another inherent weakness of the previous economic system, namely, underdefined, or unstable, property rights. In fact, the unintended result of the changes implemented under the post-communist governments has been that property rights, already greatly diluted, have become even more confused, creating a sort of "property vacuum," which, to a degree, canceled out the potentially positive impact of the tight monetary/fiscal policy.

Charemza (1992) also adopted a supply-side position in his recent article explaining not only why the economy entered into a recession but why it has been unable to eliminate inflationary expectations. The shock therapy of 1990 took Poland's economy out of "shortageflation" to stagflation, in large part, as the argument goes, because the abolition of state controls over public assets created an information gap, which prevented rational expectations. Since convergence to rational expectation equilibrium is a time-consuming learning process, the transition to this state involves losses in economic efficiency and causes additional instability (as enterprises reduce their production involvement and raise prices in the face of uncertainty).

It follows that for the economy to recover, it would be helpful to clarify property rights, i.e., locus of control over assets and legal titles of ownership. This is exactly the point made by Sachs, who claims in this volume that, in fact, the slow pace of privatization—turning responsibility for assets over to individuals—is the single greatest threat to otherwise successful stabilization. He believes that quick divestment of state assets does not present a major practical problem if only proper methods for transfer of property are selected; these include sales at nominal prices, free-of-charge distribution, and setting up investment funds.

However, one cannot escape the impression that while stabilization of the economy has been undermined by slow privatization, it is the stabilization itself that has, in many ways, harmed the divestment process. Gajdeczka stresses one important aspect, namely, that the high inflation of early 1990, administered by the government to bring all prices in line with real costs, turned the private sector (including households) into net creditors to the state sector, and reduced the former's ability to purchase state-owned assets. This has been the case, even though households expected that under the existing "implicit contract," they would have a reasonable claim to publicly owned means of production.

Of course, the pace of privatization is not determined by the financial condition of potential buyers alone. Even if, for example, the entire stock of public capital were instantly divided among citizens (or some select group) for free, such a transfer would not amount to much. A simple transfer of legal titles would not improve the efficiency of capital use as long as the new owners were not better prepared to allocate resources than the managers of state enterprises. Transfer of rights represents—as Charemza calls it in the book—only a narrow-sense privatization, in contrast to broad sense privatization where assets are actually put into more efficient use by private agents operating in a conducive environment.

For privatization to assist the economy in getting out of recession, the government would have to go beyond the current policy of finding users for state assets and offering discount sale prices or giveaways. It must also stress supply-side enhancing policies which would allow newly established private entities to be effective. Such an activist—as opposed to a hands-off attitude (shock therapy)—policy should include, according to Charemza, selective credits to assist production restructuring, strengthening of the informational base to assist private investors in long-term projects, and also an effort to demonopolize markets (i.e., create contestable markets).

The issue of privatization is also touched upon by Murrell in his broad discussion of the advantages of an evolutionary over a radical approach. His working assumption is that enterprises are able to react productively to only a limited amount of change due to informational constraints, i.e., ability to decode economic signals. To operate under such constraints, enterprises—like any other organization—develop so-called routines, or automatic responses. State enterprises formed such routines under the command system of the past—and any effort to radically change the environment which surrounds them and, in particular, a quick transfer of property rights—can only damage these routines, causing economic losses.

It is not just that routines can only be changed without loss slowly, but also the tacit knowledge accumulated in existing state enterprises cannot be easily transferred to the emerging private sector. As this knowledge is germane to the old command economy, there seems to be little doubt, as Murrell argues, that countries in transition have to allow the existence of a dual economy in the initial—not necessarily brief—period. Thus, the private sector will have to develop mostly by itself, on the basis of knowledge generated and enhanced by the entry-exit process—one involving high rates of attrition. No- or slow-growth in the state sector and rapid expansion in the private one is going to eventually tilt the balance towards private-type activities, i.e., capitalism.

It appears that by its nature, transition from one "extended order" to another (as opposed to fine-tuning of an existing economic system) requires the existence of an impure, dual (or mixed) solution. Transition is characterized by transitory arrangements rather than the instant application of an ideal (in light of economic theory) set of rules. The real demand on policymakers thus seems to be to resist the temptation to reach directly for ultimate, best solutions and to learn to live with the imperfections of second-best arrangements. In other words, the right approach seems to be to work on immediate "dirty" problems and accept marginal improvements instead of chasing an ideal and expecting instant cures.

In this spirit, Kochanowicz argues that while the ultimate goal of transition is to reduce the state role in the economy, there is a need for bureaucracies to retool—change their modus operandi—rather than execute their own self-destruction. There is a strong resentment among the post-communist reformers against any kind of direct involvement, a sentiment that, among other things, prompts them to privatize public capital immediately. Not only do they view such direct involvement as a source of economic waste but also see them as a threat that the movement away from authoritarian rule might be reversed. The reality of transition is such, however, that the state cannot absolve itself of all responsibilities instantly.

In addition to theoretical arguments for preserving the activist state, one may produce historical material to support this view. Kochanowicz refers to a well-known sequence of latecomers to the industrial revolution (Germany, then Italy, and next Russia), with each country in turn requiring ever stronger government involvement in promoting growth. The experience of the newly industrializing countries that entered the industrial stage even later seems to point to the same conclusion. One would like to add that pre-communist Poland, as well as the rest of the Eastern European region, operated not only with a large public sector but was typified by etatist—and protectionist—policies as well.

This brings us to the issue of how states should manage the foreign trade sector during the transition. The 1990 program chose to subordinate trade policy to the needs of price stabilization, a fact reflected in the decision to fix the domestic currency at a below-equilibrium level. This nominal anchor was expected to free domestic currency from inflationary pressures for about half a year, but the depth of devaluation was such that the anchor worked for one-and-a-half years. Only then did the government allow for periodic devaluations, to finally turn from a fixed regime to a managed—floating—one, with the result that the exchange rate has again became mainly a tool of foreign trade policy.

The choice of a fixed, rather than floating, regime has been criticized by some economists as responsible for creating a trade surplus in an economy that, given the enormous extent of decapitalization in the industry, would benefit more from a trade deficit. Other economists also questioned the desirability of the fast currency convertibility with which Poland elected to move ahead in 1990—unlike other transforming economies where many state controls have been maintained, as in Hungary, where households were excluded from free exchange, or in Czechoslovakia, where the currency market was even more restricted. Among the objections has been the point that defending currency in a highly inflationary disturbed economy, such as that of Poland, costs too much in terms of high interest rates and credit restrictions, and thus leads to additional production losses.

McKinnon attributes much of the rapid industrial decline in Poland, and in the former East Germany in 1990, to the switch to full current account convertibility as well as to the hasty adoption of free arbitrage between domestic and foreign markets. As he sees it, no matter how the exchange rate is set, most of the production in these countries will, in the short run, exhibit negative value added at world market prices. While trade opening is helpful in bringing domestic prices to the world level (a precondition for economic efficiency under the condition of extended negative-value), this operation is bound to drive high-cost producers—possibly whole industries—to bankruptcy.

Consequently, McKinnon suggests avoiding the "cold turkey" approach to free trade and centralizing (or recentralizing) foreign exchange allocations until the domestic financial controls necessary for supporting a market economy have been established. A gradual program is based on temporary tariff protection and assumes that once made explicit, the highest tariffs in the cascade can be phased down step by step to a low uniform level. This operation should be scheduled over a pre-announced five to ten year time horizon. Moreover, it should be combined with repricing material inputs so as to separate industries that could survive in the long run from those not so able.

If slow freeing of foreign trade is really the right way to go during the initial stages, then the question arises: What should have been done about the regional trade once formed in the CMEA structure? This structure was allowed to collapse in 1991 after the Soviet decision to dispense with ruble-based transactions and abolish intergovernmental agreements. Of course, Poland's decision of 1990 to introduce "internal" convertibility and to abolish state monopoly in trade in favor of private sector involvement did not help to extend the CMEA regime, even in a greatly modified version. Still, as Rosati documents in his statistical analysis of Poland's trade with the CMEA in 1990, the real collapse in regional volumes occurred only in 1991.

Rosati, like many other critics of the CMEA, argues that there was no rationale for maintaining the regime as it was or even in some modified version, since it was this regime which was largely responsible for producing distorted, irrational specialization patterns. Since the main objective of transition is to free Poland's economy from production patterns which do not reflect its true comparative advantage, extending the life of the CMEA would only prolong ill-directed allocation of resources. Thus, there is also no reason to replace the CMEA with any new scheme to facilitate trade financing, including a "payments union," which was helpful in the postwar reconstruction of Western Europe but has little relevance for post-communist Poland or other East European economies.

This position is challenged by van Brabant, who argues that the degree to which the CMEA members engaged in uneconomic trade seems exaggerated by many of its critics. Frequent references to the pre-communist past—such as the interwar period, when regional trade was minimal—miss the point that transactions were conducted then under substantial disequilibria (e.g., political disturbances, excessive trade barriers). But even if the volume of trade was extensive, this does not mean that the former CMEA members could not benefit from a payment facility on their way to less intense regional trade. Such a union, as a purely temporary device, would help to achieve full convertibility at the smallest "transition cost."

As the CMEA bureaucratic structure was dismantled in 1991 and since no regularized procedures—such as a payment regime—have been put in place, the former members have been left with many uncompleted transactions for lack of liquidity. The universal lack of hard-currency available to finance contracts with former suppliers and customers has rather indiscriminately hurt those who should continue and those who have little chance of survival, given their excessive costs or unacceptable quality. In this sense, the sudden collapse of the CMEA, as Murrell points out (see also Poznanski, 1992), has made the situation worse—providing another example of the need to temporarily reemploy the old, even if not very effective, institutions.

A purely economic assessment of Poland's shock therapy, as offered in this collection, discounts the political aspect of the program. In reality, shock therapy has been as much a political maneuver as an economic cure. All key economic choices made have had political implications for major social groups. Moreover, many of the economic choices had to take into account certain political constraints that seemed insurmountable—at least within the time frame available for affecting the economy. This intimate relationship between economics and politics makes it difficult to determine whether in the case of Poland's transition politics has dominated economics, or the other way around.

Let's take monetary stabilization, where the choice of shock-approach rather than a gradual phasing out of price controls and producer-subsidies seemed to be strongly influenced by political calculations. The government of Mazowiecki was aware of the fact that the defeat of the communist party created a window of opportunity through which austerity measures could be pushed, even though they had been rejected by the population before. The other calculation was that even the great popularity of the newly elected government might wear off quickly, so that it made sense to concentrate as many painful measures in as short a time span as possible. The government also hoped that by quickly reducing inflation and removing shortages—always welcome by the population—it could gain support for its other less appealing programs.

Politics has also had influence in another important element of the economic strategy of 1990—the extinction of almost all direct interference in production (except for wage setting) at the enterprise level. While further decentralization of authority seemed imperative for eliminating the economic waste characteristic of the command system of the communist party, it also reflected political reality, namely, that the new government's ability to act was negatively affected by the power transfer, as some less-experienced people replaced disaffected or compromised officials from the past. In addition to being unable to engage in extensive direct control over production, the post-communist bureaucracy also wanted to distance itself from the struggling enterprises and thus reduce political pressure on itself.

While instrumental in forming a capitalist market, the privatization process has also been heavily influenced by political concerns, many of them similar to those that motivated the government to cut enterprises loose. The point is, removing direct controls has not been enough to lift political pressure from enterprises—their workers and managers. As long as the state continued to have a legal claim on the labor collectives, it has been difficult for the government to refuse some assistance—financial favors—to them. Thus, to encourage workers to negotiate their wages with managers, and to force managers to negotiate funds with banks, the government has had to transfer its property rights over to private parties or to labor collectives, in fact, to anybody but the government itself.

Foreign trade liberalization has been very much a political issue as the government clearly has had a choice of either buying support by protecting overconcentrated and technically obsolete domestic producers or exposing them to bold import competition at a political cost. It could be that the actual deprotection of industry since mid-1990 was not intended, but one can also speculate that the opening of the economy was allowed in order to undermine certain important sectoral interests which emerged during the communist past. One of these was private farming, perceived by the government as underspecialized and over labor-intensive. Another such interest group is the miners, found by the government to be oversubsidized. Both groups were exposed to imports (while mining was also subjected to below-equilibrium state-controlled prices and export limits).

Clearly, Poland's transition to capitalism is a great puzzle, hard for social scientists to decipher and put into a cohesive analytical framework. Importantly, it is equally hard for policymakers to understand the reality of transition, which means they are often forced to make uninformed choices and move ahead with half-ready projects. With so much experimenting going on in real life, scholars should be forgiven—perhaps even appreciated—for coming up with preliminary, rather than conclusive, assessments. They should also be recognized for taking some unconventional avenues, i.e., experimenting on their own and if necessary giving a critical account of the post-communist reality—even though this reality is so far superior to the failed communist utopia.

Bibliography

Berg, A. and J. Sachs. 1992. "Structural Adjustment and International Trade in Eastern Europe: The Case of Poland," *Economic Policy* (April).

Charemza, W. 1992. "Market Failure and Stagnation: Some Aspects of Privatization in Poland," *Economics of Planning*, vol., 25, no. 1.

Kolodko, G. 1991. "Inflation Stabilization in Poland: A Year After," Working Papers M 17, Institute of Finance, Warsaw.

Kornai, J. 1992. "The Affinity Between Ownership and Coordination Mechanisms: The Common Experience of Reform in Socialist Countries," in Poznanski, K., ed., *Constructing Capitalism*, Boulder: Westview Press.

Svejnar, J. 1991. "Microeconomic Issues in Transition to a Market Economy," *Journal of Economic Perspectives*, vol. 5, no. 4 (Fall).

PART ONE

Stabilization Program and Economic Recession

1

Poland's Transition to Capitalism: Shock and Therapy

Kazimierz Z. Poznanski

I argue in this chapter that the radical set of measures[1] introduced in 1990 has produced very mixed—if not, on balance, disappointing—initial results (compare with Berg and Sachs, 1992). Bringing down inflation has been an achievement, though the rates of price increases have continued to be high through 1992. Maintaining internal convertibility, despite stubborn inflation, has been an unquestionable success as well. The convertibility of domestic currency has been enhanced by a strong export expansion to Western markets, combined with multiplication of foreign currency reserves. All these improvements have helped Poland to obtain substantial debt cancellation from Western governments and triggered an inflow of fresh money.

However, the radical transition program has also produced some negative results, the most significant of them being a lengthy recession and rapidly rising unemployment. Deflationary policies typically lead to a short-term slowdown in output growth, but in Poland they have been followed by a drastic and lasting decline in absolute production level. I suggest here that the main reason for the failure of the radical program is that it has not turned state enterprises into cost-sensitive and demand-responsive entities. In a way, the program produced a "bad equilibrium,"[2] or, in other words, it was a case of an extensive "shock" with limited "therapy," i.e., without a quick positive change in the microeconomics of enterprises (though there has been considerable improvement in households' behavior).

The stabilization package created not only the sought-after downward pressure on prices but also caused an immediate liquidity crisis, since inherently inefficient banking choked even viable enterprises. The initial trade deprotection of cost-ineffective, low-quality domestic production, which was designed to rapidly extinguish inflation, has resulted in further damage to production. Additional harm to the economy has also come from chaotic systemic reforms and the resultant "property vacuum" or imperfect markets (see Charemza, 1991). The level of uncertainty created by this vacuum has forced state enterprises to withdraw from production, and, unlike the macroeconomic policy errors contained within the reform package, this "property vacuum" has been difficult to rectify.

The first signs of economic recovery, led by the construction sector and registered in early 1992, do not necessarily mean that shock therapy, though with a lag, finally produced the expected results. Instead, this development could be attributed, in large part, to the fact that many shock therapy policies have been softened, if not reversed. Not only did the 1991 return to a large budget deficit represent such a reversal, but so did the abandonment in the same year of a fixed exchange rate for managed-floating currency depreciation and the return to more protective tariffs in early 1992. The 1991 stalemate in the experimental program for mass privatization—through vouchers—could have had a positive impact by putting managers/workers on more solid ground, and the so-called enterprise pact offered by the government in mid-1992 may have had a similar stabilizing effect.

Radical Macroeconomic Stabilization

When the government of Mazowiecki displaced the communist regime at the end of 1989, the Polish economy was suffering from a number of economic difficulties, which was reflected in macroeconomic imbalance, both internal and external. The internal disequilibrium manifested itself in monetary overhang and a high rate of inflation, combined with extended shortages, while external imbalance was evidenced in a staggering, only partially serviced, foreign debt. Since these aggregate imbalances were interconnected, it seemed only appropriate for the post-communist government to cope with them simultaneously.

Deflationary Measures

The highest priority for Mazowiecki, when he embarked on the shock therapy program, was to halt inflation, which was perceived as a serious drag on production expansion and potentially highly destabilizing for domestic politics as well. In this choice, he echoed the communist policymakers, who were also preoccupied with removing inflationary overhang. With extremely high rates of inflation came shorter contract periods and reluctance to invest in long-term projects with high social yield. There were also adverse welfare effects, i.e., disincentives to productivity and income redistribution (since inflation divides households into those protected from price rises and those not so sheltered from inflationary erosion of their incomes; see Lipton and Sachs, 1990).

The depth of the 1990 anti-inflationary package was indeed enormous, as real wages were instantly reduced by almost 35 percent, while for the whole of 1991 they declined by 31 percent. At that early stage—at least through mid-1990—enterprises did not even meet the upper limits of wage payments permitted by the government. The central budget deficit, which was close to 2.8 percent of the gross domestic product in 1989, was replaced by a budget surplus, the first since 1979, which equaled 1.3 percent of the gross domestic product by the end of 1990. This was accomplished primarily by cutting state sector subsidies from 11 percent of the gross domestic product in 1989 to 7 percent at the end of 1990, and by drastically reducing the state's investment program as well.

The freeing of state-controlled prices, even though they represented only about 20–30 percent of total sales (see Kolodko, 1991) actually created a "corrective" inflation of nearly 80 percent in the first month of 1990. The deflationary package, however, allowed for a very successful reduction of price increases, because state enterprises encountered a demand barrier soon after the measures were implemented. Thus, monthly inflationary rates were reduced to 2–3 percent in mid-1990, but then through the rest of the year price increases accelerated, and oscillated between 5 to 6 percent on a monthly basis. Still, the average yearly rate of inflation for the whole of 1990 was close to 585 percent, more then twice the average price increase of 244 percent reported in 1989 (see Table 1).

Moreover, since the success in arresting inflation helped to greatly strengthen the domestic currency against the dollar, the notorious black market operations were virtually eliminated, further reducing inflationary pressure. As a result, domestic currency regained its dominant role in the cash holdings of households.[3] During the high inflation of 1989, households kept more than 70 percent of their liquidity in dollars. At the end of 1990, however, less than 30 percent of cash holdings were denominated in dollars (state enterprises quickly reduced their dollar holdings as well, mostly to take advantage of the zloty devaluation).

Table 1 Main Economic Indicators for Eastern Europe, 1988–1991 (annual rates in percent)

	Poland	*Bulgaria*	*Czecho-slovakia*	*Hungary*	*Romania*
			Net Material Product (Produced)		
1988	4.9	2.4	2.3	–0.5	-2.0
1989	–0.2	–0.3	0.7	–1.1	-7.9
1990	–14.9	–11.5	–1.1	–5.5	- 9.9
1991	-9.0	-25.7	–19.5	–10.0	–14.0
			Industrial Output		
1988	5.3	2.2	0.8	–2.3	3.1
1989	–0.5	2.2	0.8	–2.5	-2.1
1990	–23.3	–14.1	–3.7	–5.0	–19.8
1991	–14.2	-27.3	-23.1	–19.1	-18.7
			Gross Fixed Investment		
1988	5.4	4.5	4.1	-9.1	-2.2
1989	–2.4	–10.1	1.6	0.5	–1.6
1990	–10.0	–12.0	7.7	–8.7	-35.0
1991	–8.0	–49.3	-36.0	–11.0	–16.8
			Rate of Inflation (Cost of Living)		
1988	59.0	2.4	–0.4	15.5	1.7
1989	244.1	6.2	1.4	17.0	n.a.
1990	584.7	19.3	10.0	28.9	n.a.
1991	74.5	385.8	60.4	35.8	197.6
			Foreign Trade Volume (Exports)		
1988	9.1	2.4	3.2	5.0	7.4
1989	0.2	–2.3	–2.0	0.3	–10.8
1990	13.7	–24.2	–4.2	–4.3	–46.0
1991	–1.4	n.a.	–20.0	–10.7	n.a.

Source: Economic Bulletin for Europe ECE, New York: United Nations; Economic Survey of Europe 1990–1991, New York: ECE,. United Nations.

Severe Crisis

Although high inflation was eventually reduced to late 1988 rates,[4] this was accomplished only at a certain cost. The deflation contributed to an initial decline in industrial production of about 23 percent throughout the entire state sector, with the light industry and machinery sectors suffering the most (e.g., textiles reported a 34 percent decline and machinery a 38 percent loss). The depth of the early 1990 production slump greatly exceeded the decline expected by the government. An even greater surprise, however, was that industry failed to show any signs of quick recovery. In the face of prolonged stagnation, monetary/fiscal policy was relaxed[5] in late 1990, though without a positive effect, and the year closed with the net material product down by 14.9 percent (see Table 1).[6]

In early 1991, the government, now led by Bielecki, returned to a highly restrictive policy. While production in the state sector registered further declines, the government continued its anti-inflationary policy. Although only nominal gains were being made in the fight against inflation, the government showed little concern for reviving industrial output. State-sector industrial output declined by another 14.2 percent for 1991, while the gross domestic product decreased by 9 percent for the whole year. With all sectors of state industry registering lower output, it became clear that the economy was slipping into a general recession, or depression, rather than just undergoing a temporary structural adjustment.

The downfall in production had badly shaken the labor market, which moved quickly from no unemployment, which was characteristic of the communist period, to high rates of unemployment. By the end of 1991, the unemployment rate, with 2 million people out of work, was close to 11 percent (despite the fact that real wages continued to stay below the prestabilization level). Some urban centers, such as Poznan or Warsaw, with a rate of unemployment in late 1991 of less than 2.5 percent, have fared better than the nation as a whole. A few major industrial cities, however, have encountered extremely difficult times (e.g., the coal mine area of Walbrzych or the textile city of Lodz),[7] and in many less-developed regions the rate of unemployment has moved above 25 percent.

Interestingly, the employment level has not declined as steeply as the level of output. While industrial production declined by at least 25 percent in 1990, state industry employment declined by around 5.6 percent. In 1991, with the fall of output in the state industry at 12 percent, the rate of decline in employment was 8.5 percent. As the state enterprises have continued to retain workers, the source of these striking unemployment figures must be newcomers to the labor market.[8] This means that despite a severe recession, labor productivity in industry has declined, and that even under the greater financial stress imposed upon them by the shock therapy program, state enterprises have, as in the past, continued to be heavily overmanned.

The private sector, however dynamic it may have been, was not only too small to single-handedly lift the economy out of the depression, but also unable to fully escape the slump in the state sector. Although the private sector was able to resist recession better than the state sector, its performance was negatively affected by restrictive policies and external shocks. In 1989, industrial output in the private sector increased by 22 percent, but in 1990 the respective rate was 8 percent. Investment by the private sector increased by 2.6 percent in 1989, but declined by 3 percent in 1990. Only in employment was there no negative change—in both years the number of workers increased by almost 27 percent.[9]

Vicious Circle

By instantly provoking such a severe, "unhealthy" recession, the radical stabilization program has eventually proved self-defeating. While the 1990 slump in production initially helped to curb high inflation, it backfired in 1991, and increased the pressure to raise prices. The major reason for renewed inflationary pressures was that the recession in the state sector had caused a sharp decline in tax revenues. With dwindling tax revenues, the fiscal surplus of 1990 [10] was replaced by a small deficit in early 1991, which reached as high as 4–5 percent of the gross domestic product by the end of the year. That was a higher deficit than the level reported at the outset of the stabilization program.

Desperate for budgetary revenues, the government has continued to tax state enterprises at a high rate while exempting the private sector from some tax payments and tolerating massive tax evasions by that sector as well.[11] As a consequence, state enterprises have been taxed out of their rapidly falling profits. During early 1990, profits in state enterprises were taxed at 47 percent, a level not unusual for an industrial country. In early 1991, however, 91 percent of profits were taken in taxes, and, apparently, in mid-1991, the budget collected 110 percent of the reported state enterprise profit.

While helpful in solving short term fiscal needs, this policy has been detrimental to the long-run budgetary situation because, lacking the needed profits and access to "easy" credit, and deprived of budgetary funding, state enterprises had to reduce their capital investment. Specifically, gross investment declined by 10 percent in 1990 and by 8 percent in 1991, bringing the total reduction since 1989 to about 20 percent.[12] With this withdrawal from capital expansion, the level of investing in real terms was brought substantially below the pre-1979 crisis level. This reduced investment activity has undermined enterprises' ability to restructure their production and manage their way out of contraction, and with this to expand the tax base for the government as well.

This policy of taxing enterprises out of their profits has also resulted in a sharp increase in the number of state enterprises classified as insolvent. While very few of the larger state enterprises have failed thus far, the number that is technically bankrupt has been growing very rapidly. According to the most recent reports, in early 1992 more than 50 percent of the 8400 state enterprises defaulted on their debts to state banks (Financial Times, February 7, 1992). Consequently, the budget has also found itself under increasing threat that at one point it would have to bail out—or write-off—bad loans owed by state enterprises. It would be difficult, at least for political reasons, for the government to refuse such financial assistance, though it would further strain the state budget.

Policy Priorities

The most common explanation for the deep recession following the 1990 stabilization program is that both priorities of halting inflation and strengthening the domestic currency were right in theory but wrong in execution (see Kolodko, 1991, p. 22). For instance, some economists have argued that because the anti-inflationary policy lacked resolve, the government prematurely relaxed restrictions only to find itself in a sequence of contradictory moves (see Crane, 1991). Others reject indecisiveness as a cause and stress instead that production collapsed due to a deflationary overdose brought about by the government's refusal to ease its tight monetary policy in time (Dabrowski, 1992).

I would fully agree with the overdose thesis if not for the fact that there are serious doubts as to whether making inflation the main target of economic policy in 1990 was the only rational option available to the non-communist government. There was at least one other viable target—the economic recession. When Mazowiecki assumed power in mid-1990, Poland not only suffered from high inflation but was also well into a recession. Industrial output and investment spending had both already been registering negative rates for a few months,[13] while domestic output was stagnant[14] (or as other sources report it, had declined by .5 percent) for the whole of 1989 (Kolodko, 1991, p.29).

Although at first glance the recession of 1989 did not appear very dramatic, it was in fact a very worrisome signal, given that the national economy had just emerged from a sharp crisis in 1979–82. While there were no signs that the economy might be turning around on its own in late 1989, there were strong indications that inflation had been receding (due to budgetary restrictions implemented in late 1989; Milanovic, 1991), which made the decision to downplay the recession even more surprising. It appears that rapid, out-of-control inflation was over before it was attacked, and Mazowiecki was confronted mostly with the sudden resurgence of inflation caused by price-freeing in 1990 and the upward corrections of the remaining state-controlled prices (e.g., coal, rents, utilities) by his own government.

While retaining some state price-fixing may not be a "clean" solution, there is substantial empirical evidence that it may be an acceptable halfway-house arrangement for economies in transition to the capitalist market. As an example, China's utilization of dual-pricing and parallel markets in the post-1978 reforms have not resulted in high inflation. Not only has inflation been reasonably low, seldom moving into the double-digit range, but China's production has experienced a very high rate of growth (see Lardy, 1991; Naughton, 1992). Hungary, as another example, has operated since 1968 with partially liberalized prices without causing significant damage to its economy (and it has definitely emerged from the communist years with the strongest economy in the whole of Eastern Europe).

Wage Control

Aside from the issue of whether the economy of Poland required such deep deflation, another debatable aspect of the shock therapy program was the choice of the particular wage policy selected to combat inflationary tendencies. Mazowiecki, and then Bielecki, decided to continue the policy of the outgoing communist party/state, namely, to index wages while imposing severe taxes on any excessive increases in wages above the legal limit. Among economists, this latter element is very controversial, with many arguing that by allowing only similar wage increases for all state enterprises, regardless of differences in their financial conditions, the state was stifling labor mobility and thus preventing structural adjustment in production.

Rather than imposing strict wage/price schedules upon the workers, the government could have utilized another procedure—some form of a "wage contract." The signing of a wage contract was the avenue the leadership of Mexico adopted in 1988, under conditions quite similar to those found in Poland in 1989, namely, the existence of a labor-based government and powerful unions.[15] Such a combination is a recipe for uncontrollable inflation unless both sides, the government and the workers, sign a truce. The advantage of such a contract is that by specifying potential future wage rates and the circumstances under which both parties can renegotiate their mutual obligations, wage bargaining can proceed in an orderly fashion. In fact, Mexico's 1988 accord has greatly helped reduce that country's wage-price spiral and thus has contributed to a remarkably strong economic recovery as well (Edwards, 1992).[16]

Since the government expected that wage taxes would not be well received by the workers, it unloaded one more weapon—a tight credit policy. The government assumed that by making public enterprises financially responsible, the enterprises would be forced to cut labor. This has turned out to be a rather dubious disciplinary device since enterprises quickly realized that the majority of them are financially troubled, so that falling into deeper wage-related debt carried little risk of punishment by the government, which was unprepared for massive plant closures. In this manner, state enterprises tested the government in early 1991 and have since decided to face enormous penalties for going beyond wage ceilings and borrowing to meet their needs. Real wages increased by 2 percent and real income by even more in 1991 (possible only because real investment declined sharply).

Imposing strict wage-price schedules upon the workers proved not very practical, contributing to both labor unrest and political destabilization. Popular anger was responsible for the collapse of Mazowiecki's government, and not a personal squabble involving Walesa, as suggested by some scholars (e.g., Gross, 1992). Walesa's motivation to begin a so-called war-at-the-top was mainly to regain his rapidly eroding popularity by removing Mazowiecki. The next government, led by Bielecki, was also dismembered by voters frustrated with falling living standards and disappearing job opportunities. The successor to this government, the cabinet of Olszewski, the first to be produced in free elections, engaged in dismantling the shock therapy program (by putting on hold the radical privatization program, perceived by the workers as a threat to their jobs, and by reducing the wage-tax progression, etc.).

Moreover, Poland has been drifting toward a wage-contract system. In mid-1992, under mass pressure, the government of Suchocka, successor to Olszewski's cabinet, accepted in principle the idea of replacing the existing central control of wages through indexation and progressive taxes with collective bargaining. In July 1992, the government sent the unions its proposal for a so-called pact with the state-owned enterprises. In this pact, an excess-wage tax would be maintained but the upper limit for wage increases (free of excess tax) would be negotiated between the government and union representatives. Also, the rate of tax progression would be reduced from 500 to 300 percent (with costs of worker training and social programs such as child care for employees to be excluded from taxation).

Financial Aftershock

Although the imperfect wage-control segment of the shock therapy program has contributed to inflation, workers' wage increases can neither be viewed as the major cause of the post-reform price spiral nor as the source of the shock-related depression. Far more damaging to production than the initial reduction of wages has been the credit squeeze, which was expected not only to help remove labor slack as indicated earlier, but also to strengthen domestic currency (Kozierkiewicz, 1992). To be more specific, preoccupied with these policy objectives, the post-communist government has kept high interest rates (relative to real return on capital) for much too long at the expense of production needs.

The credit squeeze has been aggravated by the fact that this stringent measure was applied to an economy lacking the infrastructure necessary for such macromanagement. In particular, the economy has been functioning without a developed credit or banking system.[17] Indeed, a two-tiered banking system that separated central bank functions (e.g., money emission) from commercial lending was first established in 1988. There were only 16 state banks in operation in 1990, a great improvement from 1987 when only 5 were in place, but still only a minuscule number given the size of Poland's economy. The credit market has remained deeply segmented, with a weak connection between households and enterprises, rudimentary interbank operations, and little cross-border capital mobility.

Although the government expected the credit squeeze to hurt the inefficient public enterprises, it did not anticipate that the banks would not only resign from selective credit policy but that they would also refuse to lend for investment to viable applicants. The more successful private sector has not been receiving credit either, in large part due to the lack of a reliable credit recording or bank rating system.[18] The practice of asking borrowers for huge collateral has become very common, with banks often retaining two-thirds of any loan value to secure interest payments.[19] After decades of passive financing—following state directives—banks have little or no experience in the market evaluation of credit requests,[20] not to mention a severe shortage of personnel to deal with these requests.

The combined effect of the initial reduction in credit availability through state-controlled measures—interest rates and credit ceilings—and independent actions by the lending institutions resulted in a very sharp decline in credit-money supply in 1990. Bank credit was almost instantly reduced by 30 percent, and by the end of the year its stock was 50 percent less than in 1989 (Calvo and Coricelli, 1991). This was a financial shock that very few economies are capable of enduring let alone an economy like that of Poland, whose state enterprises traditionally have had low equity values.[21]

Convertibility and Trade Liberalization

When deliberating on the content of the shock therapy program, the government of Poland had to decide whether radical economic stabilization in a monetary sense should be accompanied by trade liberalization. Economists have not yet agreed on whether pursuing simultaneous deflation and liberalization is the best strategy. The potential benefit of adopting both policies at the same time is that while deflation increases pressure on financial discipline, trade opening helps to break up domestic monopolies and reduce price distortions. However, because supply rigidities may prevent the economy from achieving a quick adjustment, an opening of trade could cause domestic producers to lose internal market shares to foreign imports, thus worsening the overall economic situation. Faced with this choice, Poland chose to combine deflation with trade liberalization.

Trade Effect

The 1990 devaluation of the zloty against the dollar—by almost 600 percent—and other hard currencies should have provided a positive stimulant for exports and a negative one for imports. The decisive factor, however, was the collapse of the domestic market for both consumer and capital goods. Confronted with falling internal demand, enterprises were forced to look for foreign buyers while cutting their imports. The response by state managers was very strong—a clear display of their ability to respond to market signals. Exports to hard currency markets, an area difficult to penetrate, increased by more than 35 percent in 1990 to about $12 billion. Since imports were cut at the same time, a trade surplus close to $2.7 billion was generated that year, compared to a $0.5 billion surplus in 1989.[22]

The economy has been unable, however, to sustain this remarkable export surge on the hard currency markets. The government reacted to the export slowdown with an official devaluation in mid-1991, the first since the announcement of the shock therapy program.[23] After this intervention, however, the currency was still 35 percent above the equilibrium point, which was not enough to stimulate exports and yet too little to reverse the sudden increase in dollar imports. In late 1991, as the government decided to abandon the fixed exchange-rate system and replace it with a floating rate, with marginal drifts allowed, exports still continued to be sluggish. In 1991 Poland incurred a trade deficit of roughly $.3 billion, its first in many years, and returned to a negative current account balance as well.

To revive faltering exports and rebuild foreign trade surplus, the government instituted another one-time substantial devaluation in early 1992. As before, the economy responded to this correction with lower import levels and additional exports, another sign that state enterprises have become sensitive to this macroeconomic instrument. This measure has not resulted in any visible acceleration of inflation—it continued to demonstrate a downward trend. By mid 1992 the trade surplus was reported to have reached a cumulative value of more than $.5 billion, so that if this trade trend were to continue, then the yearly trade surplus would be likely to exceed $1 billion.

The expansion of exports to hard currency economies came at the right time, for it coincided with the collapse of the traditional market in the former CMEA. Regional trade within the CMEA framework, already in trouble in 1989, developed into an open crisis in 1990, in large part due to recessionary tendencies in the region (see Brabant, 1991). Trade turnover had sharply declined, while the Soviet Union registered huge trade deficits with many of its traditional partners in Eastern Europe. Poland's 1990 exports to the Soviet Union were down 14.5 percent in volume terms, while ruble imports declined in value by 38.9 percent, which produced a surplus of R 4.8 billion.

In 1991, following the CMEA's shift to dollar financing and the abolition of bilateral protocols, Polish trade with the Soviet Union was further damaged. The Soviet Union either stopped purchasing Polish goods or kept some imports without making payments. Exports to the Soviet Union and to other former CMEA members (particularly East Germany), in volume terms, declined very sharply in 1991 and this trend continued through 1992. At this stage, the major source of contraction was the collapse of Russia's demand; while Russia's total trade turnover during the first half of 1992 was down 27 percent, with the former CMEA the negative rate was 73 percent (*Financial Times*, August 18, 1992).

This "trade destruction" could have been avoided, at least to a degree, if the CMEA had managed to continue to exist in some effective alternative form, as a temporary solution and possibly as a basis on which a substitute regional regime—some form of custom union—could be built. There was some interest among leaders in such an approach, so that in 1990, when the Soviets signaled their lack of interest in preserving the CMEA, Poland, joined by Czechoslovakia and Hungary, advocated a slow phase-out of the regime (see Brabant, 1991; Poznanski,

1992). But in 1991, after the unilateral Soviet decision to abandon the CMEA, with all East European members concentrated on building ties with advanced capitalist economies, the trade regime was allowed to quickly collapse.

Problem Surplus

Although Poland's 1990 hard-currency trade surplus greatly exceeded the government's expectations, some economists are doubtful whether the abrupt buildup of net exports was desirable (see Kozierkiewicz, 1992). Under other circumstances, Poland's surplus would have been a blessing, but in this case, it seems that it was not, for it worsened the decline in domestic absorption. Because of this, the utilized domestic product fell by 17 percent in 1990—or 5 points above the reduction in the produced domestic product, as reported earlier—which constrained consumers and producers even more, i.e., beyond the limitations resulting from an internal monetary squeeze.[24]

Of course, Poland's substantial trade surplus of 1990 should have improved its financial standing, i.e., its creditworthiness. However, to strengthen its currency, the government decided to suspend most of its huge debt repayment in 1990,[25] and did not resume it until late 1991.[26] This only added to the already excessive foreign debt, which increased from $40.8 billion in 1989 to $46.1 billion in 1990, or by $5.3 billion (with one half of that increase related to dollar depreciation against other hard currencies). About three fourths of this outstanding debt was in the category of official debt to governments (or guaranteed by governments), of which as much as 25 percent was owed to the German government.

Some experts have argued that if there were no other payoffs from the recent surplus, at least Poland gained by having about 30 percent of its official debt forgiven by western countries (including up to 50 percent of its debt to the United States) in mid-1991. It should be kept in mind, however, that Poland had not serviced its official debt since 1980, and, as demonstrated earlier, had only partially paid its commercial debt to private banks. In exchange for a reduction of the nondebt to foreign governments, Poland had to agree to some restrictions on its policies because the official debt reduction was structured as a multiyear program that was contingent on Poland meeting certain macroeconomic conditions set by the lenders.[27]

Poland's commercial debt still stood at $11–12 billion in 1992, which was very close to the level reported in 1979, when the economy first entered its financial crisis. The Polish government, meeting with a consortium of western banks representing the various holders of

Poland's debt, sought to negotiate a debt reduction but with little success (though a Brady-type deal is still a possibility). The consortium was reluctant to make any concessions, as it was perceived that the forgiveness of some of Poland's official debts had made cash available for the repayment of its commercial debt (see Brainard, 1991). Furthermore, the accumulation of foreign currency reserves during 1990–91 [28] has made it more difficult for Poland to argue that it has no available funds with which to service its obligations to these banks.

The trade surplus with the Soviet Union has not been very helpful either. Before 1988, Poland had accumulated a very substantial trade deficit with the Soviet Union, which the latter turned into "trade credits" at a low interest rate. The Polish communist government had tried, to no avail, to make the Soviet Union reschedule this debt. With the post-1989 trade surpluses, Poland has actually paid back its outstanding debt to the Soviet Union long before it intended to do so. Incidentally, as a result of this accelerated debt repayment, Poland sacrificed leverage that it might have had in its negotiations with the Soviets, in which Poland demanded fair (properly valued) compensation for its participation in joint projects on Soviet soil.

Industry Deprotection

Not only was the initial strongly pro-export bias of dubious value, but so was the subsequent deep deprotection of the economy through 1991 currency overvaluation and erosion of tariffs, which was particularly substantial during mid-1990 and late 1991. This eventual deprotection has created an economic threat to import-competing producers, for so many of them operate in negative value-added ranges. McKinnon (1991) estimated that between 30 to 40 percent of domestic industry in Eastern Europe[29] falls into this category, meaning that their production costs recalculated at prevailing world market prices exceed the prices paid for their products worldwide. Considering this structural weakness, McKinnon and many others have advocated the application of very high, barrage tariffs as a medium-term solution.

One factor that proves deprotection has hurt domestic producers and thus contributed to the recession is the strong correlation between the relative import exposure of particular industries and the depth of cross-sector output decline. For example, the textiles and electromachinery industries—the sectors most severely affected by the recession—have experienced some of the highest exposure to foreign competition, as evidenced by their import-penetration ratio. While this ratio for Polish industry as a whole increased from 16 percent to 25 percent during 1990–91, it rose from 18 to 26 percent and from 25 percent to 38 percent for textiles and electromachinery respectively (Coricelli and Revenga, 1991, p. 20).

Premature deprotection has also harmed national output by discouraging foreign investment, which is needed to somewhat offset the withdrawal from production by domestic enterprises. Allowing cheap imports during the initial stages of the transition to capitalism, when the risk-level for foreign investors is particularly high, the government has endangered potential profit margins for foreigners. This has been particularly detrimental for investors interested in producing for the internal market, which happens to be the very target of most potential investors from abroad. Contrary to the arguments in favor of immediate trade liberalization,[30] there is ample evidence that in the case of Poland, the opening of trade has had some negative consequences for foreign investment.

The negative impact of rapid trade liberalization can be observed, for example, in Poland's automobile industry, which for years has been in great need of capital injection to repair its severely outdated equipment. General Motors, while waiting for the Polish government to secure a 35 percent tariff on the import of cars for a five- to ten-year period, stalled negotiations on the potential acquisition of a large auto plant near Warsaw. French Citroen, a competitor for the acquisition of that same factory, made a similar request, and Fiat's earlier negotiations for that same Warsaw facility were terminated when Poland refused to ensure full exclusivity for Fiat to supply the domestic market with cars manufactured by this facility.[31] General Motors signed a contract in mid-1992 only after receiving a governmental commitment to impose higher duties.

Progress in Privatization Program

In the governmental strategy, the stabilization program was perceived as only a necessary precondition for restoring the capitalist economy, in particular for the privatization of public assets, which accounted for more than 90 percent of total capital value outside of agriculture. It was also assumed that stabilization could not succeed in the long run as long as there was no proprietary interest in maximizing the value of capital. Thus, Mazowiecki decided to apply both deflationary policy and pursue full-scale privatization simultaneously, with the latter to be completed as promised within two to three years (see Poznanski, 1992). As if the two shocks of deflation and deprotection were not enough, the government chose to administer a third, which, I believe, has proved very detrimental to the economy.

Changing Priorities

The decision to privatize in 1990 came as something of a surprise, since as late as the roundtable negotiations of 1989 the opposition had continued to press for a labor-managed form of control, patterned after Yugoslavia. A labor-managed model was most consistent with the long tradition in Poland of worker self-organization (e.g., worker councils set up for the first time in 1956). Reversing itself, however, the opposition, after assuming power, rejected the idea of self-management. This was part of an overall shift towards aggressive liberalism, which was inconsistent with the soft ownership formula inherent in the Yugoslav model.

When the privatization program was announced in 1990, the formula adopted was that of a public offering or sales of shares in state enterprises to be supervised by a specially created ministry. This proved to be a frustrating approach that offered little chance for quick completion. Moreover, certain forces within the power center had not totally given up the idea of turning workers into proprietors. The parliament, dominated by union-backed forces and former communists, forced the government to make concessions, both in terms of stripping the new ministry of many powers and opening the door for methods of divestment that would directly benefit the workers.

Accordingly, in mid-1990, a new formula was given priority, namely democratic capitalism, which would allow, especially for smaller, defunct enterprises, leveraged buy-outs by both managers and worker collectives. A higher priority was even given to the idea of a free distribution of shares to the entire populace through so-called vouchers. The shares would then be managed by special investments or mutual funds. This concept gained momentum in mid-1990 when the government of Bielecki, the successor to Mazowiecki, decided to speed up privatization by targeting 400 large enterprises for a fast track procedure, while announcing that about a dozen funds would be set up not only to control the portfolios of shares but also to manage the respective enterprises.[32]

While the idea of vouchers seemed to provide a great attraction to workers and their families, the public response to Bilelecki's push for quick privatization was very unreceptive (similar to the reaction given by Czech workers to the voucher scheme announced in late 1991). For the government to proceed with the fast track, approval by the targeted enterprises was required. Most state enterprises, however, decided to abstain from the process. The divided parliament, still dominated by former communists, made it even more difficult for the government to act. Because the elections to parliament that were held at the end of 1991 paralyzed the government, the voucher program as well as other reforms were put on hold.

Despite its great commitment and readiness to take shortcuts, such as the vouchers scheme, the government had little success in its privatization effort. The only impressive results of privatization have been registered in transportation, where more than one-third of the trucks were already privately owned in 1991, and in retail trade, where roughly seventy percent was in private hands at that time (and about forty percent of wholesale trade). Of the 8,400 state-owned enterprises in the industrial sector, however, only 880 have been privatized so far, none of them in the category of the large state enterprises that still account for the 70–80 percent of total capital value outside of agriculture (see Sachs, 1992). Significantly, of those 880 that have been privatized, more than 80 percent were divested through leveraged buy-outs, which involved the majority of workers employed at these enterprises.

Many economists have complained about what they consider the current slow pace of privatization, including Sachs (1991), who has lamented that piecemeal privatization hampers the transition process by locking Poland into a market socialist system where prices are free but property belongs to the state. Kolodko (1991) complains that the shock therapy program, while excessive regarding deflationary measures, has lacked decisiveness with respect to divesting public capital. What these views imply is that privatization could have proceeded faster if not for lack of resolve, while, most likely, the process has been slow because of the enormous complexity and scale of the whole operation. Consequently, such calls for acceleration of divestment may lead to unnecessary haste in decision-making and risky experiments.

Great Gamble

The principal weakness of Poland's program for privatization of the state sector has been that despite its declared commitment to minimizing risk of reform by trying proven, well-tested solutions, the government has, to the contrary, experimented on a large scale. When it was discovered that the classic methods of public offerings, such as those utilized by Chile or Great Britain, were too time consuming, the policymakers began to invent substitute schemes, the most favored of which had never been used before. Both the voucher scheme and massive buyouts by managers/workers, as instruments of building a capitalist economy, fall in that category. At best, these concepts bring to mind some of the ideals or utopias early socialists dreamed of, which is a great irony, given the rather conservative political makeup of the current leadership of Poland.

The idea of a giveaway distribution of shares was presented to the public as the most effective way of bypassing the greatest financial obstacle to privatization, the lack of personal savings with which to purchase public capital. By giving assets away, however, the government risked the possibility that some, if not most, shares would be given to recipients who were both unqualified to make decisions and unprepared to take reasonable risks. Furthermore, financial intermediation is needed not only to scrutinize potential owners of assets, but also to prevent dispersion of capital, so that it is prudently controlled (putting funds in charge of capital allocations, as proposed by the government, would not help much).

One cannot avoid an impression that the voucher program was promoted by the government mostly because of the damage created by its own stabilization measures. Specifically, the drastic confiscatory deflation of 1990, as well as earlier efforts by the communist regime to remove "monetary overhang," have left households with no available funds to purchase state assets.[33] The stabilization efforts have taxed households out of their excess, and possibly even pushed them below an equilibrium level of money holdings (they were first shifted to state enterprises, only to then be confiscated by the state budget; see Gajdeczka, 1991).

Another supposed advantage of the voucher system is that it would help buy public support for privatization, as it is likely that workers, who perceive state enterprises as their own, would expect some financial compensation for giving up control. It is a great illusion, however, that workers are going to give up their power at the enterprise level in exchange for freely distributed shares. In fact, receiving shares might further strengthen their interest in controlling the enterprises directly. Because such economic chaos exists in Poland now, workers mostly fear that they will lose their jobs and fall into poverty. As a result, no form of security offered through a share package of very uncertain market value would provide the workers with the incentive to yield control at the enterprise level.

Property Vacuum

The common displays of dissatisfaction voiced by economists concerning the slowness of the privatization campaign has obscured the fact that dramatic changes in property rights have actually occurred in Poland since mid-1989. While it is true that very little has been transferred to private owners, the government's announcement of its intent to quickly divest public assets has nevertheless had a very dramatic impact on property rights. The initial declaration in mid-1989 that privatization would take only a few years and that it would include the majority, if not all, of the existing enterprises had the appearance of a credible policy. Even though few real changes have followed, this policy declaration by itself has had a very strong effect on the actual "users" of public assets.

Poland's declaration that it would execute a radical privatization program was announced at a time when public property rights had already been greatly diluted. Without going into detail, suffice it to say that during the labor unrest of 1980–1981, workers had effectively taken control of state enterprises, only to surrender this control in 1982 to the military "commissars." With the relaxation of military rule in 1984, managers and workers began to share power. With the transfer of authority from the party/state to the opposition in mid-1989, however, the balance of power within enterprises shifted from managers to workers. By declaring its intentions for a quick privatization in 1990, while refusing to directly intervene in production, the non-communist government had essentially stripped the managers of the remnants of their protection against the workers (Portes, 1991).[34]

It is not surprising, then, that in this peculiar "property vacuum," the managers, the only group capable of assuring efficient use of resources, lost interest in maintaining capital value in their enterprises.[35] Not only do they have less leverage against the workers, but they are also unsure as to whether the new owners will allow them to keep their positions. Consequently, they have developed a strategy of abandoning the enterprise, except for the healthy, manageable piece of it that they wish either to acquire for themselves or to hand over to a resourceful partner in exchange for the retention of their positions. In any case, it makes perfect sense for managers to run the enterprises' capital down since it would lower the purchase price for these entities.

The situation is even more dramatic: not only do managers have an incentive to deplete resources, but the factory workers themselves are interested in decapitalization. Workers have been closing their eyes to massive sales of equipment to cover their wage payments. Moreover, as indicated before, workers have become interested in acquiring shares in their enterprises in order to secure their jobs and possibly enhance their personal income. Stripped of savings by inflation and paid little, they have perceived it as to their advantage to drive the value of capital assets down, much like the managers, with whom they have, in fact, often become allies (this has been taking place even though such depletion of capital represents a threat to their future employment and wage levels).

It is not even certain whether those state enterprises that have already privatized feel any more secure in their rights than those awaiting divestment. The whole process is so confusing, with so many conflicting regulations and opportunities for financial abuse, that many new owners actually have serious doubts as to whether or not they will eventually be investigated by the government. In fact, the "nomenklatura" enterprises acquired by the communist elite have been subject to frequent questioning by the legal authorities while being threatened with both forced closures and confiscation of assets. Moreover, it is still unclear whether the general public will at some point react violently to the recent acquisitions of national assets.

Alternative Options

Certainly, it would be ideal to quickly—or better yet, instantly—create a market based upon private property while simultaneously establishing financial discipline. However, even with the greatest commitment possible, it would take the government many years to introduce effective property rights. The slow pace of privatization in Poland, as I see it, reflects the fact that such a process has to be slow if it is to succeed; the pace is not slow because somebody has failed to act in a proper way. Calling for an acceleration of privatization (see Sachs, 1991) would simply invite more confusion into the already greatly diluted ownership structure.

It is not that the government had no choice but to announce all-out privatization. In a situation as complicated as that inherited from the communist rulers, the simplest solutions may well be the most effective ones. At this point, for instance, consolidation of power by managers was probably the most logical choice. The government could reclaim enterprises by turning them into treasury-owned, joint-stock companies and then put managers on performance contracts. The sale of enterprises under firm governmental control would definitely be easier than divesting assets simultaneously claimed by a number of different parties, as has been the norm to date.

Furthermore, a viable alternative to the governmental policy of destroying the state sector and creating a private one would be to let the public industry struggle in a level playing field with the private businesses, while allowing fair competition to decide who prevails and under what circumstances. One could even envision a policy that would allow a reasonable level of survival for the state sector along with a complete opening of the private sector, as in China (see Poznanski, 1991). In this latter approach, the state sector would not be destroyed but simply marginalized, as the more efficient private sector grows at a faster rate than the state sector. Recently, in China, more than 50 percent of the national product was generated by the nonstate sector (i.e., cooperative, private, or municipal), all without privatizing a single major enterprise (Lardy, 1991).

Moreover, there are some less controversial methods of buying workers' support for privatization than simply giving away shares or leasing at a nominal price. One alternative, adopted by Mexico, would offer a suitable model because the political scene in Mexico, as in Poland, is dominated by strong trade unions and a populist government. Rather than endorse the concept of popular capitalism as pursued by Poland, Mexico decided that proceeds from sales would be put into a special fund that finances local projects—school, hospitals, roads—in the most needy areas. Interestingly, due to the strong appeal of this program, the government's popularity has been historically high.

Destabilizing the state sector so drastically, as in Poland, has had to create some opposition to reform. That economic problems are adding to political volatility has been reflected in subsequent elections. In the presidential elections of late 1990, Mazowiecki received 18 percent of the vote (and 11 percent of the eligible electorate). Bielecki, or rather his liberal-oriented party, obtained less than 8 percent of the vote during the parliamentary elections of late 1991. Moreover, during the elections of 1990, the forces of Mazowiecki lost to a completely unknown right-wing candidate, while the former communists emerged as the second strongest party during the latter elections.

Summary

Thus, in an effort to quickly stabilize the domestic economy, the governments of Mazowiecki and Bielecki have pushed the country into a vicious circle. Contributing greatly to this disturbing spiral has been the policy priority of balancing the budget at almost any cost. Anti-inflationary restrictions have badly hurt production, which in turn has worsened the state budget while adding to the inflationary price spiral. However, while the swing from a budget deficit in 1989 to a surplus in 1990 was quite large, it does not fully explain the production collapse, nor the persistence of that slump, since similarly deep budget shifts experienced by other countries have not caused similar declines in production (see Crane, 1991, p.6).[36]

An additional factor at work has been the choice of a fixed exchange rate policy for the initial stage of shock therapy, which was motivated by the government's desire to support stable prices. Introducing this regime rather than floating currency near its real value (i.e., purchasing power parity) has proven costly to the Polish economy. The undervaluation of early 1990 damaged the import-dependent sectors, while the subsequent overvaluation—combined with tariff reductions in mid-1990—overexposed the import-competing industries. Only with the 1992 rebuilding of higher tariffs (but without quantitative restrictions) the conditions have somewhat changed.

Another reason why the stabilization program turned out to be destructive is that it was imposed on an economy exhausted not only by years of underinvestment, but also suffering from the obsolete institutional setting inherited from the communist past. In this primitive institutional setting, the deflationary measures produced, as an aftershock, a particularly severe "liquidity crisis," since banks have not been in a position to select good-risk projects for financing. Given Poland's crude economic system, industry could have been better off if the government had applied not only a milder dose of deflation but also if it agreed to some halfway solutions as well (e.g., retaining control over certain prices, stepwise removal of subsidies).

The post-communist Poland has slipped into a recession, or even a depression, without achieving the desired deep structural adjustment, because the harsh measures applied by the government were unable to work under conditions of a property vacuum. The traditional state-controlled system of directives has for the most part been eliminated, but the ills associated with it continued to plague the economy. Unhealthy state enterprises have not been declared bankrupt, while overmanning persisted because, as in the past, workers have won effective control over their enterprises. Furthermore, after a brief pause immediately following the imposition of shock therapy, enterprises overborrowed with little fear of punishment from the commercial banks, which for all practical purposes continued to operate as agencies of the state.

Notes

Kazimierz Z. Poznanski is with the Henry Jackson School of International Studies, University of Washington. Comments by Wojciech Charemza, Przemyslaw Gajdeczka, and David Kemme are acknowledged.

1. Such a simultaneous, three-way economic program was not tried before except by Chile after 1973, and even there the starting conditions seemed more favorable than those in 1990 Poland. See more in Edwards, 1992.

2. A "bad equilibrium" is defined by Calvo and Frenkel (1992, p. 113) as one ". . . in which growth is low and incentives to undertake efficient investment are stifled" or, to put it differently, one ". . . in which socially profitable long-term

investments are crowded out by less profitable short-term investments" (Ibid., p. 114).

3. Moreover, very high interest rates were introduced on domestic currency deposits, effectively in excess of 60 percent in 1990 (mostly because the exchange rate between zloty and dollars was kept constant).

4. Charemza (1991, p. 1) estimated that between March 1990, when "corrective inflation" was already over, and March 1991, the average rate of inflation was 5.4 percent per month, equivalent to an annual rate close to 88 percent.

5. By mid-1990, the government relaxed monetary restrictions to reverse the economic decline. The interest rate on credit was lowered (from 4 percent to 2.5 percent monthly) and credit limits for banks were increased. Government expenditures were expanded to reduce unexpected budgetary surplus. Moreover, real wages were allowed to increase in the second half of 1990. The economy responded to this aggregate demand expansion with a visible upturn in production, but at the same time, inflation accelerated.

6. The loss in output should be distinguished from the welfare effect, the latter being less than the former. Elimination of shortages wiped out the welfare loss related to the extended search for goods (proportional to the price gap between official and black market, see: Lipton and Sachs, 1990). Quality of goods has improved due to expanded import of consumer goods (though many substandard products have been shipped in as well).

7. Textile industry employment, mostly concentrated in Lodz, declined by 50 percent through mid-1992.

8. Hidden unemployment in the state industry was estimated at .9 million in 1951. This means that if the excess labor were eliminated, the rate of unemployment would almost double.

9. See Informacja Statystyczna GUS, January 8, 1991.

10. Monthly deficits showed up in the second part of 1990.

11. The share of all tax burdens in the total value of production in the state sector was 46.2 percent in 1991 (and 32.9 percent in 1989) while the respective share for the private sector was 7.9 percent in 1991 (and 14.1 percent in 1989).

12. Investment in Western machinery has been particularly hurt, with the share of capital goods in total imports only at 15 percent in 1990 and 17 percent in 1991.

13. In the last month of 1989 the industrial output was 10 percent below the respective month in 1988.

14. In 1989, gross national product increased by .2 percent but net national product declined by .2 percent.

15. Among Eastern European countries, Czechoslovakia adopted a wage contract, Austrian-style, within which workers agreed to some losses in real wages in exchange for generous unemployment payments (see Brada, 1991).

16. Edwards (1992, p. 8) evaluates Mexico's policy of wage de-indexation as a positive experience and generalizes that a fairly democratic society can successfully bring down inflation by working not only through the exchange rate but also by working in the direction of wages and other contracts and by sup-

porting exchange rate anchors through income policies. Others also stress the benefits of "social pacts" but in the context of Western European experience, particularly that of Austria. Limitations of such arrangements are stressed as well, suggesting that due to these limitations, the popularity of social pacts has been on the decline in the region. However, it could be that Eastern Europe is recently at a stage of development comparable to that of Western Europe in the time when such contracts were relatively useful.

17. Calvo and Frenkel (1991) argue that it is essential for successful transition to put in place effective capital markets before other major steps are made. They stress that if price liberalization is executed in the absence of working capital markets, a negative supply-effect is very likely. Higher prices of inputs will reduce working capital that will be difficult to build up since lending institutions won't be able to assess the creditworthiness of their clients.

18. It is estimated that the private sector received only 2.7 percent of the total credit issued during 1990 (see Lipton and Sachs, 1991). In 1991, the respective share increased to approximately 10 percent of the loan portfolio held by state banks. The private sector has been forced to rely on funds available from family members or friends, and the rapidly expanding "grey" sector is still turning only limited amounts of finance.

19. Svejnar (1991, p. 133) makes a similar observation about banks' reluctance to lend, given the lack of reputation and limited collateral by domestic enterprises. He argues, "In this situation, there is strong economic justification for the government to step in and provide credit insurance."

20. In the absence of an efficient financial market, the central bank was practically left with one instrument to control "credit creation," namely, reserve requirement ratio, which changed several times in 1990 alone.

21. Not only did the banks restrict lending to an amount less than was allowed, but public enterprises have been forced to reduce their nonbank, interfirm lending as well. Throughout 1989 the latter interfirm network expanded rapidly, primarily because the central bank was willing to supply credit to overexposed enterprises. While interfirm lending was not without risks for the financial system, this arrangement was essential for its survival. By the end of 1989, interfirm credit was twice the size of the bank credit for working capital (Calvo and Goricelli, 1991, p.17). After the state banks' sudden withdrawal of insurance against losses, the volume of interfirm credit declined by 40 percent for 1990 as a whole (Ibid.).

22. In fact, the 1990 surplus was the highest ever in more then a decade, including the previous decade of Poland's trying to pay back its debt, when surpluses were around $1.5 billion.

23. In mid-1991, the currency was reportedly overvalued by at least 40 percent, which brought with it strong disincentives to export.

24. Furthermore, the huge trade surplus added to inflationary pressures, since the surplus resulted in a sharp increase in the money supply in mid-1990, which the government had a hard time sterilizing for lack of the necessary instruments. When the stabilization program was applied, there was no bond market in place. That market was set up only in mid-1990, and it took time to

make it work at all. It has thus been very difficult for the government to finance the budgetary deficit through bond flotation. Instead, fiscal deficits have been financed mostly by printing money. Specifically, the government covered roughly two-thirds of its deficits with credit issued from state banks.

25. In 1990 Poland owed about $7 billion in debt payments, which would have taken as much as 60 percent of hard currency export revenues to finance. The actual payments were about $.7 billion, in part facilitated by the decision of the official-debt holders to allow for deferred obligations. Payments to commercial banks were officially suspended with unrefinanced interest owed to the banks exceeding $1 billion.

26. In 1991 Poland owed $10.6 billion in arrears plus another $1.2 billion in interest arrears to about 500 private banks (*Financial Times*, June 21, 1991). Poland was to pay $3.9 billion on its hard-currency debt (compared to $3.5 billion in 1989) but only $.5 billion was actually paid (while in 1989, $1.1 billion was spent to service the debt).

27. Importantly, under the new, most restrictive arrangements, Poland will have to pay at least half as much annually as before the agreement, when it resumes payments, possibly increasing the payments from $1.6 billion during 1986–1988 to $2.5 billion a year (see Raczkowski, 1991).

28. Poland's hard-currency reserves were estimated at $6.2 billion at the end of 1991.

29. Similar results are reported in Charemza (1991), with the shares for Poland falling below the 30–40 percent range.

30. The opponents of postponing trade liberalization for the sake of attracting foreign capital argue that such inflow of capital may result in appreciation of currency and overexpose domestic industry to imports.

31. The threat from imports is greatly aggravated by the fact that massive numbers of Poles have been buying second-hand cars from abroad. Large quantities of stolen cars are also brought into the country, some of them to be then shipped to the Soviet Union. Apparently, about 250,000 used cars have been brought in over the course of 1991, of which 20,000–30,000 were stolen cars. Some sources indicate that the true number of imports was close to 400,000 (plus large quantities of auto parts).

32. The other response was to let small- and medium-scale state enterprises be privatized without careful scrutiny by the government. Rather than examine case by case and determine the proper sale value, the government decided to shift much of its authority to local agencies. The government's decision to sell assets was made with the hope that their value would improve under new ownership rather than with the expectation that the sales prices will reflect the true market value of capital.

33. The rate of savings in communist economies is typically very low, since there are very few financial instruments and very unattractive interest rates.

34. According to Portes (1991), Poland's government considerably delayed systemic institutional change, while spending most of 1990 trying to stabilize the economy. Consequently, state enterprises have assumed a form of tutelage in which agents are left without principals.

35. Excessively taxed and deprived of access to long-term credit, state enterprises have also been denied a modern legal framework that would not only force really insolvent units into bankruptcy but also allow them to buy some time for restructuring. Enterprises have been left with an obsolete bankruptcy law, that makes the state budget carry the burden of unpaid debts, since the state continues to be the owner. Moreover, this law lacks provisions that would allow endangered state enterprises to seek protection from creditors and work out some reasonable repayment schedule.

36. The official interpretation of the recession has made it very difficult for critics of the stabilization program to make their point heard. The size of the loss has been downplayed on the grounds, for instance, that much of the output gone represented goods unsalable in the past.

Bibliography

Bauer, T., 1991, "The Microeconomics of Inflation under Economic Reforms: Enterprises and their Environment," in: Commander, S., ed., *Managing Inflation in Socialist Economies in Transition*, Washington, D.C.: The World Bank, Economic Development Institute.

Baumol, W. and Benhabib, J., 1989, "Chaos: Significance, Mechanism, and Economic Applications", Journal of Economic Perspectives (Winter).

Berg, A. and J. Sachs, 1992, "Structural Adjustment and International Trade in Eastern Europe: The Case of Poland," *Economic Policy* (April).

Brabant van, J., 1991, "Convertibility in Eastern Europe through a Payments Union," in: J. Williamson, *Currency Convertibility in Eastern Europe*, Washington: Institute for International Economics.

Brada, J., 1992, "Political Economy of Eastern European Soviet Trade: Rethinking the Past and Searching for the Future," in: Poznanski, K., ed., *Constructing Capitalism: The Reemergence of Civil Society and Liberal Economy in the Post-Communist World*, Boulder: Westview Press.

_______, 1991, "The Economic Transition of Czechoslovakia from Plan to Market," *Journal of Economic Perspective*, Vol. 5, No. 4 (Fall).

Brada, J. and King, A., 1991, "Is There a J-Curve for the Economic Transition from Socialism to Capitalism?" Princeton (conference paper).

Brainard, L., 1991, "Reform in Eastern Europe: Creating a Capital Market," *Economic Review*, Federal Reserve Bank of Kansas City (January/February).

Calvo, G. and Frenkel, J., 1991, "Credit Markets, Credibility, and Economic Transformation," *Journal of Economic Perspectives*, Vol. 5, No. 4 (Fall).

Calvo, G. and Frenkel, J., 1992, "Transformation of Centrally Planned Economies: Credit Markets and Sustainable Growth," in: G. Winkler, ed., *Central and East Europe Roads to Growth*, Washington: IMF.

Calvo, G. and Coricelli, F., 1991, "Stagflationary Effects of Stabilization Programs in Reforming Socialist Countries: Enterprise-Side vs. Household-Side Factors," Washington: The World Bank (mimeo).

Charemza, W., 1991, "Market Failure and Stagflation: Some Aspects of Privatization in Poland," Department of Economics, University of Leicester (May) (mimeo).

Coricelli, F. and Revenga, A., 1991, "Wages and Unemployment in Poland: Recent Developments and Policy Issues," Washington, D.C., The World Bank (mimeo).

Crane, K., 1991, *Poland's Economic Performance in 1990: Taking Stock of the 'Big Bang'*, Washington D.C.: PlanEcon, Inc.

Dabrowski, M., 1992, "Stabilization Program in Poland, 1990–1991," Warsaw: Batory Foundation (mimeo).

Edwards, S., 1990, "The Sequencing of Economic Reforms: Analytical Issues and Lessons from Latin American Experiences," *The World Economy*, Vol. 13, No. 1 (March).

_______, 1992, "Central and Eastern Europe in Transition," *Contemporary Policy Issues*, vol. X (January).

Friedman, M, 1953, The Effects of Full-Employment Policy on Economic Stability: A Formal Analysis, in: *Essays in Positive Economics*, Chicago: University of Chicago Press

Gajdeczka, P., 1991, "Inflation Tax, Household Wealth, and Privatization in Poland," International Monetary Fund, Washington, D.C. (mimeo).

Gomulka, S., 1986, *Growth, Innovation and Reforms in Eastern Europe*, Madison: University of Wisconsin Press.

_______ 1991, "The Cause of Recession Following Stabilization," *Comparative Economic Studies*, vol. XXXIII, No. 2 (Summer).

Gross, J., 1992, "Poland: From Civil Society to Political Nation," in: I. Banac, ed., *Eastern Europe in Revolution*, Ithaca: Cornell University Press.

Hare, P. and Grosfeld, I., 1991, Privatization in Hungary, Poland and Czechoslovakia, *European Economy*, No. 5.

Kolodko, G., 1991, "Inflacja i stabilizacja," in: *Polityka Finansowa, Stabilizacja, Transformacja*, Warsaw.

Kolodko, G. and Rutkowski, M., 1991, "The Problem of Transition from a Socialist to a Free Market Economy: The Case of Poland," *The Journal of Social, Political and Economic Studies*, vol. 16, no. 2.

Kornai, J., 1980, *Economics of Shortage*, Amsterdam: North-Holland Publishers.

_______ 1990, *The Road to a Free Economy: Shifting from a Socialist System*. New York: W.W. Norton.

_______, 1992, *The Socialist System*, Princeton: Princeton University Press.

Kozierkiewicz, D., 1992, "Exchange Rate Policy and Economic Growth," conference paper, Institute of Finance, Wilga (10–12 July).

Lardy, N., 1991, *Redefining U.S.-China Economic Relations*. NBASR Analysis, No. 5.

Lipton, D. and Sachs, J., 1990, "Creating a Market Economy in Eastern Europe: The Case of Poland," *The Brookings Economic Papers* (January).

McKinnon, R., 1991, "Stabilization Programs in Post-Communist Eastern Europe," Seattle (June) (conference paper).

Milanovic, B., 1991, "Poland's Quest for Economic Stabilization, 1988–1991," World Bank, Washington, D.C. (mimeo).

Montias, M., 1991, "The Romanian Economy: A Survey of Current Economic Problems," *European Economy*, No. 5.

Murrell, P.,1991, "Can Neoclassical Economics Underpin the Reform of Centrally Planned Economies?," *The Journal of Economic Perspectives*, vol. 5, No. 4 (Fall).

Naughton, B., 1992, *Growing Out of the Plan: Chinese Economic Reform, 1978–1990*, New York: Cambridge University Press.

Newbury, D., 1991, "Reform in Hungary: Sequencing and Privatization," *European Economic Review* (April).

Portes, R., 1991, "Introduction," in: *The Path of Economic Reform in Central and Eastern Europe*, vol. 2, in the series *European Economy*.

Poznanski, K., 1986, "Economic Adjustment and Political Process: Poland Since 1970." In: E. Comisso and L. Tyson, eds. *Power, Purpose, and Collective Choice*. Ithaca: Cornell University Press.

_______, 1989, "The CPE Aversion to Technical Innovation," *Economics of Planning* (October).

_______, 1992, "Market Alternative to State Activism in Restoring Capitalist Economy," *Economics of Planning* (January), vol. 25, no. 1.

_______, 1991, "Decline of Communism, Rise of Capitalism," *Center for European Studies Working Papers*, No. 15, Harvard University.

_______, 1992, "Pricing Practices in the Authoritarian Trade Regime of Eastern Europe: A Reappraisal," University of Washington (mimeo).

_______, 1992, "Privatization of the Polish Economy: Problems of Transition," *Soviet Studies*, vol. 44, no. 4.

Roczkowski, S., 1991, "Comment," in: Kolodko, G., ed., *Polityka Finansowa: Stabilizacja, Transformacja*. Warsaw: Instytut Finansow, pp. 235–239.

Sachs, J., 1991, "Accelerating Privatization in Eastern Europe: The Case of Poland," World Bank (mimeo).

Svejnar, J., 1991, "Microeconomic Issues in Transition to a Market Economy," *Journal of Economic Perspectives*, vol. 5, no. 4 (Fall).

2

Poland's Quest for Economic Stabilization, 1988–1991: Interaction of Political Economy and Economics

Branko Milanovic

Poland's stabilization program of January 1990 has attracted widespread attention.[1] It is so far the boldest attempt to transform a socialist economy suffering from a high degree of instability (inflation, shortages) into a stable capitalist economy. It thus involves two separate components: macroeconomic stabilization and systemic reform. In this chapter we shall be concerned with the first component. This chapter is organized in four sections. In the first two sections we examine, respectively, the Price and Income Operation of February 1988 (the so-called second stage of reform) and the change in policy that ensued under the Rakowski government, including the removal of food subsidies in August 1989. The third section discusses the January 1990 Stabilization program.

As we demonstrate, the 1990 Stabilization program, however impressive, cannot be considered in isolation. Prior to the January 1990 stabilization there were at least two years of intensive attempts at reform. Reforms failed, either because no minimal social consensus could be achieved, or because they were badly designed. However, they hold lessons for other countries that may engage themselves along the same road as Poland. Their failure also paved the way for a much more ambitious project that took place in January 1990.

The Failed Price and Income Operation, November 1987–October 1988

In the last forty years Poland has experienced several attempts to reform its centrally planned economic system. They have all been at best moderately successful and the system has shown a remarkable tendency, once the initial impetus of the reform movement slackened, to drift back to its old modus operandi. In the 1980s, the reform effort commenced in 1982 and 1983 under the very difficult circumstances of the State of War. Since the economy, due to intense shortages, was at that juncture in a nearly chaotic situation, the first reflex of the government was to increase central controls. Meanwhile, the government clearly expressed its view that recentralization should only be temporary, and that its strategic orientation remained a movement toward a more market-oriented system where enterprise decision-making would be to a large extent free from state interference. Some important changes were realized in these years, notably the slashing of subsidies and the price readjustment,[2] but the reform soon ground to a halt.

In October 1987, in an effort to inspire the reform movement with renewed energy, the government under Prime Minister Messner and with strong economic guidance from the Deputy Prime Minister and Head of Central Planning Commission, Professor Sadowski, inaugurated the so-called second stage of reform. It was complete with an ambitious and detailed timetable for administrative reorganization as well as with legal and policy changes to be implemented. The reform was supposed to deal with one of perennial problems in all centrally planned economies—price distortions. The reform had a long list of predecessors, the major ones being price reforms of 1970, 1976, and 1982. A number of prices in Poland were "social prices," deliberately held below equilibrium levels in order to protect consumers. This was the case with food, agricultural inputs (fertilizers, pesticides), all types of energy inputs, transportation, and rents.

The government decided, in the second half of 1987, that it needed to move decisively in the price area, and, in order to enlist public support, it submitted to a popular referendum the plan on sharp price increases for most of the subsidized products. In the referendum held in November 1987 the proposal failed to receive the required 50 percent majority of all eligible voters, although among those who voted the proposal was accepted by a 2 to 1 margin. In face of the result of the referendum the government decided to scale down its initial plans, and to proceed with a more cautious price reform. Macroeconomic developments in 1988 were dominated by what became known as the Price and Income Operation. It represented not only the key plank in government economic strategy for the year but the key element of the reform process as well. As we shall see, for a number of reasons, the operation went awry and eventually failed. Yet its reverberations, and the developments to which it gave rise, dominated the economic scene in 1988, and, to some extent, all the period up to the Stabilization program of January 1990.

The essential idea behind the Price and Income Operation launched in February 1988 was to raise prices of foodstuffs, household energy, rent, and alcohol and tobacco, and to compensate (most) workers for the increase in the price index net of the part due to alcohol and tobacco. The government tried to achieve several objectives: (1) to tackle the sensitive issue of relative prices and to eliminate some of most egregious disparities that have serious effects on the allocation decisions both in consumption and production (e.g., low coal prices); (2) to proceed to a somewhat hidden reduction in real wages (by not compensating for the entire change in the price index), and thus to reduce excess aggregate demand; and (3) to improve its fiscal position by raising more taxes (via increased prices of alcohol and tobacco), and by lowering subsidies.

The price and income operation, together with other actions of the government (creation of the commercial banking system, reorganization of the state administration, reduction in the scope of central planning, and liberalization of the trade system) was supposed to restart the economic reform, stalled in the period 1984–87. In the event, the government failed to achieve its objectives. The main cause of the failure lay in inability to stem extremely high "compensatory" wage demands that followed in the wake of raised prices. Vocal demands by workers, reinforced by strikes, led the government to allow substantial wage increases that were already by March 1988 running ahead of inflation.

The March wages in the socialized sector, measured on a month-to-month basis (March 1988 to March 1987),[3] were 67 percent higher while prices (measured the same way) increased by 57 percent (see Figure 1). The gap remained unchanged after strikes in May 1988, and then after a series of fresh strikes in August 1988 increased to more than 20 percentage points.[4] In the last months of the year the gap grew further and by the end of 1988, wages had increased by 156 percent and retail prices by 73 percent.[5] Instead of a decline in real wages and reduced excess demand the very opposite situation ensued. Price disparities had remained more or less unchanged. The real amount of subsidies increased by 2 percent and the share of total subsidies remained at the high level of 15 percent of GDP. Among the subsidies, food subsidies, which were to be curtailed, increased 56 percent in real terms.

FIGURE 1 Monthly Rate of Inflation

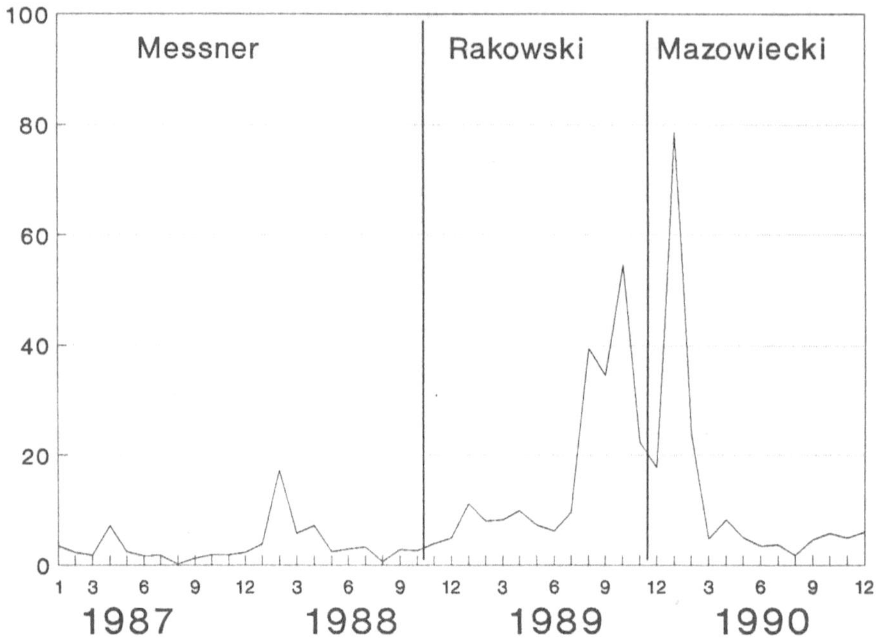

The mismatch between the purchasing power of the population and the availability of goods, often at controlled prices,[6] resulted in growing shortages. The supply of consumer goods in particular could not keep pace with the increase in incomes: While retail sales increased by 3 percent in real terms, total incomes of the population (composed of wages, social benefits, agricultural incomes, and nonagricultural private sector incomes) went up by almost 15 percent.

Since price controls were not removed, inflation was not allowed to mop up the entire amount of excess liquidity. Excess money balances found their outlet in the parallel market for foreign exchange. The parallel exchange rate of the zloty with respect to the dollar soared in the year by 160 percent. The official exchange rate broadly kept pace with increase in prices until August 1988 but then fell increasingly behind. The ratio between the parallel and the official rate, which during the previous year and a half fluctuated between 3.5 and 4.5, increased in August 1988 to 5, and reached almost 7 by the end of the year. Some devaluation of the parallel rate was due to political events and fear of instability at the time of each major strike movement. Most of the increase, however, was attributable to rapid rise of incomes.

With a shortage of goods, few opportunities for private investment, and negative real interest rates on zloty deposits, foreign exchange proved to be the safest way to protect savings.[7] A simple regression for the period 1987–88 (on monthly data) shows that each percentage increase in real wages was associated with 0.9 percent real devaluation of the parallel exchange rate.[8] In normal instances the effect of the increase in real wages on the exchange rate would be only indirect: through an increase in domestic costs and worsening trade balance. In the Polish situation the impact was almost immediate since foreign exchange served as the main store of value. Excess liquidity also exerted a negative impact on external equilibrium. In the last months of the year imports increased (partly as a result of the government's decision to increase the supply of consumer goods in order to alleviate shortages) while export growth, due to an easy home market and real appreciation of official exchange rate, decelerated.[9]

In May 1988, faced with a situation that already seemed to be running out of control, the Sejm gave to the government extraordinary powers. The principal objective of that move was to stem the accelerating rate of inflation. This was to be accomplished mostly by administrative means: more difficult access to credit for enterprises that increased wages excessively, dismissal of managers by the government, expansion of the obligatory price increase notifications, lengthening of the approval period, etc. These measures were directly antithetical to the avowed aim of economic liberalization. The government was yet again obliged to move in a vicious circle: Starting with piecemeal liberalizations that should have been a prelude to a comprehensive liberalization, it was led by events to a position where it needed to reassert its role in the hope of reversing negative trends in the economy, and was thus undermining the original intent of the reform.

Most of the granted extraordinary powers were never used, nor were government decisions always implemented. For example, viewing domestic disequilibrium with alarm, the government decided in May 1988 to press enterprises to increase their deliveries to the domestic market. It decided that only enterprises that kept their domestic deliveries at the level at least equal to the one achieved in 1987 would enjoy export incentives. The measure originally created some stir among export-oriented firms, but was never seriously implemented. It was in addition directly in conflict with another objective of the government policy—increase of convertible currency exports. Similarly, the existence of wage increase thresholds, which were supposed to trigger punitive tax rates, was quietly forgotten.

It seems that originally the government had a relatively coherent policy in mind and tried to steer the economy in a definite direction; after May, despite its enhanced powers on paper, it was mostly reacting to events, and to some extent drifting. This became even more obvious when the next rounds of strikes occurred in August 1988. The worsening economic situation led in October 1988 to the replacement of the Messner government and resignation of the main architect of the Price and Income Operation, Professor Sadowski. The new government was led by Mr. Rakowski, heretofore secretary-general of the Polish Communist Party.

The failure of the Price and Income Operation can be traced to several causes, the relative importance of which is difficult to determine. It can be argued that the operation itself was bound to fail as it was not comprehensive; notably, the exchange rate issue was left practically untackled,[10] the trade regime was unchanged, price controls remained pervasive, and the interest rate was starkly negative in real terms. The whole operation had a whiff of administrative tinkering about it.

However, it can be argued that the main cause of failure lay in the government's inability to resist wage increases and willingness to underwrite them through credit subsidization of enterprises (see Figure 2). The average interest rate charged on credits to socialized enterprises was 11 percent, that is –30 percent p.a. in real terms. The room for burgeoning wage payments was thus created thanks to implicit subsidization of credits.[11] Transfers through implicit interest rate subsidies were estimated at 10.3 percent of GDP (4 percentage points higher than in 1987).[12] Responsibility for the interest rate policy lay with the National Bank of Poland (NBP), whose relations with the main architects of the reform was strained. Reformers were not able to control the policy of the NBP.

Furthermore, enterprises continued to cumulate arrears against the banking sector, and the amount of inter-enterprise credit increased by one-fourth in real terms. The financial position of enterprises improved (gross profits increased by 10 percent in real terms). All of that plus inadequate depreciation allowances permitted enterprises to raise wages without relation to productivity. This was all the easier because of the existence of significant ex post subsidies (and taxes) that tended to equalize the performance of profitable and unprofitable firms.[13] Since negative interest rates entailed only a minor explicit subsidization by the government, the fiscal picture appeared good. The government deficit that amounted to 2.5 percent of GDP in 1987 was practically eliminated in 1988, thanks mostly to buoyant tax revenues (driven by increased profitability of enterprises).

FIGURE 2 Real Wage Level (quarterly average)

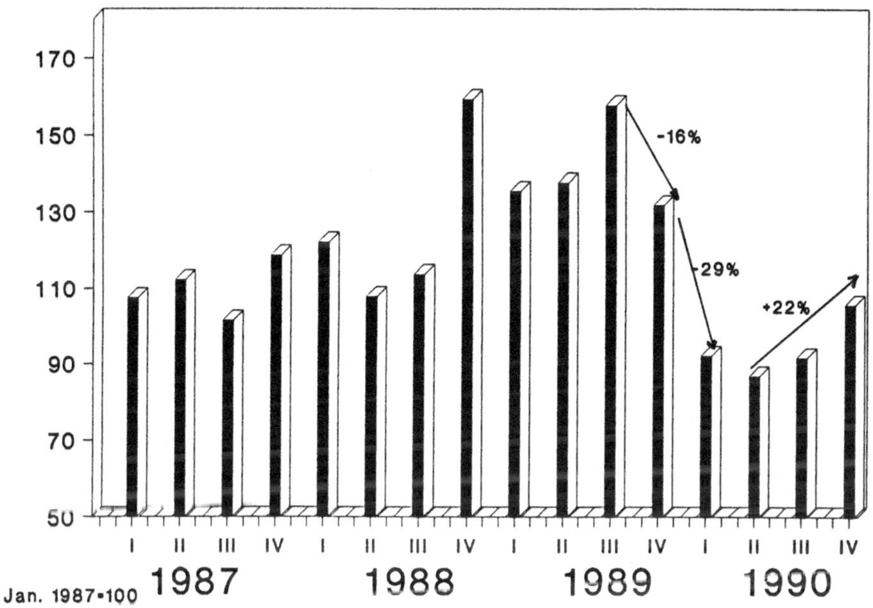

This means that there were two components to the failure of the February operation: (1) letting wages rise and (2) paying this higher wage bill out of implicit credit subsidies. This is very similar to the inflationary mechanism that by 1988 was quite common in Yugoslavia.[14] As a number of authors have argued (Pant and Lahiri, 1988; Mates, 1987; Rocha, 1989) these channels were inadequately understood until the Yugoslav Stabilization program of December 1989. It seems that the IMF, who throughout most of the 1980s had stand-by programs with Yugoslavia, was similarly unaware of the problem. Being concerned primarily with the objective of external equilibrium, the IMF might have emphasized devaluation without realizing sufficiently its impact on implicit exchange rate subsidies and thus on inflation.

In other words, in addition to the usual channels whereby devaluation causes inflation (cost-push), there was in Yugoslavia also the implicit subsidy element that proved an even more potent source of inflationary pressure. The question may be raised whether sufficient attention was being paid by the IMF to a similar mechanism operating via interest rate subsidies in Poland. It is difficult to determine conclusively whether it was or not. However, there is a marked contrast, in terms of the attention paid, between the need for external adjustment (achieving current account balance in convertible currencies) and the discussion of macro-economic mechanics at work. There is no evidence that dangers of subsidization that would ultimately derail the program and undermine the objective of external adjustment were fully comprehended.

The program definitely got unstuck in August following a series of strikes. The inability to resist the wage push resided in lack of political strength of the government: It feared social disorder. Thus the failure of the Operation was inevitable so long as workers were unwilling to accept a decline in real wages, and the government was too weak to hold the line.

The Decomposition of the System, October 1988–September 1989

Significant changes in the economic system already started under the Messner government. They included phasing out of the central planning system, decentralization of the banking system, introduction of the first drafts of laws that equalized treatment of all forms of property and allowed private individuals to purchase and issue bonds and shares and thus to create joint-stock and limited-liability companies. Most of these laws were adopted by the Sejm under the Rakowski government, often in a more liberal version. For example, the draft bill on Undertaking Economic Activity at first limited private sector employment to 50 workers; under the Rakowski government the limit was removed. The draft Law similarly envisaged greater number of areas to be closed to the private sector. The number of "forbidden areas" was later reduced (publishing, for example, was originally on the banned list).

The legacy of the Rakowski government is ambiguous. It is positive in the area of institutional change, since almost all impediments to private sector development were then lifted. The three fundamental laws—on undertaking economic activity, on foreign investments, and on banking—were passed during the Rakowski government. Limited internal convertibility of the zloty was introduced in March 1989. Purchases and sales of foreign exchange between citizens, which in the past were legally prohibited even if tolerated, were legalized and private individuals were allowed to open foreign exchange offices. "Spontaneous privatizations" also started in the first half of 1989. The importance of central allocation of inputs decreased. Central allocation concerned only a handful of essential items (coal, coke, crude oil, paper pulp, etc.), in contrast to about 22–25 percent of total intermediate inputs in 1988. Finally, a major operation of lifting of food subsidies was also executed at the end of the government's tenure in August 1989. In the area of macroeconomic management, however, the legacy is almost entirely negative since the economic situation deteriorated markedly.

Macroeconomic instability became worse in the last months of 1988 and continued on in 1989. Monthly increases in the retail price index that in 1988 oscillated between 3 and 7 percent (with the exception of February when the Income and Price Operation was launched) accelerated to about 10 percent in the first half of 1989. Real wages continued to outdistance prices and were by July 1989 about 25 percent higher in real terms than a year before. The official exchange rate appreciated in real terms between January and September by 9 percent (see Figure 3). Real interest rates became even more negative: The highest interest rate charged on enterprise credits in the first half of the year was –36 percent p.a. in real terms; interest rate on credits to the government proper for the financing of state budget was –53 percent p.a. The rate of growth of industrial output steadily declined and by midyear reached zero.

The fiscal position of the government deteriorated sharply due to several factors: (1) acceleration in inflation reduced real tax revenues;[15] (2) tax reform combined with stagnation of output generated lower revenues; and (3) expenditures increased as food subsidies due to higher agricultural procurement prices snowballed.[16] The fiscal deficit, which in the nine months of 1989 amounted to more than 10 percent of GDP (at annualized basis), was financed mostly by National Bank lending to the government.

Shortages were exacerbated and the ratio between parallel and official exchange rate stayed between 6 and 7. Currency substitution already present in 1988 became more widespread; the result was that two-thirds of broad money consisted of dollar-denominated deposits held by enterprises and the population.[17] The economy was thus exhibiting all typical features of accelerating inflation (increasing velocity,[18] declining stock of real zloty) and was threatening to burst into hyperinflation. As output was stagnant, the gap between the purchasing power of the population and supply of goods was increasing. This was the situation of shortage-stagflation.

The external position that began to worsen in the last quarter of 1988 slipped further. Trade surplus with convertible currency area was halved: from almost \$1.1 billion in the first ten months of 1988 to \$570 million for the same period a year later. The deterioration occurred in response to real appreciation of the official exchange rate, but also due to deliberate government policy of increasing imports in the months prior to June 1989 elections (the first multiparty elections since 1947). Soaring imports of consumer goods were also supposed to mop up some of the excess liquidity.

FIGURE 3 Official and Parallel Real Exchange Rate (January 1987 = 100)

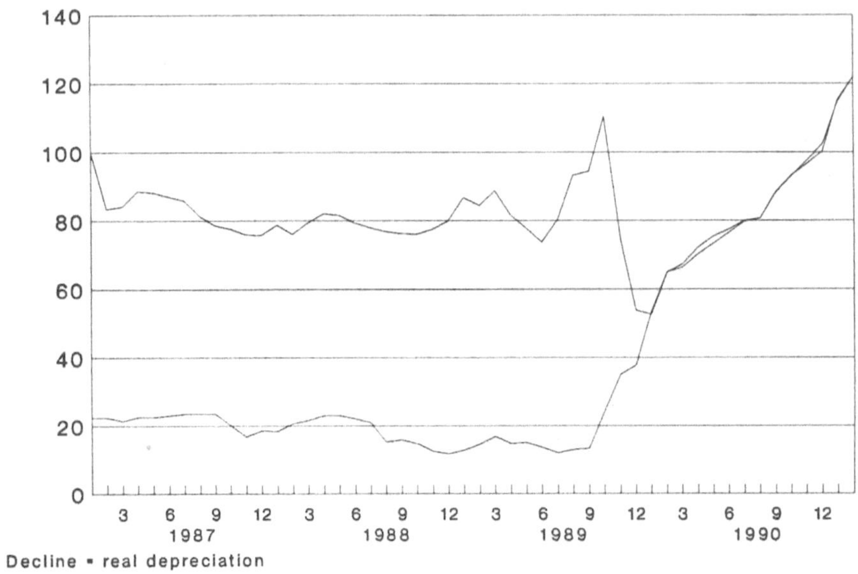

The question arises, why did the Rakowski government allow the economic situation to deteriorate in such an unambiguous fashion? Different views were advanced. In part, government hands were tied since the "Roundtable" talks between the government and the opposition. These talks lasted throughout the first quarter of 1989 and introduced the principle of wage indexation (at first at 80 percent of price increases). It was difficult for the government—which did not enjoy more popular support than its predecessor—to renege on that. Secondly, the government continued with the earlier strategy aimed at changing relative prices. This necessitated particularly sharp increases in prices of energy inputs (electricity, heating, and fuels). It also proceeded to further price liberalization so that about 50 percent of retail prices were free.

According to a different view, the Rakowski government deliberately pursued the policy of high inflation. Because of elections the government let wages increase even faster than was implied by the indexation formula[19] (thus in June alone real wages increased by 9 percent). Also, the government might have held that only through inflation could it effect structural changes. Since it assumed that most prices were inflexible downward, it concluded that higher relative prices of some products inevitably required a generalized increase in the price level. It probably overlooked the fact that when inflation so quickly threatens to degenerate into hyperinflation, all signals about relative profitability are lost in a cacophony of rising prices, and relative price changes become indistinguishable from the changes in the overall price level. The economic situation in July 1989 (after the electoral defeat of Communists) reached its nadir. Amid growing shortages (including those of food), the inflation rate for the first time since 1982 reached, on a month-to-month basis, a triple-digit level, while the cumulative growth in industrial output was 0.2 percent.

The last decision of the Rakowski government was a courageous one. With very little to gain from it, the government decided in August 1989 to proceed with an action that had eluded all previous governments: to practically eliminate food and agricultural input subsidies in one fell swoop. The two were quid pro quo. Output prices could be liberalized only if farmers accepted that their input prices be raised as well. The decision took place in conditions of food shortages and its immediate effect was the doubling of food prices and an increase in the rate of inflation (39.5 percent in August alone). It was ironic that the decision that eluded the Communist government and cost several of them their office (after disturbances in 1970, 1976, and 1980) was finally executed in the last month of Communist rule in Poland. On September 16, Mr. Mazowiecki from the "Solidarity" party became the Prime Minister.

In the political arena, in particular, the legacy of the Rakowski government is subject to different interpretations. It can be argued, I think, that the lack of success of the Price and Income Operation, coupled with similar failures in the past, convinced the Rakowski government that it essentially had two options. Either it needed to define a new economic policy designed to stimulate private sector growth or it had to proceed with political liberalization. Under the first option, liberalization would be limited to the economic sphere. Since most social groups were already alienated from the government, the nascent private sector would be the stratum on which the government could count. The idea found favor with economic liberals[20] even if the new policy were to benefit not only the legitimate private sector but, possibly even more, the nomenklatura, which sought to convert its political clout into economic power.

As Walicki (1989, p. 362) wrote, "[liberals] distinguish between the post-totalitarian economic system and the post-totalitarian ruling group, seeing the latter . . . as thoroughly de-ideologized, deeply disappointed with the existing system, and no longer identifying their personal and group interests with its maintenance." Liberals were ready to support consistent marketization holding (probably rightly) that it would quickly lead to depolitization of economic life and the reemergence of the rule of law. The Krakow Industrial Society exemplifies this attitude. Liberals also believed that the second option, immediate political democracy, was too risky and held a strong promise of populism. Following Hayek, they might have also thought that, if choice needs to be made between economic and political freedom, the former was more important because more fundamental and more relevant for the everyday life.

One of the mysteries that remains for political scientists and historians to solve is why did this option fail, despite strong support, based on a coincidence of interests by the official circles of reformers, economic liberals, and one part of the opinion-making elites? To many observers, the ending of the roundtable talks—which resulted not only in legalization of Solidarity but in partly free elections—foreshadowed the failure of this option because it ushered in political democracy that was incompatible with preservation of the Communist party in power. But there are indications, too, that the Communists thought that they would succeed in squeezing an honorable electoral result, which would thus allow them (with rules giving them an almost instant majority in the Sejm) to retain power.[21]

To a spectator, it seemed at times that Communists viewed roundtable talks and free elections as another maneuver in co-optation of society without realizing that they were actually putting their power at stake. Maybe the long reign, which was punctuated by numerous carrot-and-stick operations and designed alternatively to cajole and to menace the population, made Communist leaders almost impervious to the idea that power could be lost. Believing that they are involved in another of the periodic thaws, Communists effectively connived in surrendering power. When the outcome became clear, their demoralization and "fatigue of governing" prevented them from taking measures that they indubitably would have some twenty years ago. The period of economic liberalization permitted one part of the nomenklatura to find relatively lucrative positions: They had less to fear from the change of the system and thus less to defend.

The Rakowski government vacillated between the two options: economic liberalization alone or democratization. As Ryszard Bugaj (quoted in Dryll, 1990), recently put it, "I wonder whether the Rakowski government opened the door to a new Poland or it made the attempt, the last attempt, to prevent Poland's transformation."[22] The bill on responsibility of the Rakowski's government for marked deterioration in the economic performance states essentially the same: "Mr. Rakowski's government in its short tenure undertook efforts at partial modernizations of the social and economic system. However, attempts to modernize economic rules were not accompanied by social conditions facilitating economic change." It seems that the Rakowski government originally opted for the first solution (economic liberalization alone) but was then, often reluctantly, pushed by the unfolding events toward the second option: democracy.

The Balcerowicz Stabilization Program, January 1990–January 1991

The most important developments prior to the introduction of the Stabilization program (that is, in the period September–December 1989) were the decline in real wages and real devaluation of the official exchange rate. During the last quarter of 1989, real wages decreased by about 16 percent. About one-third of the eventual real wage reduction was already achieved by January 1990. The real (official) exchange rate was steeply devalued between October and December: It went from 1775 zloty per dollar in October to about 5200 zloty in December, i.e., the number of zloty per dollar increased by a factor of 3 while retail price index increased by 44 percent.

The program included substantial fiscal adjustment. Subsidies were further streamlined[23] with the objective of bringing them to a level of some 5 percent of GDP (as against 15 and 12 percent in 1988 and 1989, respectively). Total extent of planned fiscal adjustment was around 6 percent of GDP: From a deficit of 7 percent of GDP in 1989, the government planned to achieve a 1 percent deficit in 1990. Aggregate demand was also reduced through the wealth effect. Unification of the official and parallel market rate produced an important real appreciation of the parallel rate (see Figure 3). Population (and enterprises) whose holdings of foreign exchange amounted to probably $7-8 billion incurred substantial capital losses.[24]

Interest rate policy was to be entirely overhauled. Net domestic assets of the banking system (the IMF performance criterion) were supposed to increase by 20 percent in nominal terms in the first quarter of 1990. As the price jump in January proved much stronger (79 percent) than expected, monetary policy turned out to be even more restrictive than originally anticipated.[25] The real interest rate (measured by the discount rate) became positive in March 1990. From the beginning, the intention was to reduce rates in nominal terms in line with the declining rate of inflation.

If one compares the Balcerowicz program with the Price and Income Operation of February 1988, it emerges that the Balcerowicz program was both more comprehensive (e.g., foreign trade reform was hardly mentioned in 1988) and more consistent. It included a substantial up-front real devaluation of the official rate, which deliberately represented somewhat of an overshooting. This was done in order to avoid over-valuation later, when inflation inevitably continues for a few months. Parallel and official exchange rates were unified (as the current account convertibility of the zloty was introduced) almost exactly at the mid-point between the two rates (see Figure 3).

In drawing positive parallels between the Balcerowicz program and its predecessor, one must give due acknowledgment to differing political circumstances. We have argued above that possibly the key reason for the failure of the Price and Income Operation was political unwillingness (or impossibility) to resist wage increases combined with inability of those who designed the program to control accommodating policy of the National Bank. The Balcerowicz program was helped by: (1) the willingness to tolerate unemployment that inevitably appeared as restrictive fiscal and monetary policy began to take hold, (2) the ability to extract real wage decreases, and (3) the existence of the $1 billion stabilization fund to defend the zloty. In February 1988, the first two elements were politically unacceptable, and the third did not exist.[26]

The two much-quoted negative effects of stabilization are unemployment and a drop in industrial output. The number of the unemployed reached 1.2 million by the end of the year, three times as much as the original government forecast. The state sector industrial output dropped by about 25 percent (in comparison with 1989) immediately after the introduction of the program and stayed more or less there since. As employment in the socialized sector decreased by about 10 percent, productivity per worker also declined.

While one part of the decline in output is statistical (the growing private sector is statistically poorly covered, retailers might have over-reacted to initial decrease in demand by drawing down stocks and delaying new orders, etc.) or is irrelevant (a number of products were really unwanted or of very bad quality), the severity of the decline was greater than anticipated. A possible explanation may lie in the monopolistic nature of the Polish economy, where a cut in output by one—and often only one—buyer or supplier affects a number of downstream and upstream enterprises, which must also reduce production. Massive trade liberalization that was part of the stabilization program helped by providing alternative sources of supply and by stimulating exports, but the time left to domestic producers to adjust to foreign competition was probably too short.

The output decline was most important in production of investment goods. This was due to weak investment demand; demand, in turn, was low because of high interest rates (at least relative to the past) and, more importantly, because of unsettled questions of industrial ownership. Workers and managers were understandably reluctant to invest since they could not be sure that assets may not be taken over by the state and sold to outside investors. Centralized state investment has, due to numerous earlier decentralization measures, become quite small (e.g., accounting for only 2 percent of GDP in 1989) and was, because of the fiscal situation as well as the ideological preference of the new government, to remain so. New private investors were too few to make a difference to overall investment demand (and they too were affected by uncertainty and high interest rates).

Rapidly declining real wages, unemployment, and a drop in industrial output were juxtaposed with overly optimistic promises of "prosperity around the corner" that were made by some Solidarity leaders at the time of Solidarity resumption of power. By mid-1990, this situation had led to the first open signs of dissatisfaction both in the media and among workers. The first strikes also appeared at that time. The rumblings of dissatisfaction, combined with the distancing of Mr. Walesa from the Balcerowicz program amid signs that the presidential campaign may be in the offing, might have persuaded the government to somewhat relax its monetary stance (increase in credits to the state sector) and allow for wage increases.[27] Restrictions on wage growth were thus relaxed in July.

Still these were small improvements (from the immediate perspective of the population) and they proved insufficient to prevent convincing defeat at the November 1990 presidential polls of Mr. Mazowiecki. Elections were widely seen as a referendum on the first post-Communist government in Poland, and in particular on its economic policy. Mr. Walesa, who has a reputation for sensing well the swings in popular moods (which led to accusations of latent populism from his opponents) might have, in this case too, gauged well the public sentiment by laying emphasis on acceleration of systemic changes and by sounding some populistic economic themes.

At the time of the induction of the Bielecki government, the "integrity" of the 1990 Polish stabilization program faced renewed pressures, both domestically and externally. On the domestic side, the problems included a continued drop in industrial production, stubbornly persistent inflation oscillating between 4 and 5 percent per month (it rose to that level after the July 1990 monetary relaxation), slow privatization, and an increasingly appreciated real exchange rate of the zloty (in February 1991 some 10 percent higher than the official rate at any time since 1987).

On the external side, the situation substantially worsened in comparison to January 1990. Recession and disorder in the Soviet Union led to a decline in demand for Polish exports. These exports have very few alternative outlets as some Polish enterprises have been exporting to the Soviet Union (and according to Soviet specifications) for years. Furthermore, the terms of trade with the USSR strongly moved against Poland in January 1991 when Polish-Soviet trade switched to convertible currencies, which also implied that Poland must pay world prices for natural gas and oil. The Polish government expected that the switch to dollar trade would be preceded by several years of adjustment. It is estimated that the 1991 annual terms of trade loss for Poland amounted to $3 billion.

German unification has led to cancellations of the already concluded deals between the previously East German firms and Polish companies. Finally, the Gulf crisis had multiple negative effects on Poland. Iraq is a net debtor of Poland (owing some $400 million); Polish firms have been involved in construction works in Iraq; increased oil prices cost Poland an additional $300 million in 1990 alone. The only significant bright spot is forgiveness of some 30 percent (and possibly 50 percent if the IMF targets are observed) of Polish debt to official Western creditors. However, in cash terms, the current account improvement due to forgiveness was minimal since Poland was servicing only a fraction of its debt anyway. The key advantage of forgiveness is to facilitate new foreign investment and lending.

Conclusion

In the economic sphere the beginning of the end of Communist rule in Poland probably started with the Income and Price Operation in February 1988. Even if this was a better thought out and a more comprehensive operation than the previous ones (1976, 1980, 1982), its eventual failure showed that the country could not be governed without an agreement with society. Significant changes of systemic nature, both in economics and politics, were thus clearly seen as a sine qua non for the solution of the crisis. The Rakowski government was aware of this, and its approach was, it seems, two pronged. In the economic arena, it proceeded to a number of deep institutional changes, virtually eliminating all limits on the private sector activity; it began with privatization of state enterprises, introduced limited internal convertibility of the zloty, and created a two-tier banking system.

In the political arena, its actions were more tentative, and it will be doubtless difficult, if not impossible, to ever determine how far Mr. Rakowski and Communist elite in power were willing to go in that direction. It can be argued that they were unaware where exactly their concessions would ultimately lead them or even that they simply held a too optimistic view of their own popularity. In any event, the succession of events overtook those in power, and they had, however reluctantly, to surrender power. Mr. Rakowski's vow at the time of his induction as Prime Minister—that, if he failed in his duties, he at least expected to "fall from a tall horse"—was fulfilled, although certainly in a manner different than he envisaged.

The debacle of the Communist party in the Polish elections and the accession of the first non-Communist government in eastern Europe in September 1989 had far reaching consequences for the rest of the region. The domino theory at its best, democracy in Poland stimulated similar demands in countries where until that moment Communists were unwilling to envisage any power sharing (Czechoslovakia, Bulgaria, East Germany, southern part of Yugoslavia, Albania and, indeed, Romania); at the same time, it made a return one-party rule almost impossible in countries where Communist parties already transformed themselves into Social-democratic parties and, at that stage, at least verbally, accepted the idea of political pluralism (Hungary and the Yugoslav republic of Slovenia). Politically, the example of Poland was of crucial importance.

Notes

Branko Milanovic is affiliated with World Bank, Washington, D.C.

This paper expresses only the author's personal views. A modified version of this paper was published in *Soviet Studies*, 44 (3), 1992. The author is grateful for very useful comments provided by Luis de la Calle, Alan Gelb, and Witold Walkowiak. The usual disclaimer applies.

1. To mention only two excellent papers: Sachs and Lipton (1990), Rocha and Coricelli (1990).

2. In 1982, a number of retail prices were raised in an attempt to mop up excess liquidity. The relative prices of energy inputs were also increased. The inflation rate reached 105 percent, and real incomes of the population declined by 20 percent.

3. This measure is used in order to adjust for fluctuations due to uneven monthly payments of bonuses.

4. To make matters worse, agricultural procurement prices were raised in July in order to maintain parity between rural and urban incomes.

5. On an average yearly basis, the gap is somewhat less: real wages increased some 15 percent. The conventionally calculated increase in real wages, however,

overstates the real improvement in the standard of living because shortages became more acute in 1988. The same issue, but in reverse, reappeared during the stabilization in 1990.

6. There were three types of prices at that time: official prices, which were fixed by the government; contract prices, which were supposed to reflect relations of supply and demand but for which the government either set a limit or imposed obligatory notification before the increase; and free prices. The proportions of output sold at different prices were respectively 45, 35, and 20 percent.

7. The average interest rate paid on household deposits was 22 percent: With an average annual inflation of 60 percent, this yields a real interest rate of about –24 percent. The yield differential between the zloty and foreign exchange was startling: Real annual yield on the US dollar was +28 percent (valued at the parallel rate).

8. The equation is:

$$\log PER = 8.789 - 0.898 \log W$$
$$(0.00) \quad (0.00)$$

with $R^{-2} = 0.553$, where PER = real parallel exchange rate and W = real wage. Values under the coefficients show the significance level at which null hypothesis is rejected.

9. In the last quarter of 1988 (compared to the same period of 1987), convertible currency imports of foodstuffs increased by 38 percent; imports of medicines and other consumer goods by 51 and 133 percent, respectively. Convertible currency trade was in balance compared to a $226 million surplus in 1987.

10. There were some modest attempts to increase the percentage of foreign exchange kept by enterprises and to broaden the scope of foreign exchange auctions at which enterprises could freely sell and buy foreign exchange.

11. At times, enterprises used working capital loans to pay higher wages.

12. See "Poland: Economic Management for a New Era," *The World Bank Report*, No. 7999-POL, p. 8.

13. While pretax (and presubsidy) profit rates of socialist enterprises may be widely different, negotiated subsidy and tax settlements considerably narrow this range, and often turn money losers into profitable firms. See Kornai (1986) and Schaffer (1990).

14. The difference, however, is that in Yugoslavia, subsidization of the enterprise sector took place through coverage of the exchange rate risk.

15. The tax burden of the socialized sector decreased from 30.8 percent of GDP in 1988 to 20.1 percent in 1989.

16. As the then Deputy Prime Minister Sekula explained in a recent testimony to the Sejm, procurement prices were raised to avert farmers' strikes. Quoted from Dryll (1990).

17. Dollar deposits are converted into zloty at the parallel exchange rate (for household deposits) and the auction rate (for enterprise deposits). The stock of foreign exchange deposits kept on increasing continuously: from about $4

billion in 1987 to $6 billion by mid-1989. But even more important for boosting money balances was real devaluation of the parallel exchange rate.

18. Income velocity of zloty held by the population increased from a stable level of 2.4 in the 1980s to 3.4 in 1988, and was 4.75 by September 1989 (the last month of the Rakowski government).

19. The whole dispute about the indexation formula at that time has a slightly surreal touch. Arguments raged as to whether the coefficient should be less or equal to 1 while real wages were clearly rising and the government was manifestly unwilling to restrain them.

20. The word "liberal" is used in its traditional (European) meaning: to favor the extension of private sector freedoms and a minimal role for the government.

21. There are at least two signs that can be interpreted to mean that the Communists assessed their position relatively favorably: The Communists argued for the majority voting system even if it distinctly penalizes small parties; and in the summer 1989, after the overwhelming electoral defeat, General Kiszczak was still seriously considering forming a new government, not doubting that the Communists' erstwhile allies (Peasants' party and Democrats) would change sides.

22. Quoted in Dryll (1990).

23. Most important were the halving of medicine subsidies, the reduction of subsidies to loss-making enterprises, the nominal freeze on subsidies to coal mines, and the elimination of non-CMEA export subsidies.

24. Foreign exchange deposits in banks amounted to about $6 billion in December 1989, four-fifths of which were owned by the population. It was estimated that, in addition, between $1 and $2 billion were kept at home (see Krzyzkiewicz, 1989, p.29). Between January 1990 and December 1990, price level increased 95 percent while the parallel exchange rate (now equal to the official rate) devalued by about 4 percent. Real loss to foreign exchange holders (measured in domestic currency) was thus between $3.3 billion and $3.8 billion (about 6 percent of GDP).

25. See Rocha and Coricelli (1990, p.14).

26. Since the origin of the third was also political, it could be argued that all three elements were practically political.

27. According to many analysts (including Professor Gomulka, a chief government economic adviser), there is an intimate relationship between monetary and wage policy. In socialist economies, both restrictive monetary policy and incomes policy may be needed to curb wage growth.

Bibliography

Dryll, Irena, "Spor o Rakowskiego," Zycie Gospodarcze, August 5, 1990, p. 3.

Gelb, Alan, Erika Jorsensen and Inderjit Singh, "Life After the Polish 'Big Bang': Episodes of Enterprise Behavior," in Arye Hillman and Branko Milanovic (eds.), Transition from Socialism in Eastern Europe, 1992.

Hayek, Friedrich A, The Road to Serfdom, Chicago: The University of Chicago Press, 1944 (reprinted in 1972).

Lewandowski, Janusz and Jan Szomburg, "Property Reform as a Basis for Social and Economic Reform," Communist Economies, No. 3, 1989, pp. 257–268.

Kornai, Janos, "The Hungarian Reform Process: Visions, Hopes, and Reality," Journal of Economic Literature, December 1986, pp. 1687–1737.

Krzyzkiewicz, Zbigniew, "Uwarunkowania polityki" pieniezno-kredytowej," Finanse, No. 10–12, 1989.

Lipton, David and Jeffrey Sachs, Creating a Market economy in Eastern Europe: The Case of Poland, *Brookings Papers on Economic Activity*, No. 1, 1990, pp. 75–147.

Mates, Neven, "Some Specific Features of Inflation in a Heavily-indebted Socialist Country," Economic Analysis and Workers' Management, 1987.

Pant, Chandrashekhar and Ashok Lahiri, "Monetary Policy and Stabilization in Yugoslavia," Europe, Middle East, North Africa Department, World Bank, mimeo, 1988.

Rocha, Roberto, "Inflation and Structural Adjustment in Yugoslavia," Europe, Middle East, North Africa Department, World Bank, mimeo, August 1989.

Rocha, Roberto and Fabrizio Coricelli, "A Comparative Analysis of the Polish and Yugoslav Programs of 1990," mimeo, September 1990.

Schaffer, Mark, "State-owned Enterprises in Poland: Taxation, Subsidization, and Competition Policies," Paper prepared for the PHARE Project, European Communities, School of European Studies, University of Sussex, February 1990

Walicki, Andrzej, "Totalitarianism and Liberalism: Rejoinder to Mizgala, Critical Review, Spring 1989, pp. 355–368.

3

Taking Stock of the "Big Bang"

Keith Crane

This chapter assesses Poland's economic performance in the first two-and-a-half years after the introduction of the "big bang" of January 1990, the simultaneous introduction of a set of economic policy measures designed to quickly create a market economy in the country. It describes the key economic policies that were embodied in the "big bang," or "shock therapy," and then traces the economic consequences of those policies through 1991 and 1992.

The "Big Bang" Program

The Solidarity government that came to power in the fall of 1989 inherited an economy with high, accelerating inflation and declining industrial output. The government faced two separate tasks upon taking office: first, to stabilize the economy; and second, to create the institutional and policy framework needed for a market economy. The "big bang" was designed to help achieve both these tasks. In many respects, it was a standard set of stabilization policies such as have been adopted by other countries with high rates of inflation.

The main components of this program were: first, increased interest rates and the imposition of credit controls; second, reductions in budget expenditures and some tax increases to balance the budget; third, price liberalization; fourth, trade liberalization; fifth, introduction of a pegged exchange rate for the zloty and partial domestic convertibility; sixth, imposition of a very severe incomes policy through punitive wage taxes on wage increases above a set fraction of the inflation rate. Below I evaluate how these policies worked in practice.

Monetary Policy

The government used interest rates and credit rationing to control the money supply in 1990 and 1991. Interest rates were raised in January 1990 and have been repeatedly adjusted since. However, in many months rates were not set above the nominal rate of inflation, i.e., the rates have been negative in real terms. The government adopted this policy because it was concerned that an abrupt rise in rates would quickly force many Polish firms into bankruptcy. Polish firms, like their counterparts elsewhere in Eastern Europe, have virtually no equity. All of their operations were financed by bank credits so they were highly vulnerable to changes in interest rates, rates that were traditionally below the rate of inflation. The government also argued that after liberalizing prices, which would be recorded as a one-off adjustment in the official prices indices, inflation would decline rapidly.

In this case, interest rates that were less than the rate of inflation in January, for example, would substantially exceed the inflation rate by March. Thus, the government chose to set rates in line with its expectations of the future rate of inflation and not at rates exceeding current inflation levels. However, because interest rates were not set at market-clearing levels, the government was forced to ration credits. Credit rationing proceeded at two levels. At the top level, the central bank rationed credits to the commercial banks, the former regional banks of the National Bank of Poland, split off in 1989. The commercial banks, in turn, rationed credits to their traditional clients on an ad hoc basis.

These policies were unsuccessful in controlling money creation adequately in 1990. Zloty deposits by households and enterprises increased 345.7 and 514.8 percent, respectively. The increase in the stock of money reflects the weaknesses of the Polish financial system as well as the failure of the government to control the money supply. Initially the government lacked financial instruments to withdraw money from circulation. The Finance Ministry only began to issue its own bonds and bills several months after the stabilization program began operation. The central bank actually felt compelled to create its own bills in order to withdraw liquidity from enterprises because the Finance Ministry was so slow to react.

Moreover, high interest rates implied that fairly large sums of nominal zlotys were earned by savers, which immediately entered current and savings accounts. Aside from money created by the central bank, enterprises have also created money as they have extended credits to their hard-pressed clients and delayed paying bills to their suppliers. The government also injected money into the system because it lacked the instruments necessary to sterilize the large hard currency inflows that were converted into zlotys because of the dramatic increase in Poland's foreign trade surpluses.

The government has also had to grapple with the problems of a two-currency economy. In the 1980s the Poles began to hold most of their savings in dollars. In 1990, this trend reversed as the government paid monthly interest rates of 7 percent in January, falling to 4.2 percent a month on three-month accounts in December. As the exchange rate for the dollar remained the same for the entire year, in hindsight end-year interest rates were equivalent to paying 64 percent per year on dollars. Polish investors who took the plunge did extremely well in dollar terms in 1990.

Despite the increases in the stock of money in 1990, inflation declined dramatically. The year-on-year increase in the retail price index fell from 640 percent in 1989 to 250 percent in 1990. However, despite this impressive decline, progress in controlling inflation was somewhat disappointing. Inflation declined rapidly in the first half of the year. The retail price index increased by 79.6 percent in January 1990, decelerated to 23.8 percent in February, and fell to 5–7 percent per month in April and May to reach a low point of only 1.8 percent in August. However, inflation quickly returned to the 5–6 percent per month range for the rest of the year (Table 1).

Producer prices followed a different pattern. After doubling in January, producer prices actually declined in March and continued to grow at low rates through June, 1990. At that point they began to accelerate, peaking at a 4.9 percent increase in October, 1990. Inflation continued to be a problem in 1991. It hit 12 percent in January, double the government's hopes. It declined to less than 6 percent in February. However, in July and August it fell to less than 1 percent per month. Inflation returned to a rate of 3–4 percent per month in the fall of 1991.

Such high rates of inflation impose substantial costs on the economy. They make it difficult for enterprise managers and consumers to accurately gauge relative prices, as prices play leapfrog with each other. They also impose costs on the government as citizens substitute low inflation currencies like the Deutsche Mark or dollar for local currencies thereby reducing the benefits to the government from seignorage. Given Poland's proximity to such a low inflation country as Germany, the government needs to bring inflation rates down dramatically so as not to pay an exorbitant price in terms of real interest rate differentials to keep people's savings in zlotys.

Why has inflation been so slow to decline? Part of the problem stems from the nature of the Polish consumer price index. Some of the increase

TABLE 1 Developments in Key Price Indices, January 1989–November 1991 (Percentage Change on Month-to-Month Basis and Total Percentage Change for the Year)

	Jan	*Feb*	*Mar*	*Apr*	*May*	*Jun*	*Jul*	*Aug*	*Sep*	*Oct*	*Nov*	*Dec*	*Total*
						1989							
Production Prices													
Industry	11.8	6.1	5.2	8.9	5.9	6.7	5.4	34.4	29.5	43.8	34.8	37.9	653.0
Construction	10.3	13.3	21.5	7.2	6.8	7.0	3.3	27.9	25.3	31.7	36.1	41.4	680.5
Transaction Prices													
Export	5.3	1.7	5.8	12.8	12.6	10.1	0.1	14.6	21.8	34.7	56.6	71.7	701.8
Import	1.2	0.2	12.0	5.4	14.6	13.7	0.4	4.2	16.6	39.8	42.8	61.7	514.2
Retail Prices of Consumer													
Goods and													
Services	11.0	7.9	8.1	9.8	7.2	6.1	9.5	39.5	34.4	54.8	22.4	17.7	640.3
Food	5.7	8.0	8.1	14.4	9.8	4.3	7.1	80.4	44.5	65.1	17.4	11.6	876.4
Alcohol	2.2	8.2	7.5	4.0	2.0	10.6	24.0	32.4	35.0	92.2	16.6	9.5	658.6
Non-food	15.7	8.8	7.4	8.4	6.7	7.4	8.2	17.2	27.6	40.1	29.6	27.8	530.6
Services	15.9	4.6	10.8	9.8	6.8	2.8	8.2	29.2	22.6	25.3	30.3	20.2	444.6
						1990							
Production Prices													
Industry	109.8	9.5	–0.2	2.1	0.6	1.5	3.3	2.9	2.7	4.9	3.6	3.3	191.8
Construction	48.9	20.8	12.6	1.4	3.7	1.8	6.0	2.3	1.7	3.6	2.1	2.5	159.2
Transaction Prices													
Export	85.8	2.7	0.1	–0.1	–0.8	1.0	1.7	–1.1	3.0	3.0	8.1	–7.2	104.7
Import	110.2	3.2	4.5	2.9	4.6	–0.4	4.2	2.4	8.5	–3.1	–9.0	6.3	163.7

(*continues*)

Table 1 ***(continued)***

	Jan	*Feb*	*Mar*	*Apr*	*May*	*Jun*	*Jul*	*Aug*	*Sep*	*Oct*	*Nov*	*Dec*	*Total*
Retail Prices of Consumer													
Goods and													
Services	79.6	23.8	4.3	7.5	4.6	3.4	3.6	1.8	4.6	5.7	4.9	5.9	249.3
Food		82.8	17.2	–0.2	10.8	5.1	1.8	0.8	0.2	3.5	5.1	5.8	7.7
Alcohol	42.4	27.3	1.4	3.0	0.8	2.2	1.4	2.3	1.0	3.3	1.1	2.5	118.7
Non-food	70.7	32.5	9.1	5.9	3.3	3.4	2.7	3.0	5.7	6.3	5.2	5.6	268.5
Services	139.9	17.6	5.0	6.1	9.9	8.5	14.8	2.0	6.2	6.4	3.9	4.1	436.3
						1991							
Production Prices													
Industry	9.8	5.4	1.4	1.0	1.6	3.1	2.1	1.6	1.6	2.1	1.6		35.7
Construction	8.3	5.5	5.0	1.4	1.9	1.8	0.7	1.7	1.1	1.8	1.6		35.1
Transaction Prices													
Export	–0.6	1.7	13.1	–5.8	–4.4	2.6	12.6	8.2	–7.4	–4.2	N/A		14.2
Import	–16.5	16.7	1.2	–6.3	–6.1	10.2	–7.0	10.9	–4.1	0.1	N/A		–5.3
Retail Prices of Consumer													
Goods and													
Services	12.7	6.7	4.5	2.7	2.7	4.9	0.1	0.6	4.3	3.2	3.1		55.4
Food	10.5	3.8	3.0	0.5	–0.8	1.9	–4.5	–3.2	6.4	4.2	5.2		29.4
Alcohol	26.6	15.8	0.8	7.0	13.5	1.6	3.2	2.7	1.6	1.3	0.2		99.2
Non-food	12.0	6.5	4.5	3.4	3.5	3.4	2.6	2.9	3.0	3.3	2.2		58.3
Services	16.2	12.3	10.1	5.4	5.9	15.6	4.4	3.6	3.5	2.4	1.6		115.9

Preliminary data reported after the Ministry of Finance and the GUS in Polish economic press. January-October index for prices where November indices were unavailable.

Source: Biuletyn Statystyczny GUS (Monthly Statistical Bulletin of the Polish Main Statistical Office).

in the consumer price index (CPI) in 1990 was exaggerated. In past years, the Polish consumer price index has been biased downwards as many prices used in black market and private market transactions were not captured. Although prices on basic goods quadrupled, some black market and private market prices fell or rose very little in 1990, so the average cost of a more representative market basket would not have increased as rapidly.

Another major reason has been the inefficiencies of the Polish system. Poland suffers from the lack of an efficient commercial banking system. Traditionally, the government had gathered deposits through the postal bank and banks designed specifically to gather hard currency deposits. These funds were then redistributed through the national bank, which loaned funds to enterprises, and a special bank that subsidized the construction of housing.

Despite the creation of a two-tier banking system in 1989, most savings in 1990 continued to be channeled through this state-owned banking system. The state-owned banks continued to channel funds to state-owned enterprises, many of which were making losses. Private entrepreneurs found it extremely difficult to get credit from state-owned banks and turned to private money lenders or their families instead. The resulting capital market was extraordinarily inefficient.[1] Many entrepreneurs have found it extremely difficult to expand as rapidly as they otherwise could because of the shortage of finance.

Although bond and equity finance could provide some capital for the new private sector, this type of finance is a very partial, inadequate solution. Most households prefer to maintain savings accounts for at least part, if not most of their savings. They have little knowledge of or inclination to purchase stock or bonds. Polish private businessmen also prefer to finance at least part of their operations through banks, as it is extremely difficult to raise equity finance outside small groups of friends and acquaintances, and bond finance does not exist. Even if such financing should exist, small businesses the world over find bond and equity finance expensive and "lumpy." The one-off nature of much of this finance makes it difficult to adjust levels to daily needs. Thus, Polish entrepreneurs need access to commercial banking credits. The absence of a well-developed commercial banking system to provide these credits is a severe brake on economic growth.

Fiscal Policy

After recording a 4.7 trillion zloty deficit in 1989, equivalent to 4.5 percent of NMP, or roughly 3.8 percent of GDP, the government ended

1990 with a budgetary surplus of 900 billion zlotys, roughly $95 million, less than 1 percent of GDP. This was a very substantial turnaround in the course of one year, yet the end-year figures fail to explain the depths of the Polish recession. The key to this puzzle is in the lack of stability in the budget.

As can be seen from Table 2, Poland followed a highly erratic fiscal policy in 1990. The government recorded a 2.2 trillion zloty ($230 million) surplus in the first quarter. The surplus surged another 4.4 trillion zlotys to total 6.6 trillion zlotys ($690 million) at the end of the second quarter. At this point the surplus was much higher than the government intended and was responsible for a much sharper contraction in domestic demand than planned. In the face of a deep recession, the government relaxed fiscal policy in the second half of the year, running a deficit of 5.7 trillion zlotys in the final two quarters, and ended the year with a small surplus.

The abrupt tightening and then relaxation of fiscal policy made the problem of stabilizing the economy that much more difficult. Declines in real wages led to a collapse in demand, which compounded the problems enterprise managers face in adapting to a market environment. The subsequent relaxation of fiscal policy contributed to the acceleration of inflation as part of the deficit run in the second half of the year was financed by money creation. Thus, the recession was more severe and the decline in inflation less rapid than would have been the case had the government followed a more even fiscal policy.

One of the major puzzles of the year was the unexpectedly large budgetary surplus in the first half. The surplus was the product of much higher than expected revenues from profit taxes. Despite the recession, enterprises recorded very large increases in profits during the first half, some of which were passed on to the government in the form of tax revenues. The high profits stemmed from the complex interaction of the government's income policies, the devaluation of the zloty, price liberalization, oligopolistic domestic markets and import constraints.

When prices were liberalized in January 1990, producers "overshot" as they raised prices by about three quarters. Wages hardly budged in January as concerns about unemployment and government "jawboning" discouraged managers from raising wages. Sales fell sharply, but many enterprises still found lower sales volumes at higher prices more profitable than the larger volumes sold under the old system. Moreover, many Polish enterprises were able to take advantage of the sharp devaluation of the zloty and profitably increased exports to the West. Market forces took some time to eliminate economic profits by forcing prices down. Because many producers operate in oligopolistic indus-

TABLE 2 Developments in Polish Gross Domestic Product Produced and Used, 1985–1991

	in Billion Zlotys at Constant 1984 Prices												
	1985	*1986*	*1987*	*1988*	*1989*	*1990*	*1991*	*1986*	*1987*	*1988*	*1989*	*1990*	*1991*
Gross Domestic Product	9018	9398	9582	9978	9994	8840	8133	4.2	2.0	4.1	0.2	−11.9	−8.0
Industry	3725	3884	4007	4191	4101	3197	2650	4.3	3.2	4.6	−2.1	−22.0	−17.1
Agriculture & forestry	1314	1382	1297	1318	1324	1298	1355	5.2	−6.2	1.6	0.5	−2.0	4.4
Construction	858	891	910	964	961	822	877	3.9	2.1	6.0	−0.3	−14.5	6.7
Transport & communications	455	476	503	524	533	466	372	4.6	5.6	4.2	1.8	−12.6	−20.2
Trade & other	1218	1279	1354	1450	1522	1639	1785	5.1	5.9	7.0	5.0	−0.8	8.9
Communal economy	114	121	124	129	130	116	n.a.	6.2	2.2	4.0	0.8	−10.4	n.a.
Non–productive services	1335	1365	1388	1403	1423	1418	1133	2.2	1.8	1.1	1.4	−0.4	−20.1
GrossDomestic Product Used	8884	9252	9413	9803	9845	8328	8378	4.1	1.7	4.1	0.4	−15.4	−1.4
Consumption	6543	6505	6965	7145	7050	6226	n.a.	−0.6	7.1	2.6	−1.3	−11.7	n.a.
Personal	5693	5655	6106	6286	6311	5486	5891	−0.7	8.0	2.9	0.4	−13.1	7.4
Social	850	850	859	859	739	740	692	0.0	1.0	0.0	−14.0	0.2	−6.5
Investment	2341	2446	2449	2658	2795	2102	n.a.	4.5	0.1	8.6	5.1	−24.8	n.a.
In fixed capital stock	1872	1957	2037	2161	2115	1890	1805	4.5	4.1	6.1	−2.1	−10.6	−4.5
Change in inventories	469	490	412	498	680	−212	178	4.5	−15.9	20.8	36.6	−68.9	n.a.

Notes: The official national income statistics—both for GDP and NMP—are believed to have contained an upward bias because of systematic underestimation of price increases. PlanEcon estimates based on performance of the economy in the first nine months of 1991 as reported by the Polish Main Statistical Office (GUS) in the Plan Fulfillment Report and on the January–November performance as reported by GUS in the Polish press.

Source: 1985–90: Polish Statistical Yearbook 1991.

tries, these producers were initially able to keep prices relatively high. They were assisted by the slow pace at which the government reduced tariffs, which served to protect producers from foreign competition.

The rapid decline in the budget surplus in the second half stemmed from a sharp drop in revenues in the third quarter. The government reduced taxes, including tariffs, and enterprises faced increased competition, which in turn led to lower profits and profit tax revenues. The deterioration in the budget in the fourth quarter stemmed from a sharp increase in expenditures due to higher expenditures on welfare as the number of unemployed increased and on product subsidies as the costs of producing those goods that continued to have controlled prices rose.

Fiscal policy was much looser in 1991. The government targeted a budget deficit of 4.3 trillion zlotys (about $400 million) for the year. By the end of August, the budget deficit reached 18.7 trillion zlotys (roughly $1.7 billion), over 4 times the annual target, rising by over 4 trillion in August alone. A continued decline in industrial output, due in part to the sharp fall in exports to the Soviet Union, greatly reduced revenues from the corporate income tax and dividends from state-owned companies. Proceeds from privatization were also lower than expected while expenditures on social spending have grown rapidly. Because of the budget deficit, Poland fell out of compliance with its IMF program in August and was denied additional drawings.

Price Liberalization

Price and trade liberalization have been one of the successes of the "big bang." Before liberalization, shopping in Poland was a long, difficult process, but after liberalization lines disappeared almost overnight. Import liberalization has fostered an enormous increase in variety and quality of products. The retail sector has boomed as Polish citizens have set up their own shops or purchased cooperatively owned or state-owned facilities. By the end of 1990, well over half the retail sector was in private hands. Competition has increased and speculative profits have disappeared.

The wholesale sector has evolved at a slower pace. Western companies have rapidly set up distribution networks, especially automobile manufacturers. However, the old distribution systems have been slower to adapt. Under central planning, the wholesale network was the key instrument determining the allocation of resources. Directors of these organizations relied on orders from the ministries to allocate goods. With the transition to the new system, some of these managers continued to wait for directives before making decisions on sales. Others have used their position to extract monopoly profits. For example, meat wholesalers failed to reduce prices to retailers even though they cut prices paid to farmers. However, here too competitive pressures have been at work. Many producers have started to market directly to retailers or consumers, bypassing the old wholesale networks.

Trade Liberalization and the Introduction of Internal Convertibility

A combination of tight monetary and fiscal policies, the liberalization of foreign trade, and the introduction of internal convertibility has led to favorable changes in Poland's foreign trade. Convertible currency exports rose 39.4 percent by value and 40.0 percent by volume in 1990 as Polish enterprises cut prices and aggressively sought new Western markets to compensate for the decline in domestic demand. Polish enterprises continued to push convertible currency exports in 1991; these exports rose 27.9 percent in the first three quarters of the year in comparison to the same period last year, to $9,168.4 million. Polish enterprises have increased exports much more rapidly after trade liberalization than most Polish and Western economists had expected.

Despite trade liberalization, imports increased only 4.2 percent in value and 1.3 percent in volume from convertible currency areas in 1990. The very competitive exchange rate chosen by the Polish government and the sharp fall in aggregate demand accounted for the slow growth in imports. On balance, trade liberalization probably had a positive effect on the trade balance as exporters were able to import key components more easily, facilitating their ability to improve their exports.

Convertible-currency imports more than doubled to $9,511.5 million in the first three quarters of 1991. The rate of increase in imports has slowed, however, since the current surge began in September 1990 due to the devaluation of the zloty in May 1991, continued recession, and a sharp rise in customs tariffs since August 1991. These trade policies permitted Poland to record a current account surplus of $668 million on its convertible currency current account in 1990. This was Poland's first current account surplus since the 1960s, when Wladyslaw Gomulka was First Party Secretary.

Changes in demand in export markets has resulted in the reorientation of Polish trade. The European Community (EC) became the destination of 53.3 percent of Poland's exports in 1991; the former European members of the CMEA took only 17.9 percent. As recently as 1989, the EC accounted for only 32.1 percent of Polish exports, while the

CMEA accounted for 35.1 percent. Germany has become Poland's most important trading partner, taking 22.3 percent of total exports and providing 9.6 percent of total imports in 1991. In contrast, the Soviet Union took only 10.6 percent of Polish exports, although it accounted for 15.6 percent of imports in that year.

Changes in the commodity composition of exports reflect the structural changes that Poland is now undergoing. Exports of fuels continue to decline as loss-making coal mines are being closed. Exports of hard coal, Poland's traditional hard-currency earner, have fallen 32.2 percent in volume. Poland's loss-making metallurgical industry continues to increase exports as domestic clients cut purchases. Exports of other intermediate goods, most notably construction materials and wood and paper, have also risen as domestic clients reduce orders.[2]

The government has been less successful in its policies towards ruble trade. The Polish government used the ruble exchange rate to support state-owned enterprises in 1990. Despite rapid inflation in the Soviet Union, the ruble exchange rate was pegged, making exports to the Soviet Union profitable for factories that had no other markets. Although ruble exports fell 7 percent by value and 10.4 percent by volume in 1990 because of the fall in demand in Eastern Europe, exports to the Soviet Union rose as private Polish entrepreneurs and loss-making state-owned firms took advantage of the expansion in nominal demand in the Soviet Union.[3] Ruble trade ceased in 1991 as the last remnants of the old CMEA trading system finally disappeared. Total exports through September 1991 were only 1,205 million rubles (about $228 million), 15.1 percent of the level in the first three quarters of 1990. Ruble exports have been used to pay off the remnants of obligations from previous years or mark delays in payments from previously shipped goods.

Poland's exchange rate policy has been a success in that it has permitted a rapid expansion of trade and travel. By pegging the rate at 9,500 zlotys to the dollar, the government provided a nominal anchor for the stabilization program during a period when prices were in turmoil. However, as with all nominal pegs during periods of inflation, the real value of the zloty rose, which led to a deterioration in the balance of trade. The exchange rate was adjusted in mid-May of 1991 by less than 17 percent. However, continued rapid import growth and slowing exports convinced the government to abandon a fixed peg for a crawling peg in October 1991. The shift to a crawling peg marks reduces the role of the exchange rate as an anti-inflation instrument (where it has been less than a success) and restores the primary role of the exchange rate to the more traditional purpose of regulating trade.

Income Policies

The government's incomes policy has been one of the most bitterly contested parts of its program. Punitive taxes on wage increases above a set fraction of the inflation rate called the "popiwek" contributed to much lower increases in nominal wages than in inflation in 1990. Average real wages of employees in the state and cooperative sectors fell 28 percent. Consequently, workers and their unions have pressed for a relaxation of the popiwek. They succeeded in part. The entire decline in real wages in 1990 occurred in the first quarter. Real wages remained steady in the second quarter, and rose considerably in the second half of the year, especially in the final quarter, as the government relaxed its policies.

Wage controls were maintained in 1991 so continued inflation has not led to a corresponding rise in wages. In the first nine months of the year, wages rose close to 24 percent in nominal terms but declined, according to official calculations, by about 15 percent in real terms. Because of the decline in real wages, personal consumption fell by about 24 percent in 1990. Households kept food consumption under tight control; they also spent far less on nonfood commodities and services. However, statistical data on changes in the real value of incomes or the level of consumption do not fully reveal the qualitative changes in standards of living: the elimination of shortages, the increase in the range and availability of goods, or the ease with which shopping is performed. As noted above, they also exaggerate the increase in the consumer price index. Based on past patterns, I estimate that in 1990 real per capita incomes probably declined by 16.5 percent rather than by 24 percent.

Incomes policies are supposed to balance lower average incomes for those employed with lower unemployment. Poland's experience provides some support for this hypothesis. Total employment in 1990 fell by 7.5 percent in the public sector and 14 percent in industry (approximately 950,000 and 550,000 jobs, respectively). Registered unemployment represented 6.1 percent of the total labor force by the end of December 1990. In contrast, upwards of thirty percent of East German workers were unemployed or on short-time by the end of 1990. In general East German economic policies after unification were similar to Poland's, with the exception of incomes policy.

The total number of unemployed rose to 1,971,000 by the end of September 1991—more than double of what it was a year previously. This constituted 10.4 percent of the total labor force. As an indication of the change in enterprise management behavior, the share of group lay-offs in the total increased to 21.4 percent in September 1991, up from

16.3 percent for the whole of 1990. Companies have finally begun to feel the pinch of the market environment and reacted by closing completely unprofitable lines.

The prospering private sector, excluding agriculture, added some 400,000 jobs in 1990, which initiated an important shift in the employment structure. Retail trade outlets, trading companies, and enterprises based on foreign capital provided most of the new jobs. By the end of the year total employment in the private sector was 1.9 million people, 15.7 percent of total employment outside agriculture, up from 10 percent in 1989. The total number of people employed in private retail trade rose by a factor of 2.4, and more people were employed in communications, the health and social services, and education than in 1989.

Despite the country's reputation, the number of strikes in Poland in 1990 was small (250). Although 115,700 workers participated in strikes, only 159,000 working days were lost, over one-third less than in 1989. Poland's penchant for strikes appeared to have moved westward in 1990, as almost every East German worker participated in one strike or another in 1990.

In the past, the Polish government was the prime saver in the economy. The government deprived enterprises of depreciation and retained earnings through the tax system and taxed households through inflation. Furthermore, it restricted household savings by providing few incentives or means by which to save. With the development of a market economy, the Polish government will no longer be the main source of investment funds in the economy; enterprises will have to rely on retained earnings, depreciation, and borrowing from the household sector. A key question concerning future economic development is, therefore, whether Poland will be a high- or low-saving country.

Although savings patterns are not yet established, 1990 provides some clues to future trends. In 1990, dollar savings increased by 18.4 percent, and money in bank accounts by 466.4 percent. As the year-on-year inflation rate was 250 percent, zloty savings rose 62 percent in real terms from the very low levels of 1989. In short, despite the declines in real incomes Polish households saved 16.8 percent of their total income in 1990, making them a highly parsimonious group. The savings rate was identical in 1989, making the Poles a high-saving nationality.

The "Big Bang" and the Polish Recession

To this point, I have attempted to evaluate the individual components of the "big bang" in terms of how particular policies were implemented and how they affected inflation, the balance of payments, and employment. This section assesses the extent to which the "big bang" has been responsible for the current recession in Poland, one which was first manifested in the 12 percent fell in gross domestic product (GDP) in 1990 (Table 2). This decline rivals the declines in economic output in 1981–82 when GDP fell 14.3 percent from its 1980 level (10.0 percent in 1981 and by another 4.8 in 1982). The decline in GDP in 1990 was concentrated in the state sector, in particular in state-owned industry and transport. Nonagricultural private sector activity expanded 17 percent.

Despite initial optimistic growth projections for 1991 by the Polish government, the second year of the "big bang" did not bring recovery. Output in all economic sectors continued to decline in the first nine months of 1991. Industry, transport, and construction have been the most severely affected sectors of the economy; as these sectors have traditionally heavy weights in Polish GDP, GDP declined by 7–8 percent in 1991. National income used fell 17 percent in 1990 due to record trade surpluses, industrial output plummeted 13.1 percent, and personal consumption fell 23.3 percent. Gross investment fell only 8 percent and net investment 9 percent as more and more of gross investment was directed toward covering depreciation. Inventories appear to have increased. Data on stocks held by enterprises when divided by the producers' price index show an increase of 13.5 percent in stocks in real terms.

These statistics present a number of puzzles. For example, agricultural output fell 1.4 percent in 1990, yet the output of the socialized food processing industry plummeted 25.7 percent at a time when processors faced much greater incentives not to waste inputs. Part of the answer was the rapid growth of private food processors. In general, food processing requires less capital than heavy industry; private entrepreneurs find it easier to enter this branch. Consequently, the statistics mask the growth of the private sector and overstate the decline in output. On the other hand, private entrepreneurs have not moved as rapidly into textiles. Declines in output here were 40.5 percent. In contrast, sales by the apparel industry fell 30.6 percent, yet traditionally there is substantially more private sector activity in this sector than in textiles.

Surprisingly, in 1990, heavy industry and the machine-building sector were not hurt as badly as light industry. Sales of machinery fell 19.4 percent and precision instruments by only 16.8 percent. These sectors were somewhat cushioned as domestic investment fell less than personal consumption, and exports held up surprisingly well. These sectors were hurt in 1991, however, as sales to the Soviet market collapsed. In the first nine months of 1991, industrial sales were down by another 12 percent, the worst affected branches being machine building (where output during the first three quarters of 1991 vis-à-vis the year before declined by 23.5 percent), transportation equipment (–35.6 percent), and metallurgy (–20.5 percent). Those branches of manufacturing that held up best in 1991 included wood (–1.2 percent), the paper industry (+3.6 percent), and food processing (+2.4 percent).

Energy output also slumped badly in 1990. Coal production fell sharply by 30 million tons to 147.6 million tons. The percentage decline, 16.9 percent, was twice that of 1989, when coal output fell 8 percent (by 15.4 million tons). The decline in coal output reflects the process of restructuring taking place in this industry. In the past, the government operated quantity targets for coal output, but in 1990, mines were placed on an independent basis, so that high cost shafts and mines have been closed and investment has been shifted to more profitable investments.

During 1990 a three-year trend—in which prices for agricultural produce had risen faster than prices for manufactured products required by the agricultural community for investment and production purposes—was reversed. While prices for agricultural products increased fourfold, prices of machinery increased eightfold, and retail prices for goods and services increased almost sevenfold.[4] This deterioration in the agricultural sector's terms of trade resulted in farmers' strikes and deep opposition to the "big bang" in the countryside.

Net investment in fixed assets fell 9 percent in 1990, the second year of decline; in 1989 it was down 2.4 percent. Despite the repeated assertions that socialist economies invest too much in structures and not enough in machinery and equipment, the balance moved even more heavily toward structures under the reformed economy. Outlays on construction and refurbishing fell only 3 percent while the share of investment outlays on machinery and equipment fell to 28 percent of total outlays compared to 32 percent in 1989 and 33 percent in 1988.[5]

The major reason for the declines in investment was a 48 percent drop in central investment projects and a 36 percent decrease in local authority investment. A sharp drop of 20 percent in enterprise investment also contributed to the decline. The major bright spot was a 20 percent increase in investment by housing cooperatives, as the long-repressed demand for housing is spilling over into increased construction. In the first eight months of 1991, investment fell an additional 11.2 percent compared to the 1990 level. Investment in plant and structures declined more rapidly—by nearly 15 percent. Investment in machinery and equipment fell less than 7 percent, reversing the trend of the past few years.

What has been the main cause of these sharp declines in output? Adjustment policies must take much of the blame, but other factors deserve attention as well. First, Polish manufacturers are facing enormous changes in the structure of domestic demand. Consumption of milk and bread declined sharply in 1990 with the removal of subsidies. Households have been substituting purchases of fewer higher quality goods, some of them imported, for more purchases of lower quality goods (especially apparent in sales of clothing). Producer goods industries are also facing a shift in domestic demand. After the "big bang," manufacturers have had little problem hiring labor, so as to utilize machinery for two or three shifts. Manufacturers are also now turning to Western imports of highly productive machinery. The recession has been deeper because managers of state-owned enterprises have been slow to adjust to the new system. Although they have been quick to search out new export markets in the West, they have delayed layoffs, allowed inventories to accumulate, and had difficulty in revamping product lines.

Next, the slow pace of "commercialization" and privatization of state-owned firms has also slowed restructuring. In Western market economies enterprises facing bankruptcy are often sold to new owners that can provide an injection of capital as well as new management talent. The failure to pass a revised foreign investment law until well into 1991 and the slow pace of privatization rendered it extremely difficult for state-owned enterprises to obtain injections of capital or to change their ownership. Moreover, as noted above, the extreme rigidities in the Polish financial system appear to have made the costs of adjustment more severe as the economy still lacks mechanisms for efficiently allocating savings and selecting investment projects. Moreover, the state, the initiator of most large investment projects in the past, has abandoned this role. State-owned enterprises have not picked it up because they lack the resources and, in many cases, the authority to initiate substantial investment projects. Thus, it is no surprise investment has fallen sharply.

Finally, the disappearance of ruble trade had a severe impact on the Polish economy in 1991. In the past, ruble exports accounted for 8.1 percent of GDP. Exports to this area in 1991 were less than half 1990's levels, i.e., the decline in exports was equivalent to a fall of 4 percent in GDP. Furthermore, Poland has suffered a very sharp decline in terms of trade with this area. In the past it received much higher prices for its machinery and other exports on this market than it did on convertible currency markets while imports were relatively cheaper. After the transition to convertible currency trade, Poland estimates its terms of trade with this region have declined 55 percent, equivalent to a decline of 2 percent in domestically utilized GDP. In short, almost three quarters of the projected decline in GDP in 1991 can be traced to declines in exports to the former ruble trade region and the deterioration in terms of trade with this region.

Signs of Recovery

Despite political instability at the top, the Polish economy has started to show the first signs of improvement. In the four months of 1992, industrial output and construction began to rebound, all this without fueling inflation, providing hope that given the right policy mix, this recovery should last. Industries that survived 1991 in better shape seem to be staging a come-back. In the first quarter of the year, the food processing, wood and paper processing, and construction materials industry have increased their output from month to month. Output in metallurgy and most of machine building industrial branches is still declining, however. Overall, monthly industrial sales increased by 17 percent in March over February. As of April industrial output in the first four months of 1992 was only 6.3 percent less than the same period of 1991. April itself was up 4.5 percent over the previous April's. The March figure showed no change from a year earlier, while in January and February, industrial output has been substantially less than in 1991.

A strong rebound in construction continued from the second half of 1991 into the first quarter of 1992. While investment in new construction has not recovered, demand for renovation and refurbishment work primarily from private firms continues to rise. As a result of these trends, output of construction rose by 11.2 percent in the first three months of 1992 compared to the same period a year ago. Growth in private sector output exceeded 40 percent as increasing numbers of new private firms and joint ventures become operational. In the first quarter of 1992, the private sector accounted for close to 70 percent of overall construction output, up from 29 percent at the end of 1990.

Following a 7.5 percent increase in the consumer price index in January, primarily due to adjustments in government-controlled prices, prices in February and March rose by only 1.8 and 2.0 percent, respectively, despite a 12 percent devaluation of the zloty. The consumer price index rose 3.7 percent in April and possibly at an even higher rate in may due to the introduction of new turnover taxes and another round of utility price increases. Nonetheless, the threat of triple digit inflation has greatly receded. Assuming that the government can avoid monetizing the budget deficit, inflation in 1992 should fall to less than 40 percent.

The case for strong growth rates over the medium-term is very strong in Poland. The deceleration in the rate of inflation serves to provide a much more stable environment for investment, domestic as well as foreign. The accompanying declines in nominal interest rates should serve to reduce the cash-flow problems of Poland's larger enterprises. Reducing uncertainty and lower interest rates should serve to spur investment, especially in housing.

Moreover, the gradual emergence of a corporate structure and the emergence of markets in almost all sectors has changed management incentives and improved performance. Anecdotal evidence indicates that many managers are focusing on profits; gross output and gross sales targets are things of the past. Poland's strong export performance, layoffs and other cost-cutting measures and the disposal of loss-making assets by state-owned companies indicate that managers are pursuing profits (or at least attempting to avoid losses) rather than pursue output or sales targets.

The recent rise in industrial output appears to have been made possible by bringing unused capacity back on line. Although many of the production lines closed over the past three years will never be used again, as in other economies recovering from severe recessions, Poland stands ready to benefit from a strong surge in industrial output made possible by reemploying these unused capacities and making some small capital investments. Importantly, Poland has been slowly developing a modern financial system that should serve to allocate savings more efficiently than the old system. Low levels of capital productivity were a major problem in the past system. The new system should soon serve to improve investment selection.

With the passage of the foreign investment law in 1991, Western firms are finally beginning to invest substantial sums in the Polish market. The purchase of FSM by FIAT, a $2 billion investment, and the signing of a letter of intent with GM to purchase FSO are only the most prominent signs that foreign investment is beginning to flow into Poland on a substantial scale. Although foreign investment rarely contributes a substantial share of gross investment within a country, in the case of Poland these investments bring with them technologies, management and financial systems and links to marketing networks which should serve to speed the integration of the Polish economy with the rest of the world.

There are also some reasons for concern about the Polish economy, however. Poland has not yet conquered inflation, which will cause some problems. To integrate into the EC, Poland will eventually have to enter this system, but this is impossible, unless inflation rates move to West European levels. If Poland fails to reduce inflation to these levels, it will pay a cost in extending the period of integration. Moreover, if Polish inflation rates are persistently in the 40–70 percent range, the range of the past two years, the country will pay substantial costs in terms of lost seignorage and very high real interest rates needed to encourage citizens to hold zlotys.

Poland could still experience a sharp decline in the money supply, if the government does not handle its enterprise debt problem correctly. Currently, massive amounts of bad debts exist on the accounts of banks and suppliers. The Polish government will have to create a policy for dealing with these debts that does not lead to the widespread bankruptcy of potentially solvent enterprises due to a collapse in credit. One should be concerned about inconsistent policies towards foreign investment. Western investors still complain about an extremely slow decision making process; agreed points frequently come undone and negotiations go in circles. Decisions about privatization have been concentrated in the Ministry of Privatization; the resulting system is bureaucratic and arbitrary. If this system does not become more efficient, we are concerned that investment flows and, hence, economic recovery, will be significantly retarded.

Conclusion

To this point the results of the "big bang" have been mixed. On the positive side, private sector activity has soared in Poland. Private entrepreneurs are becoming established in the manufacturing and construction sectors, as well as in retail trade and services. This sector has cushioned declines in output in the state sector and created a substantial number of jobs. Because of the lack of adequate data collection systems, much of this output has not been captured in the official statistics, thereby causing Poland's performance to appear bleaker than it actually was.

Poland performed much better in terms of foreign trade than expected. The country ended 1990 with its first convertible currency current account surplus since Gomulka's reign. All the improvement was due to increased exports; convertible currency imports registered a modest increase. Exports in 1991 also hold up well, as imports have increased very rapidly. The creation of a convertible zloty also must be ranked as one of the finest achievements of the reform program.

The key focus of the program, the reduction in the rate of inflation, has been achieved, but to a lesser extent than hoped and after a longer period. Poland still recorded a year-on-year inflation rate of 250 percent in 1990. Less fiscal discipline in the second half of the year, the undervaluation of the zloty in the first half, and problems in sterilizing foreign trade surpluses led to more rapid increases in the money supply than hoped, which led to much more rapid rates of inflation in the fourth quarter than planned. Although inflation continued to decline in 1991, to monthly rates of less than one percent in August and July, lack of fiscal discipline keeps threatening progress to date.

The major failures of the program have been much sharper reductions in real incomes than expected and a concomitant decline in industrial output as consumer demand collapsed. In hindsight, the declines in real incomes and output in the first half of 1990 would probably have been less severe if the government had not devalued the zloty as sharply, had not pursued such a tight fiscal policy, and had reduced tariffs more quickly, so as to provide more immediate competition for domestic firms. By the same token, the government would probably have had better success controlling inflation in the second half of the year if fiscal and monetary policies had been tighter and the relaxation on wage restraint less abrupt.

Despite these caveats, the "shock therapy" provides a number of worthwhile lessons for other countries undertaking such reforms. One, given an appropriate exchange rate, domestic convertibility can be established overnight. Two, despite a monopolized production sector and state ownership, markets can be created and operate in these systems just by making it legally possible for them to function. Three, inflation takes a substantial, lengthy political commitment to conquer. Four, despite costs associated with "overshooting" as prices and exchange rates adjust, the "big bang" approach leads to substantially better economic performance than policies that seek to delay the introduction of markets.[6]

Notes

Keith Crane is Director of Research at PlanEcon, Inc.

1. While state-owned companies were paying negative interest rates, some private entrepreneurs were paying interest rates of over 5 percent per month on fully collateralized dollar, not zloty, loans.

2. The composition of imports is also changing. Imports of food products have more than doubled as have those of wood and paper products. As exports of wood and paper products have also grown, figures indicate the development

of trading patterns common in the developed West: countries import and export products in the same commodity category.

3. During the course of the year the government adopted a three tier exchange rate regime; exporters that were not able to export within prenegotiated trade quotas received 100 zlotys to the ruble as opposed to 2100 for other exporters. Nonetheless, Poland racked up a current account surplus of over 7121 million rubles as imports from ruble areas fell 35 percent by value and 33.7 percent by volume.

4. Farmers sharply reduced purchases of fertilizers, pesticides, and fungicides; between July and December 1990, for example, only 588,000 metric tons of fertilizer were sold—67 percent less than in the same period of 1989.

5. Despite the declining share of machinery in gross investment, there were substantial changes in the source of machinery. Imports of investment goods from the ruble area in constant prices fell 46 percent in 1990; imports from convertible currency areas rose 6.8 percent in real terms, one of the few categories in which imports actually rose last year.

6. Despite many bleak statistics, Poland's economic performance was substantially better than Romania's or Bulgaria's in 1990 and 1991 and the Soviet Union's in 1991. While Poland is currently poised for a modest recovery, the Soviet Union is continuing to experience rapid declines in output as market mechanisms have yet to replace the old system of central planning.

PART TWO

Foreign Trade Sector: Reform and Policies

4

The CMEA Demise, Trade Restructuring, and Trade Destruction in Eastern Europe: Initial Assessment

Dariusz K. Rosati

The traditional CMEA system of trade and payments in Central and Eastern Europe was dismantled in 1990. The political and economic changes that swept through the region paved the way for abandoning the centralized state trading regime and adopting market rules in mutual trade relations. Although economists and policymakers seem to agree that the switch to a market system will ultimately bring about substantial gains in efficiency, they also recognize that the short-term costs of transition are likely to be high, which would adversely affect levels of trade, output, income, and employment in the former CMEA countries. If not addressed in an adequate way, negative spill-over effects may cause serious deterioration in the economic situation in the region and even put the whole transformation process in jeopardy.

The foundations of the traditional system of trade and payments among the CMEA countries were established as early as the beginning of the 1950s and had changed little until 1990. The system was based on barter-type bilateralism in mutual trade, with central government authorities deciding on detailed trade flows in five-year intergovernmental agreements and annual protocols. The role of market and monetary instruments was negligible. The bureaucratic trade system of the CMEA, together with a highly autarchic development strategy inevitably led to a misallocation of resources on a large scale in member countries, which resulted in a heavily distorted structure of the national economies. External sectors of the CMEA countries were characterized by a generally low degree of international openness, strong bias toward CMEA markets—mostly the USSR—and distorted trade structure that was broadly inconsistent with the pattern of comparative advantage.

The deficiencies of the traditional system had been commonly known for a long time to the specialists in this particular field of research, but no serious reform attempts to overcome them were undertaken until 1989. Any market-oriented reform in external trade would have required fundamental changes based on central planning and domination of state ownership in the domestic economic systems of the CMEA countries. It was, however, impossible to challenge these paradigms for many years. Only after "perestroika" reforms had started in the USSR and sweeping political changes had taken place in other CMEA countries in 1989 did the renegotiation of the CMEA regime become possible; moreover, the rapidly deteriorating economic situation in the region, and especially in the Soviet Union, made the task of the CMEA reform very urgent.

Although bilateral and multilateral negotiations on the CMEA reform started in 1988, the real breakthrough came in 1990. Initially, the member countries contemplated a gradual transition to a market trade system, with various interim mechanisms and "shock absorbers" protecting mutual trade against the impact of the new, market-oriented regulations. That was the core of the Polish proposal to the CMEA summit in Sofia in January 1990, when the Soviet delegation suggested abandoning settlements in transferable rubles (TR) and switching to convertible currencies. The Polish proposal was accepted in principle by all CMEA delegations (except for Cuba). But after the balance-of-payments position of the USSR worsened sharply in the first half of 1990, the Soviet government made a unilateral decision to dismantle the traditional trade system and switch to trade in convertible currencies at world market prices (ECE, 1991, p.42). On 24 July 1990 President Gorbachev issued a decree "on introducing changes into the Soviet Union's foreign economic relations," which committed the Soviet government to bringing about a transition in economic relations with other CMEA countries, beginning 1 January 1991. This decision left little choice for smaller CMEA members—they had to accept the reality.

Gorbachev's decree marked the end of four decades of the CMEA, at least in its traditional form. It also signaled the radical change of the Soviet attitude toward its former allies: short-term (if not short-sighted) balance-of-payments needs took the upper hand over possibilities of longer-term economic cooperation. Faced with the fait accompli, in the second half of 1990 the CMEA countries concluded bilateral agreements among themselves and established the new institutional framework of trade relations. The transferable ruble would be replaced by convertible currencies (mostly U.S. dollars), artificial CMEA prices by world market prices, and detailed annual protocols by general agreements that were supplemented by "indicative" lists for selected commodities.

It was widely expected that the change of the trade system would immediately result in a sharp increase of relative prices of commodities such as energy, fuels, and raw materials, and a decline of trade in industrial goods within the CMEA. The Soviet Union, being the only large net exporter of commodities in the region, was supposed to be the main, if not the only, winner, while other countries were expected to run large trade deficits vis-à-vis the Soviet Union. Of course, the economic rationale for the reform was that in the long run all parties involved were expected to gain from better allocation of resources and mutually beneficial trade based on principles of comparative advantage. In the short run, however, substantial costs of the transition were expected, which raised serious concern about the ability of Eastern European economies to adjust to the new external environment.

At the earlier stage of the discussion on possible repercussions of the new trade and settlements system, three main scenarios of adjustment were contemplated. Under the first one, smaller CMEA countries would reduce sharply their imports from the Soviet Union and maintain external balance at the cost of a deep domestic recession. This scenario was seen as the last resort because—in view of highly inelastic demand of East European countries for fuels, energy, and raw materials imported from the USSR—the required contraction could have been socially and politically intolerable. The second possibility was to run large deficits with the Soviet Union, while trying to make them up with increased exports to the West at any cost, even dumping prices and pressing western countries for increased financial assistance. This scenario was perhaps most likely, but for obvious reasons raised concerns among western countries. The third possibility was to establish an arrangement for multilateral payments in central and eastern Europe, essentially similar to the European Payments Union (EPU) of 1950–1958.

The latter possibility received a lot of attention and generated interest among economists and politicians. In a number of studies, authors advocated the idea of establishing a Central European Payments Union (CEPU); the union was aimed at alleviating problems with trade and payments in the CMEA region, and would be supported by western financial contributions from the European community or elsewhere. Although the idea has some important merits, the CEPU seems neither politically feasible nor economically justified. Instead, other comprehensive measures are urgently required to address the present crisis in Eastern Europe.

I will develop this argument in several stages. First, I will examine foreign trade developments in Poland and other CMEA countries in

1990. I will show that although the switch to a new system would clearly entail a dramatic change in economic conditioning for trade, no major restructuring took place in trade of the CMEA countries in anticipation of this "shock" in the external environment. This section also highlights the collapse of CMEA trade in the first quarter of 1991 and discusses possible scenarios. Our view is that there is little potential and justification for maintaining much of the CMEA trade.

The Demise of the CMEA: Facts and Figures

Adjustment in the CMEA Trade in 1990

The economic performance of Eastern Europe in 1990 was affected by a multiple combination of external and domestic factors. Because the CMEA transformation was only one of them (although a very important one), it is quite difficult to isolate and estimate its impact. In response to a variety of shocks, foreign economic relations of the CMEA countries have undergone substantial changes. The official trade statistics reveal two main tendencies: a general decline in total foreign trade, and a diversion of trade of individual countries from East to West. Export volumes fell in 1990 in all CMEA countries (with the notable exception of Poland) by an average of 13 percent, with Romania and Bulgaria registering the biggest slump (by 46 percent and 26 percent, respectively). The decline of exports to CMEA markets was in all countries stronger than exports to other markets. Table 1 gives a detailed overview of trade results in 1989–1990.

The decline in exports in 1990 had different causes in different countries. In Bulgaria and Romania, the decline was due mostly to supply-side constraints that resulted from the disintegration of the domestic economy. These constraints were exacerbated by attempts to secure subsistence levels of supplies of goods and services in the domestic market, which increased the external disequilibrium. Czechoslovakia and Hungary (and to a lesser extent the USSR) in turn managed to increase convertible currency exports while they sharply reduced their CMEA trade. Hungary performed relatively better because of more restrictive financial policies at home and more advanced institutional reforms. On the average, in 1990 five smaller CMEA countries decreased their exports to the CMEA region by 9 percent (in TR terms) and increased their exports to developed market economies by 7 percent (in dollar terms), although in some cases the actual export diversion was probably smaller than suggested by these figures (e.g., Poland).

All CMEA countries also reported a decline in imports (apparently with the exception of the USSR, but the Soviet data are still preliminary

TABLE 1 Changes in Foreign Trade Value of the CMEA Countries, 1989–1990, by Country Groups, in percent

Country and trade partner group	*Exports*			*Imports*		
	1988	*1989*	*1990*	*1988*	*1989*	*1990*
Bulgaria						
World	9.1	–6.2	–17.8	3.4	–9.2	–15.0
Socialist countries	6.5	–3.6	–25.3	–5.4	–10.2	–17.4
Developed market economies	3.3	17.2	–12.4	4.4	0.6	–26.7
Developing countries	–3.5	–35.8	4.5	81.3	–8.7	–22.6
Czechoslovakia						
World	9.2	–2.9	–16.7	5.8	–2.2	–6.6
Socialist countries	5.9	–4.7	–20.2	1.5	0.4	–8.9
Developed market economies	13.6	10.9	13.4	9.8	–1.6	28.1
Developing countries	–2.5	0.1	–10.9	—	17.0	–11.9
Hungary						
World	4.3	–3.3	–1.3	–4.9	–5.4	–2.7
socialist countries	7.9	–2.4	–13.6	0.2	–7.7	–11.1
Developed market economies	14.9	5.6	20.6	0.4	7.7	3.8
Developing countries	11.8	–6.8	–0.2	7.5	–22.0	60.9
Poland						
World	13.3	–6.6	14.9	12.8	–7.3	–15.6
Socialist countries	3.2	5.2	–10.4[a]	–3.9	1.7	–33.7
Developed market economies	18.5	5.3	40.0[b]	30.1	7.1	1.3
Developing countries	14.0	–3.6	—	12.9	–8.8	—
Romania						
World	8.6	–7.9	–49.2	–8.1	10.4	–3.4
socialist countries	9.0	–8.0	–45.3	0.3	5.4	–17.6
Developed market economies	4.6	–3.9	–45.3	–12.6	1.7	210.8
Developing countries	15.5	–15.2	–38.1	–23.4	29.0	–12.2
USSR						
World	2.7	–1.3	–8.1	11.6	6.9	5.4
Socialist countries	–3.0	–1.5	–19.2	3.0	3.0	–2.4
Developed market economies	7.8	7.8	14.3	22.6	21.1	6.1
Developing countries	2.2	2.0	–3.2	17.4	26.0	4.8

[a]"First payment area."
[b]"Second payment area."

Note: Detailed data for Polish trade in 1990 are given in the section titled "The Adjustment in Poland in 1990."

Source: Economic Survey of Europe in 1990–1991, ECE, New York, 1991, p.64.

and should be taken with caution), although the decline in imports was generally smaller than the decline in exports (except for Hungary, where the difference was rather insignificant). The reasons behind the import reduction were either domestic stabilization measures, as in Poland and to a lesser extent in Hungary and Czechoslovakia, or a foreign exchange shortage and growing balance-of-payments difficulties, as in Bulgaria, Romania, and the USSR. In the former group of countries, the decline in imports was the result of domestic output contraction; in the latter case, it was one of the underlying causes of output contraction.

As a result of disproportionate changes in imports and exports, most of the CMEA countries recorded increased deficits in their overall trade balances (or decline in surpluses). The deterioration of external balance was particularly strong in the USSR and Romania, and less so in Czechoslovakia and Bulgaria. Poland registered a record surplus, while Hungary's position remained unchanged.

Strong import diversion from East to West was observed in all CMEA countries, with the exception of Bulgaria, and it was in general more pronounced than in the case of exports. Actually, all countries except Bulgaria and Poland registered a relatively strong growth of imports from developed market economies; import growth ranged from 4–6 percent in Hungary and the USSR, to 28 percent in Czechoslovakia and 210 percent in Romania. On the average in 1990, five smaller CMEA countries reduced their CMEA imports by some 15 percent (in TR terms), and increased imports from developed market economies by 20 percent (in dollar terms).

If judged by these figures, the trade diversion effect seems to be indeed remarkable. Has this effect been precipitated by the prospective change in the CMEA trade and payments system? Can it be inferred that the smaller CMEA countries have managed to reduce their dependence on intra-CMEA trade in 1990, thereby making the switch to a market regime in mutual trade in 1991 less painful? A more detailed statistical analysis reveals that such a conclusion would need important qualifications. Such a conclusion can be derived from data on the market shares of particular regions (country groups) in trade of individual CMEA countries, as calculated from official statistics.

The share of the CMEA in total trade of some member countries has been declining since 1986–1987 and has been substituted gradually by rapidly increasing trade with developed market economies. The share of developed market economies exceeded that of the CMEA in the Polish trade in 1988 and in the Hungarian trade in 1989. In 1990 this tendency continued at an accelerating pace in other CMEA countries as well.

However, it seems more important that a significant part of the apparent trade adjustment, especially in 1989–1990, has been due to changes in the national ruble-dollar cross rates, which systematically tend to reduce the proportion of ruble trade in total trade. In addition, the apparent trade reduction in 1990 was generally greater for trade with smaller CMEA countries than with the USSR; this situation reinforced the "radial" structure of intra-CMEA trade, in which the Soviet Union is the dominant partner.

Furthermore, the apparent trade diversion does not seem to be an outcome of a consistent government policy. Domestic imbalances and problems with external payments that all Eastern European countries experienced have simply enforced cuts in less vital trade links. These cuts have strengthened the relative share of "hard" goods trade flows that concentrate in relations with developed market economies (consumer goods) and the USSR (fuels and raw materials); the primary trade losers are smaller CMEA members and developing countries. This seems to be confirmed by the asymmetry of the diversion effects: The import diversion has been much stronger than the export diversion, which demonstrates the "emergency" rather than structural character of the changes in trade patterns of the CMEA countries.

The export and import market shares are not always good indicators of the intensity of bilateral relations because they are quite sensitive to demand and supply conditions. The share of a given market (region) in a country's exports may increase as a result of a greater proportion of declining exports to other markets rather than as a result of sales expansion. Remember that in the 1980s several countries in Eastern Europe experienced more or less pronounced contraction of output and trade.

To deal with possible distortions, it is advisable to apply relative trade shares, commonly known as "trade intensity coefficients."[1] Normally, differences in trade intensity coefficients reflect geographical distance as well as historical and political ties between any two countries (markets, regions). Changes in the value of the coefficient are assumed to reflect mainly changes in economic and trade policies, e.g., establishing or dismantling a customs union. It may therefore be of interest to see whether the perspective of eliminating intra-CMEA trade preferences affected trade patterns in 1989–1990.

The analysis of trade intensity coefficients allows for some interesting observations. First, they confirm a strong bias in CMEA trade toward CMEA markets and against DME markets for all CMEA countries, but especially for Bulgaria and the USSR. In general, coefficients for intra-group trade are much higher in the CMEA than in other country groupings, such as EC or EFTA (for instance, for EFTA members the trade intensity coefficients rarely exceed 3 for intra-group trading partners). Next, the results confirm the "radial" structure of the CMEA trade, because trade links with the Soviet Union are much stronger than links with other CMEA partners (the coefficients for exports to the Soviet market are on average 1.5–2 times higher).

Finally, the comparison of coefficients for EE6 and EE5 groups suggests that the GDR was an important trade partner in the group, which is confirmed by generally lower coefficients for EE5 group than for EE6 group. The unification of Germany has left the remaining European CMEA countries with relatively weak trade links. Fourth, the role of intra-CMEA trade actually increased, or remained broadly the same, for all CMeA countries during the 1980s. Only in 1990 could a decline of trade intensity within the CMEA be observed, especially for Poland, Hungary, and Czechoslovakia. These countries also recorded some trade diversion from East to West, as illustrated by increasing values of coefficients for DMEs in 1989–1990. However, the process has not led to restored "neutral" proportions in trade: The trade intensity coefficients for DMEs are in all cases below unity.

The Adjustment in Poland in 1990

The unprecedented expansion of hard currency exports in Poland has been mainly due to a sharp reduction of domestic demand following the "crash" stabilization program in 1990 and to a deep devaluation of the Polish currency (by more than 80 percent between 1 December 1990 and 1 January 1991). Such an "expenditure switch" reaction could have been foreseen, although the actual results went far beyond expectations.[2]

By contrast, the actual picture of trade with formerly "socialist" economies is more complicated. The analysis faces insurmountable statistical and aggregation problems, especially in the case of the Polish-Soviet trade. For instance, the official trade data suggest that a major trade restructuring in favor of developed market economies took place from 1986–1989 and reduced the share of CMEA countries in the Polish trade from 49 percent to 35 percent for exports and from 55 percent to 33 percent for imports. However, a large part of this change has probably been due to manipulations in the official cross exchange rates (the steady increase of the dollar rate from 1.76 TR/$ in 1985 to 4.52 TR/$ in 1990). The aggregation and statistical problems have become especially difficult in 1990 (for an extensive discussion of this issue, see *Economic Bulletin for Europe*, vol. 42/90, Chapter 2).

Three tendencies can be observed from the figures for trade with the CMEA countries and the USSR from 1989–1990 (see Table 2). First, the transferable ruble trade declined (as expected), although in the final months of 1990 ruble exports to the USSR made a surprising recovery. Second, there was a sharp increase of convertible currency trade with

TABLE 2 Polish Foreign Trade, by Major Country Groups, 1989–1990, in Billion Zloty and in TRs (current prices)

Item	*1989 in value units*	*1990 in value units*	*1990/1989 index*
Total trade (ruble and nonruble)			
Exports (in billion zloty)			
Total exports	19475.5	128246.4	658.5
Socialist countries	7914.9	36448.1	460.5
CMEA countries	6836.7	32474.2	475.0
Soviet Union	4048.6	19809.8	489.3
Imports (in billion zloty)			
Total imports	14767.3	75372.1	510.4
Socialist countries	5955.6	25144.7	422.2
CMEA countries	4858.2	22129.2	455.5
Soviet Union	2688.9	15275.5	568.1
Transferable ruble trade (in zloty, current prices)			
Exports (in billion zloty)			
First payment area	6608.7	22793.5	344.9
of it Soviet Union	3870.8	13822.8	357.1
Imports (in billion zloty)			
First payment area	4685.4	13489.2	287.9
of it Soviet Union	2621.1	6704.7	255.8
Transferable ruble trade (in TRs, current prices)			
Exports (in million TRs)			
First payment area	12210.8	11356.0	93.0
of it Soviet Union	7231.7	6978.6	96.5
Imports (in million Trs)			
First payment area	10106.0	6568.9	65.0
of it Soviet Union	5459.0	3275.4	60.0

Source: Author's calculations on the basis of Informacje Statystyczne—Handel Zagraniczny, styczen-grudzien 1990, GUS (Central Statistical Office), Warszawa, luty 1990.

CMEA member countries, especially with the USSR. The aggregation of the two trade flows with the use of the official IBEC rate (0.65 TR/$) tends to overestimate the ruble component; use of the national cross rate of 4.52 TR/$ obviously dwarfs the ruble trade.[3] Thus, the aggregation of dollar and ruble trade figures poses a major problem.

The dollar-denominated trade partially compensated for the sharp decline of the ruble-denominated trade. Table 3 illustrates the tendency of substituting ruble transactions for dollar transactions in the Polish trade with other CMEA countries. The data in the table show that the share of nonruble transactions increased sharply in the second half of

TABLE 3 Share of Ruble and Nonruble (convertible currency) Transactions in the Polish Trade with Selected CMEA Countries, 1990 and 1991

	1990				1991
Country/transaction	*First quarter*	*Second quarter*	*Third quarter*	*Fourth quarter*	*First quarter*
USSR					
Ruble trade					
Exports	80.5	71.8	66.0	56.2	31.5
Imports	76.9	65.2	36.4	24.1	5.8
Nonruble trade					
Exports	19.5	28.2	34.0	43.8	68.5
Imports	23.1	34.8	63.6	75.9	94.2
Bulgaria					
Ruble trade					
Exports	96.8	92.3	81.4	83.0	17.6
Imports	98.6	99.0	80.6	77.2	69.2
Nonruble					
Exports	3.2	7.7	18.6	17.0	82.4
Imports	1.4	1.0	19.4	22.8	30.8
Czechoslovakia					
Ruble trade					
Exports	87.3	79.2	84.3	80.8	23.6
Imports	98.5	97.4	96.0	91.9	56.4
Nonruble trade					
Exports	12.7	20.8	15.7	19.2	76.4
Imports	1.5	2.6	4.0	8.1	43.6
Hungary					
Ruble trade					
Exports	88.2	77.9	54.5	59.8	10.3
Imports	83.3	66.7	60.2	67.3	50.5
Nonruble trade					
Exports	11.8	22.1	45.5	40.2	89.7
Imports	16.7	32.3	39.8	32.7	49.5

Source: Central Statistical Office (see Table 2).

1990 in anticipation of the switch to convertible currency trade, which was announced in Gorbachev's decree in July and planned to take effect 1 January 1991. The change was particularly strong in the case of imports from the USSR—in the last quarter of 1990 75 percent of imports were paid for with convertible currencies. Thus, we may assume that a major part of the impact from the switch to convertible currencies had been absorbed by the Polish economy in 1990.

Third, the role of the private sector in Polish-CMEA trade increased considerably in 1990. Private companies were very active in the Soviet market. However, this otherwise positive tendency produced another statistical difficulty because the rules of reporting on foreign trade transactions by various economic units in Poland in 1990 were inconsistent. While the trade of state sector enterprises was recorded on the "bill" basis ("faktura," or FE and FI documents), copies of which were transferred to the Central Statistical office, trade by private sector companies was registered on the basis of customs declarations only. As a result, it is rather difficult to come up with accurate figures on the volume of trade with the CMEA countries in 1990.

As illustrated by the data in Tables 2 and 3, the convertible currency trade expanded, although the transferable ruble trade sharply diminished, especially on the import side. However, the final outcome in terms of volume changes cannot be directly determined, as Polish statistics for 1990 do not provide separate figures on ruble and nonruble trade. Therefore, I have applied an indirect estimating procedure (details are available upon request).

The results suggest a strong decline in the volume of imports from the USSR (from –9 percent to –24 percent); but in the case of exports, results are inconclusive. The two estimates that appear to be most reliable (the "shadow" cross rate conversion and the export price deflator) show a relatively minor change in the volume of exports (between –9 percent and +6 percent), but this is probably all we can reasonably state. In any case, it is by no means certain that the Polish exports to the USSR declined in 1990 in real terms; if this was the case, the decline might have been rather small. This relatively strong export performance was due to a combination of factors, with the domestic recession, expansion of private trade, and reexports to the Soviet market playing perhaps the most important roles.

The Polish government tried to curb the excessive ruble-denominated exports to the USSR with the use of a differential exchange rate policy. On 1 June 1990 a lower ruble exchange rate of 1000 zloty/TR was established for all exports not included in the annual trade protocol. Since export expansion continued, with ruble balances accumulating rapidly, the exchange rate for "extra-protocol" transactions was reduced even further to 500 zloty/TR in August, before it was increased again to 1000 zloty/TR in September. This pushed the TR/dollar cross rate for "extra-protocol" transactions to 9.5 TR/$ (or even 19 TR/U.S. $ in August), which was far above the official cross rate of 4.52 TR/$ (not to mention the official IBEC rate of 0.59 TR/$). But these measures were not efficient enough. After a temporary slowdown in the third quarter, exports to the USSR soared again in the last quarter of 1990.

The effects of the exchange rate policy were to some extent neutralized by continuous export subsidies to the USSR. Unprofitable export transactions accounted for 20–25 percent of total exports to the USSR and were subsidized by the Export Development Fund (at an average rate of 70–80 percent), provided they were included in the annual trade protocol. Generous and largely automatically disbursed subsidies definitely weakened incentives for more radical restructuring in the state industrial sector, especially in shipbuilding, chemical, and metallurgical industries. Preliminary data for 1990 indicate that the share of exports to the Soviet Union remained basically unchanged.

It may be concluded that in 1990 there was no clear tendency to reduce Polish exports to the USSR. The policy measures to contain the excessive exports were inconsistent, and were unable to offset high export profitability stimulated by specific cross exchange rates and low quality requirements of Soviet importers. The impressive export expansion to convertible currency was mainly due to a reduction of sales on the domestic market, whereas the export diversion from the Soviet market to western markets took place only on a very limited scale, if at all.

How Big Was the Polish-CMEA Trade in 1989–1990?

The picture of trade inferred from the official trade statistics in the CMEA countries may in fact be misleading. The market shares are calculated from national statistics where trade figures are given in national currencies, which are converted from foreign currencies at official exchange rates. In the process, ruble and nonruble trade flows are aggregated at a national cross exchange rate (ruble-dollar). Depending on the level of cross rates, which are decided upon by each country independently, the ruble component of total trade may be higher or lower, and so will be the corresponding CMEA market shares.

As may be seen from the national statistics,[4] the same ruble transaction represented different dollar values for different countries. In extreme cases, cross rates differed 1.8 times in the early 1980s and 7.7 times in 1990. The impact of cross-rates differentials on trade statistics is particularly strong in the case of Poland. Poland had the highest cross rates after 1985, and therefore the real value of the ruble component of total Polish trade tends to be underestimated, at least as compared with other CMEA countries.

It is rather difficult to find the appropriate ruble-dollar cross rate that reflects the true value of the ruble trade in international market prices. It depends on the composition of trade flows, and on current prices in international markets and in the CMEA. Marrese and Vanous, in their celebrated study (1988), found that the most plausible cross rates in 1980 for Soviet exports to the CMEA and for Soviet imports from the CMEA were 0.52 TR/$, and 0.96 TR/$, respectively (for a different approach, see Poznanski, 1989). Some recent estimates made for Poland put the "real" level of the cross rates at 0.90 TR/$ for Soviet exports, and 1.11 TR/$ for Soviet imports from 1988–1989.

These results suggest that while the rates applied in the USSR and Bulgaria (as well as the official IBEC rate) are probably inflating the dollar value of the ruble trade (especially on the Soviet import side), the rates adopted in Poland from 1989–1990 definitely underestimate the dollar value of the CMEA trade (especially on the Soviet exports side). Excessively high cross rates for Poland (and to some extent for Hungary) artificially diminish the actual market shares of the CMEA region in total trade with these countries. If this is the case, then the apparent trade diversion from East to West that was observed in these countries from 1989–1990 may not have actually been so significant.

In order to verify this hypothesis, a sensitivity analysis of trade intensity coefficients with respect to various levels of the ruble-dollar rate has been prepared for Poland. The sensitivity test was run for the ruble component of total Polish trade (33.93 percent in 1989 and 16.9 percent in 1990), which was converted to dollar value under two different assumptions: (1) at the constant cross rate taken from 1988 (2.21 TR/$), and (2) at the arithmetic average rates for CMEA countries in 1989 and 1990. In both cases, the dollar value of ruble trade increases significantly, and the trade diversion effect diminishes. The results suggest that the CMEA-orientation of the Polish trade might have been not lower but higher from 1989–1990 as compared with 1985–1987, and that in reality there was no significant adjustment in the Polish trade from 1989–1990.

The Adjustment in 1991: The Trade Destruction

The trade balance turned around dramatically in 1991 when the new settlements rules were introduced in the CMEA trade. The data for the first quarter are alarming. While volumes of exports and imports declined sharply, the value of imports from the USSR rose substantially because of price changes, which turned the trade balance from surplus to deficit (see Table 4). The overall trade deficit of 3.2 trillion zl (some $335 million) in the first quarter signals a fundamental reversal in the Polish external position. In the corresponding period of 1990, Poland registered a trade surplus of almost 9 trillion zl. In 1991, despite a continuous recession (industrial output in the first quarter of 1991 decreased from 1990 by 4.3 percent), imports rose sharply while exports stagnated. The reversal was particularly strong in trade with the CMEA countries, where a surplus of 2892 billion zl in 1990 (first quarter) was replaced by a deficit of almost the same magnitude (2973 billion zl), entirely due to the huge deficit in trade with the USSR. Because the level of economic activity in the real sector remained basically unchanged,

TABLE 4 Polish Foreign Trade: Total and with the CMEA Countries, January–March 1991, in Billion Zloty at Current Prices

Country and trade partner group	Exports			Imports		
	1988	1989	1990	1988	1989	1990
Bulgaria						
World	9.1	–6.2	–17.8	3.4	–9.2	–15.0
Socialist countries	6.5	–3.6	–25.3	–5.4	–10.2	–17.4
Developed market economies	3.3	17.2	–12.4	4.4	0.6	–26.7
Developing countries	–3.5	–35.8	4.5	81.3	–8.7	–22.6
Czechoslovakia						
World	9.2	–2.9	–16.7	5.8	–2.2	–6.6
Socialist countries	5.9	–4.7	–20.2	1.5	0.4	–8.9
Developed market economies	13.6	10.9	13.4	9.8	–1.6	28.1
Developing countries	–2.5	0.1	–10.9	—	17.0	–11.9
Hungary						
World	4.3	–3.3	–1.3	–4.9	–5.4	–2.7
socialist countries	7.9	–2.4	–13.6	0.2	–7.7	–11.1
Developed market economies	14.9	5.6	20.6	0.4	7.7	3.8
Developing countries	11.8	–6.8	–0.2	7.5	–22.0	60.9
Poland						
World	13.3	–6.6	14.9	12.8	–7.3	–15.6
Socialist countries	3.2	5.2	–10.4[a]	–3.9	1.7	–33.7
Developed market economies	18.5	5.3	40.0[b]	30.1	7.1	1.3
Developing countries	14.0	–3.6	—	12.9	–8.8	
Romania						
World	8.6	–7.9	–49.2	–8.1	10.4	–3.4
socialist countries	9.0	–8.0	–45.3	0.3	5.4	–17.6
Developed market economies	4.6	–3.9	–45.3	–12.6	1.7	210.8
Developing countries	15.5	–15.2	–38.1	–23.4	29.0	–12.2
USSR						
World	2.7	–1.3	–8.1	11.6	6.9	5.4
Socialist countries	–3.0	–1.5	–19.2	3.0	3.0	–2.4
Developed market economies	7.8	7.8	14.3	22.6	21.1	6.1
Developing countries	2.2	2.0	–3.2	17.4	26.0	4.8

Note: Trade figures for "World" and "CMEA" based on "bills" and customs declarations; trade figures for individual countries based on "bills" only.

Source: Informacje Statystyczne, GUS, Warszawa, kwiecien 1991.

the reversal may be essentially attributed to the real appreciation of the zloty and to the change in CMEA trade conditions.

A number of factors influenced the Polish-Soviet trade in 1991. The most important has been the terms-of-trade effect on income of the new relative prices of imported goods. It explains the surge of import expenditures from the USSR by 175 percent, with almost no change in the value of imports from other CMEA countries. In volume terms, imports from the CMEA countries and the USSR declined only by 6.3 percent, but exports declined by 45 percent. For the unchanged volume of imports from the USSR, Poland had to pay roughly $600 million , that is, three times more in terms of zloty than in 1990. This confirms earlier estimates that a large part of imports from the USSR (fuels and raw materials) is price-inelastic.

The shift did not lead in Poland to a significant decline of the volume of imports from the USSR in 1991; the so called "soft" imports were probably already cut from 1989–1990 (the imports volume declined by 10 percent in 1989 and by 9–24 percent in 1990). But with collapsing exports, the resulting deficit in bilateral trade is to be covered by net outflow of international reserves of some $300 million. If the current account deficit persists, it may lead to even deeper domestic stagflation.

The collapse of exports to the USSR is apparently due to the shortage of foreign exchange in the Soviet Union, and not because of Soviet purchases shifting away from the CMEA markets. Thus, the second important effect was that of the foreign exchange shortage. This is confirmed by reports from other countries, such as Finland, Germany, and Austria, which are also experiencing a sudden decline in exports to the Soviet Union. The Soviet balance-of-payments situation continued to be rather difficult for the rest of 1991. The Soviet Union faces large amortizations of medium- and long-term debt, which amount to $12 billion, and the financial gap is estimated at $5.6–10.2 billion (see *The Economy of the USSR*, 1990, p. 15). Prospects for capital inflows are rather gloomy, and the foreign exchange squeeze may be expected to continue throughout the coming years.[5]

It should be noted, however, that even if no foreign exchange constraint existed on the Soviet side, it would not be possible to maintain the relatively high export levels of 1990. The substitution of rubles by dollars in mutual transactions has replaced the "soft" budget constraint (rubles) of Soviet firms with a "hard" budget constraint (dollars), thus sharply reducing the Soviet firms' demands for Polish industrial goods. However, Polish firms cannot make any more windfall profits based on the distorted ruble-dollar cross rate applied in reexport transactions. Furthermore, the level of aggregate demand in the Soviet Union was expected to fall because of the general recession, which also affected import levels.

Thus, Polish exports to the Soviet market were bound to fall anyway in 1991 because of the trade-diversion effect and domestic-contraction effect, but the degree of collapse was indeed totally unexpected. According to available information, in the first quarter of 1991, Polish companies concluded export contracts with Soviet partners in the amount of $1.1 billion and effectively delivered goods valued at $130 million but received payments of only $15 million (Rynki Zagraniczne, 20 April 1991). What has been observed is in fact neither a trade diversion nor a trade adjustment: It is a trade destruction.

The trade with other CMEA countries is in similar straits. The Polish trade with Czechoslovakia and Hungary has declined in volume terms by half, and in the case of Bulgaria and Romania, it shrunk to negligible levels ($ 5–8 million of exports to each of the two countries). However, the impact on the Polish economy is of considerably lesser significance than is the impact on the Soviet trade, not only because the share of other CMEA countries in Polish trade is much smaller (some 45 percent of the trade with the USSR from 1988–1989), but also because the export and import trade structures are similar. The switch to a market economy and the change in relative prices did not have a substantial terms-of-trade effect in the case of trade with other CMEA countries. Therefore, no major bilateral trade imbalances have emerged after the switch.

Direct income losses produced by the terms-of-trade effect in trade with the USSR necessarily have multiplying effects in the production sector. Conservative forecasts done in the fall of 1990 predicted a drop of roughly $0.5 billion in industrial output and 50–60 thousand people unemployed because of the reduction of exports to the disintegrating Soviet market. Current estimates, however, are more alarming. About 100 large Polish state enterprises have a high share of exports to the USSR in total output (more than one third). The recent analysis by the Ministry of Industry indicates that thirty-three of them are now in an extremely difficult financial position because of the collapse of ruble exports. Some of them (at least ten) will definitely have to go bankrupt in the near future, and induced unemployment may reach 100 thousand people.

Contrary to earlier assumptions, income losses also affect the Soviet enterprise sector. In the first quarter of 1991, the GNP declined by 8 percent, and industrial production by 9 percent, compared to the corresponding period of 1990. The contraction continued in April (coal output was down by 20 percent, oil production by 9 percent, timber by 13 percent, nonferrous metal products by 18 percent, and meat production by 13 percent; see "Financial Times," 15 May 1991). Although a major part of the decline may be attributed to strikes and social turmoil, growing evidence suggests that the shortage of imported spare parts and production inputs (most of them coming from the CMEA countries) is becoming an important cause of the current output contraction. In a supply-constrained economy, a reduction of imports leads to a reduction of output and consumption through a negative multiplier mechanism.[6]

Notes

Dariusz K. Rosati is affiliated with the Institute of Foreign Trade in Warsaw.

The present text is a shortened version of a study prepared for the World Bank. The author expresses his thanks to the World Bank for financial support and to the United Nations Economic Commission for Europe for providing data on the CMEA trade. Helpful comments from Josef M. van Brabant, Klaus Wittich, Peter Mihalyi, and Kalman Mizsei are gratefully acknowledged.

1. These coefficients relate the share of a market in a country's exports to the share of the same market in world exports, according to the formula:

$$T(i,j) = \frac{x(i,j)/x(i,.)}{x(.,j)/x(.,.)} \quad T(i,j) = \frac{x(i,j)/x(i,.)}{x(.,j)/x(.,.)}$$

where: x(i,j) = exports from country i to market j;
x(i,.) = total exports of country i;
x(.,j) = world exports to market j;
x(.,.) = total world exports.

The coefficient equals unity whenever the share of a market in the country's exports is the same as the share of that market in world exports. If the market itself is expanding (contracting), both the numerator and the denominator will change in the same direction, leaving the coefficient broadly unchanged (see ECE, 1990, p. 275–276).

2. The stabilization program for 1990 assumed a moderate deficit in trade with convertible currency area (of $0.5 billion). Instead, Poland recorded a surplus of more than $2.2 billion.

3. The figures published in the ECE Survey (p. 75) show a strong rise in the value of total Polish exports to CMEA countries expressed in ruble terms in 1990, which is rightly termed by the authors as "something of a statistical mirage." With convertible currency component of this trade having increased substantially in 1990, its impact on trade value is exaggerated by the strong increase of the relative dollar rate implied by the shift from the ruble-dollar rate of 2.9 in 1989 to 4.52 in 1990.

4. National ruble/dollar cross rates in the CMEA countries, 1980–1990, in TR per U.S. dollar

Year	*Bulgaria*	*Czechoslovakia*	*Hungary*	*Poland*	*Romania*	*USSR*
1980	0.66	0.67	1.17	0.69	0.67	0.65
1981	0.71	0.74	1.28	0.75	1.00	0.72
1982	0.73	0.76	1.41	1.25	1.00	0.73
1983	0.75	0.79	1.64	1.35	1.00	0.74
1984	0.78	0.83	1.85	1.59	1.24	0.82
1985	0.79	1.85	1.88	1.76	1.13	0.84
1986	0.73	1.62	1.64	1.90	1.08	0.70
1987	0.67	1.48	1.73	2.28	1.03	0.63
1988	0.64	1.44	1.94	2.21	1.03	0.61
1989	0.65	1.51	2.09	2.96	1.03	0.63
1990	0.61	1.79	2.30	4.52	1.11	0.59

Source: U.N. ECE Data file, calculated from national statistics.

5. Still, it is unclear to what extent the foreign exchange shortage in the USSR is a real macroeconomic constraint and not simply an effect of the new—apparently highly inefficient—foreign exchange allocation scheme.

6. In order to assess losses from the trade destruction it would, however, be necessary first to determine what proportion of the CMEA trade was superfluous and should be discontinued anyway. The answer to this question would require extensive studies and goes beyond the scope of this chapter, though some preliminary assessment can be done on the basis of changes in trade in from 1989–1990.

Bibliography

Marrese, Michael and Ian Vanous, 1988, "The Content and Controversy of Soviet Trade Relations with Eastern Europe, 1970–1984," in Josef Brada et. al, eds., *Economic Adjustment and Reform in Eastern Euorpe and the Soviet Union*, Durham: Duke University Press.

Poznanski, Kazimierz Z., 1988, "Opportunity Lost in Soviet Trade with Eastern Europe: Discussion of Methodology and New Evidence," *Soviet Studies*, vol. LX, no. 2 (April).

5

The New East and Old Trade and Payment Problems

Jozef M. van Brabant

The spectacular changes in the eastern part of Europe, here collectively referred to as East, since 1989 have ushered many new problems into the arena of international economic relations. Until about 1990, most of these countries[1] had been intricately interlinked within the trade and payment, and indeed pricing, regimes typical of the Council for Mutual Economic Assistance[2] (CMEA).[3] Key factors underlying the pivotal problems with the CMEA and why the latter fell apart so abruptly in 1990 without the new leadership being overly concerned about successor trade and payment regimes have been amply sketched elsewhere (as summarized notably in Brabant 1991 a, b, c, d).

Therefore, my focus will be, first, to set forth the conditions under which a payment facility, such as a payments union, would be superfluous and those under which it might constitute a useful prop for maintaining regional commerce and indeed shoring up market-based trade ties at a time of rapid structural change. Next, I will briefly present the backdrop to the proposal for renovating the cooperation mechanisms of the new East and the types of criticism that it has elicited. Several technical details of the proposal to establish a payments union are introduced next. Then I will offer a brief discussion of who could have realistically been targeted as potential members of the payments union and in what way such a course of action could have helped to avert the alarming shrinkage of trade among the ex-CMEA members observed especially in 1990–1991. I conclude with a few observations on the intrinsic desirability of establishing a payment facility in the near term.

The Need for a Payments Union

To forestall the easy critique of advocating derogations from world market conditions, let me first outline the three circumstances under which there can be no need for any special facility, such as a payments union. First, it is superfluous when countries at near-full employment adopt some form of currency convertibility that comes close to the equivalent of the stipulation of Article VIII of the Articles of Agreement of the International Monetary Fund (IMF).[4] That should at least encompass automatic and anonymous access to foreign exchange for all duly authorized commercial transactions by legitimate traders.

A second instance occurs when the potential participants in the envisaged mechanisms can redirect their trade to convertible-currency markets without incurring sizable terms-of-trade losses. In the case of the planned economies in transition, one should further require that there be no sizable export-revenue losses either, since former CMEA trade consisted of special-order goods that would be all but impossible to merchandise elsewhere.

Finally, if potential participants were willing and able to finance their intragroup trade in convertible currency, even though their own currency is for now not convertible in the sense just defined, no payment facility is required. This case would indeed entail *de facto* convertibility through quite liberal foreign-exchange allocation mechanisms that, for now, fall short of emulating relatively free markets for commercial transactions.

Although under these conditions no payment facility should be innovated, countries may still wish to explore avenues through which they could economize on scarce foreign exchange or expedite the settlement of reciprocal transactions. There is nothing onerous or particularly unusual about establishing some clearing scheme. The facilities utilized, for example, within the context of the European Communities (EC) or the Bank for International Settlements (BIS) provide pertinent examples for countries with a fully convertible currency.

From the above it follows that I favor a payments union only to assist with the establishment of market systems in thoroughly reforming countries that used to be planned in some fashion. As such, it is a purely temporary device that should help guide the former planned economies toward current-transaction convertibility in the shortest time possible and at the smallest transition cost. Note that a payments union can come to grips only with temporary imbalances. Structural deficits have to be dealt with through structural-adjustment measures.[5] These may require loans that are specifically designed to finance the envisaged adaptation of economic structures. In time, these should enable the country in question to strengthen its export base sufficiently to sustain current-account equilibrium over the medium run.[6] Note that in some cases, funds furnished for structural adjustment could be administered in conjunction with the payments union. A pertinent example for the transition economies would be gradual winding down of current account imbalances due to adjustments in energy prices for any level of derived energy imports.

Finally, my advocacy of a payments union for parts of the East makes sense only if it is thoroughly integrated in the entire design to restructure these economies through national, regional, as well as international efforts. Such a facility would minimize the inhibitions to economic integration (through a customs union or other form of economic union) among the thoroughly reforming countries of the East. An economic union without a transferable currency cannot function. A convertible currency is by definition transferable; but the reverse is not necessarily true. Short of reaching *de facto* convertibility for the national currency, a transferable currency managed within the context of a payments union may be useful.

Without being able to pursue any of the three courses under which a payment union would be superfluous, Central Europe and the Soviet Union can choose from among three genuine alternatives. One is repeating the experiences of the 1970s and early 1980s by borrowing in commercial markets (perhaps with government guarantees and assistance from the Washington financial institutions) to finance their structural change over the medium run. But commercial lenders are highly reluctant to repeat their errors of the preceding two decades. Furthermore, massive borrowing for balance-of-payments purposes may simply worsen the external-debt situation and lead to a debt crisis, as it did in the early 1980s for most of the East. It is especially difficult for commercial banks to enact effective surveillance so that the funds are indeed mobilized to restructure production in a credible way.

To counteract the reluctance of commercial markets to finance the East's needs once again, it might be possible to set up a special borrowing facility at the IMF, similar to the oil facility inaugurated in the 1970s. This, of course, begs the question of who would finance the facility at this juncture and whether it could be managed specifically for the economies in transition. One might naturally defer this assignment to IMF but it should be noted that, like other universal organizations, they encounter great difficulty in allocating funds solely for one group of countries. Also, their particular philosophy is strongly rooted in demand management applicable to market economies. In the case of the economies in transition, it will be far more important to thoroughly restructure supply, however.

The last option is to sustain a massive loss of trade, either in terms of an erosion of the country's terms-of-trade or because of the collapse of export markets. The consequences of such a policy option would be a sharp downward pressure on sustainable levels of economic activity that may in due course lead to a protracted economic depression.

The experience of trying to introduce world market conditions in the economic relations among the ex-CMEA countries since early 1991 has only accelerated the contractionary trend. In some cases, this has resulted from the utter destruction of trade, something that was already evident in 1990. It then arose because of the obstacles arising from adhering to the transferable ruble (TR) regimes, given the severe problems faced by the Soviet Union to bolster exports of fuels and raw materials. By now, very little by way of ex-CMEA trade is left. True, some new markets in the West have been conquered. Some of the export increment has been reaped by diverting trade from East to West. The vast bulk of these export gains stem, however, from three other factors.

One is the special export facilities that some Central European countries have obtained in the West, notably the EC. The other is that a substantial part of incremental exports became available as a result of the skimming of domestic markets, following the massive destruction of purchasing power in the wake of stringent demand-management policies. Finally, the countries that have embraced "shock therapy" policies should not ignore that exports to the West may appear profitable when in fact they are not. In the short run, the inflationary effect of the switch in domestic price regime is such that inputs are still available from inventory at administered prices, but public enterprises have little incentive to properly account for replacement cost.

The logical question that arose in late 1989 is whether there could have been a way to avert this economic calamity by rescuing part of the traditional trade and, at the same time, by providing a platform for rebuilding regional economic cooperation on strictly economic grounds. I maintain that there are such opportunities, though none can be immediately placed in the context of world market conditions. One possibility has been to create an interim successor regime—a payments union—to the systems anchored to the transferable ruble (see Brabant 1989a, b) to facilitate the process of integrating these countries into the world market. The outlook for reinvigorating the CMEA through the orthodox TR pricing, payment, and settlement mechanisms was never encouraging (Brabant, 1991e). Another option is the formation of mechanisms for renewing regional economic cooperation, especially among the radically reforming Eastern countries as a means of staving off economic collapse, shoring up the base from which pervasive structural adjustment can be pursued, robustly anchoring the market orientation of these countries, and thus preparing them for fuller integration into the world economy on a sustainable basis.

The Backdrop to the Proposal

Having made it clear that I am not an advocate of putting in place something akin to a new CMEA and its highly unorthodox pricing, payment, and settlement mechanisms, allow me to backtrack to the situation of late 1989. Soon after these political revolutions, the countries explicitly stated that it was their intention to strengthen their emerging democracies through market-based economic systems, thus suppressing most of the paraphernalia of central or administrative planning typical of the preceding four decades but having to come to grips with their legacies. Such market-based systems would by necessity be characterized by separating macroeconomic from microeconomic policies and institutions. This should have given full rein to the profit motive as the paramount incentive to enterprise behavior, including in the public sector, and the unambiguous recognition of the validity of all forms of property.

Among the many obstacles slowing down, if perhaps not entirely inhibiting, this transformation were several elements in the sphere of foreign trade and payments. The CMEA countries then traded between 40 and 80 percent of their commerce among themselves, when trade is evaluated at official exchange rates; at more realistic rates, this interlinkage might have been on the order of 30 to 60 percent. Whatever the proper basis of comparison one might prefer, economic interdependence in the East through trade was very high indeed.

Furthermore, the vast bulk of that trade was, in fact, conducted under very special conditions. On the one hand, there was an intricately dovetailed transportation infrastructure that had been built up over at least three decades and various forms of production specialization. The former may not have been the optimal links that these countries should have strived for and the latter may well not have been justified on economic grounds. The network of production built up through intergovernmental agreements, in fact, reserved demand in one country to supply by a CMEA partner. These and related features were bound to exert palpable legacies for how economies in transition could proceed with their structural transformation and manage the burden of massive adaptation.

In this connection, it needs to be recalled that CMEA trade had been anchored to some modified form of bilateralism based on TR prices, which were only remotely linked to world or market-clearing prices; the immediate settlement of transactions through the TR clearing mechanisms; and the carrying over of any bilateral imbalances, whether planned or not, to subsequent trading periods. These conditions are very different from those typical of world markets. Apart from world prices that on the whole clear markets, trade among market economies is as a rule conducted in a multilateral framework and based on market relations. Moreover, in world trade the automatic, immediate payment system typical of the ex-CMEA is unknown.

In spite of much grumbling about the CMEA's defects in late 1989, there was little evidence that the TR systems would soon be in complete shambles and then abruptly obliterated. The radically reforming countries would have probably abandoned these regimes in their intragroup relations in any case. But that still left the vast bulk of CMEA trade, notably with the former Soviet Union, to be dealt with through accommodations that are basically inimical to firmly rooting market economies in Central Europe—one of the fundamental twin aspirations of the political revolutions.

Under the circumstances, the reforming countries would have had no choice but to sever their TR transactions from the rest of their external, and indeed their internal, economic activities. Otherwise, the ambition to link up domestic and foreign markets through the price mechanism, including a proper exchange rate, would have been distorted by the dysfunctional aspects of the TR regimes. One had already come to the fore in the form of chronic balancing problems in 1987–1989, basically because the Soviet Union was running sizable deficits that were not quite foreseen in the *ex ante* trade agreements, and surplus countries were exceedingly reluctant to build up TR assets. Indeed, the reforming countries began to adopt all kinds of interferences with trade (such as tariffs, quotas, and other nontariff barriers, health inspections of dubious merit, exchange-rate manipulations, political invective, and outright trade denial) to forcibly compress their TR trade.

By early 1990, however, it was clear that the disappearance of the orthodox TR regimes would now only be a matter of time. By mid-1990, under Soviet prodding, it was decided to introduce in early 1991 world market, or perhaps market-clearing, prices; settlement of imbalances in convertible currency; and clearing trade at normal conditions. Such adoption of market-clearing prices of a sort would significantly modify the CMEA terms-of-trade, which would entail a sharp deterioration for Eastern Europe and a sizable gain for the exporters of fuels and raw materials, notably the Soviet Union. In contrast to the upward drift in the export prices of raw materials, and especially fuels, prices of manufactures would be under downward pressure, especially in the medium run. Initially there would not be a sharp erosion in the prices of manufactures, provided that capacity utilization would have remained high; rather, there would be a forced compression of volumes of some goods because of the changes in export and import actors, for two reasons. For one thing, the existing machine park could be restructured only over the medium run and one could also expect certain products, especially consumer manufactures, to become completely unsalable in the East (the ex-GDR's experience—with the substantial destruction of production capacity—since mid-1990 offered a vivid illustration).

Moreover, as already intimated, demand and supply schedules would change because of new microeconomic agents acting in their own interest. Given greater freedom of choice, they were highly unlikely to replicate the earlier behavior of ministerial bureaucrats. Under the circumstances, especially in the short run, the demand of the smaller Eastern countries for CMEA goods was likely to change more radically than supply, given that not all countries were reforming and there existed considerable asymmetry between the trading patterns of the Soviet Union and the rest of Eastern Europe. Also, there might initially be a tendency for Soviet surpluses to be chronic.[7] But this depended crucially on the price of crude petroleum remaining at the high levels of mid-1990 and on the Soviet Union's ability to maintain oil output levels that would have afforded an exportable surplus of at least around 65–80 million tons.[8] Neither was then very likely, as subsequent events have amply borne out.

Finally, arguably the most important impact of the change to world conditions was bound to raise the demand for convertible currency, particularly for the smaller countries. This surge in the demand for convertible currency would occur for both transaction and precautionary reasons. A rule of thumb is that it is prudent for a country to hold foreign-exchange reserves equivalent to about three months' worth of imports. Another source of demand would be the financing of private trading and so-called noncommercial transactions (especially tourism), previously all conducted at special bilateral clearing conditions. Finally, because of the asymmetry in export structures, the smaller countries would have had to grant supplier credit of 90 to 120 days for most of their exports of manufactures but they would have had to pay cash for their imports of fuels and raw materials.

Such stocks of required convertible currency can be built up by running a net current-account surplus now or in the future (if borrowing were feasible). To do this in the short run would be impossible, given the excess demand for imports. It might help to borrow, but only if the intervening years could be utilized for structural change and thus lay the foundations for a solid current-account surplus. Even if alternative financing channels could have been explored, Eastern Europe would have had to fund the borrowing cost differential.

To build up exchange reserves essentially requires an investment in financial assets that at best yield some steady interest returns and generally compares unfavorably to the rate of return that can be anticipated from, say, economically warranted restructuring. Combined with the limited ability of the economies in transition to divert their ex-CMEA trade to the West without incurring sizable terms-of-trade and export-revenue losses, or the limits to conquering new markets with products for which these economies possess a comparative advantage (chiefly items treated as sensitive in international trade), there was danger of a massive collapse of CMEA trade.

Of course, the purpose of propping up the trade among the ex-CMEA members was not only motivated by seeking to rescue what had implicitly been economically warranted in the old TR arrangements. In addition, the emergence of new markets in the East provided an opportunity to build on unexploited existing (or static) and to exploit new (or dynamic) comparative advantages ushered in together with the industrial restructuring. These should provide room for trade creation, perhaps after an initial dip in reciprocal exchanges resulting from the elimination of trade previously justified on other than economic grounds.

It is important to be aware of these existing comparative advantages in the East and to ensure that, with the orientation toward market-based decision making, they can be vigorously exploited without necessarily impeding the strategic turn toward the West. Among the dynamic comparative advantages one should include the exploitation of scale economies in potential intragroup trading activities that had earlier been inhibited. This applies notably to foodstuffs and consumer manufactures. Furthermore, dynamic comparative advantages would be built up through industrial restructuring induced by the transformation processes themselves.

In addition to these dynamic comparative advantage, there are also sizable static comparative advantages, which fall into a number of categories. Some are elusive and will disappear over time as new production structures are put in place and consumption patterns will be adapted to prevailing market conditions and vice versa. These refer to goodwill and knowledge of each other's markets as well as the existing interdependence, chiefly in the machine parks and transportation networks. These links could be eroded only by destroying capacity, as well as the associated labor skills (such as in engineering), thereby exacerbating the economic recession, or through capital replacement over time.

Some advantages were warranted even under CMEA conditions, although it proved difficult to assess their true magnitude. These include goods of the Heckscher-Ohlin type and the benefits of being in geographical proximity and interlinked through a web-like transportation infrastructure centered on intragroup relations. There are also comparative advantages that have not been sufficiently exploited, because in the past trade was overwhelmingly determined by the need to exchange manufactures from Eastern Europe for fuels and raw materials from the Soviet Union, with the remaining intragroup trade being mostly residual. Moreover, these flows were negotiated at the intergovernmental level, and economic considerations oftentimes played at best a subsidiary role in determining the level, commodity composition, and distribution of trade.

In other words, there must exist a substantial potential for trade creation in Central Europe and the former Soviet Union, with respect to both their intragroup relations and relations with the outside world once the initial weeding out of unprofitable trade has been completed. Putting in place policies, institutions, and policy instruments to capitalize on these opportunities and to minimize the admittedly confined room for external trade diversion should rank high on the policy agenda of decision makers in the East. The argument follows essentially the logic behind the first decade or so of cooperation within the context of Benelux. Central Europe today is roughly at the level of economic development of Benelux in the late 1940s, but its market size (at least 63 million individuals) is three times larger. The positive experiences of this customs union could be emulated by the reforming Eastern countries. They should not, of course, follow the discriminatory regimes that the Benelux members resorted to in 1948 and then gradually abandoned in the 1950s. Given that the region does not have much experience with orthodox commercial policy instruments, and hence does not have to combat vested interests of this sort, the adoption of a fair external tariff with a minimum of nontariff barriers should be comparatively easy.

The mechanisms that could be designed to exploit these advantages should be rooted in market-based systems. That is to say, they should enable microeconomic agents to take maximum advantage of trading opportunities without them having to worry about the level of the exchange rate or the settlement conditions, both tasks for macroeconomic governance. Because of the pressure on external balances, it was important to reassure macroeconomic policymakers that eventual imbalances incurred in intragroup trade, which were bound to widen upon trade liberalization, would be facilitated through the payments union. Note that it is anticipated, not *ex post* imbalances as Rosati (1993) contends, that may constrain the exchange regime. Fears of large current-account imbalances may indeed inhibit swift market-oriented trade liberalization. Bilateralism would only exacerbate matters. A payment facility could temporarily help out.

In short, a payment mechanism could assist decision makers in weathering eventual imbalances, in buttressing the incipient moves toward the installation of market-based economic systems, in preparing these countries in an orderly manner for disengaging themselves from the legacies of CMEA cooperation and for merging into the world economy, and indeed in eventually lodging a credible request for full accession to the EC.

Core Technical Features of the Payment Proposal

The central purpose of a payments union is to accommodate bilateral imbalances by transforming them into multilateral ones, fostering trade liberalization as part and parcel of domestic economic reforms, and ensuring that net imbalances with respect to all participants in the union remain manageable. The latter means that the union should have sufficient funds to finance reasonable imbalances and ample supervisory clout to promote mutually reinforcing trade behavior that remains on the whole in the mainstream of promoting intimate ties with other partners; in other words, eventually full integration into the world economy. Indeed, any payment facility that inhibits the rapid emergence of more rational trade and domestic prices is bound to undermine multilateral clearing, however sophisticated the technical provisions laid down may be, as past efforts in the CMEA context have amply underlined (Brabant 1987, pp. 273–8).

To promote these objectives, the payment facility could usefully exhibit the following technical features.[9] First of all, the facility should be of limited duration, approximately five years, after which sustainable currency convertibility, in the sense of approximating the IMF's Article VIII, should be attained. Next, the facility would have two organizational units. One is the Clearing Agent, which takes care of technical settlement. This task is entrusted to an existing institution, such as the BIS. Participants grant each other unlimited credit until net balances are periodically reported to the Clearing Agent; with modern telecommunications, this can be done daily, if desired. If so, only the Clearing Agent levies interest charges, using essentially the rates common in international markets. But some marginal edge may be useful to encourage surplus countries to maintain their balances with the union.

Also, transactions should be limited to those incurred on current account, but not debt-service obligations. TR loans were obtained at disparate prices and unrealistic exchange rates. A mutually agreed conversion into convertible claims that can be actually mobilized might provide additional resources to the union, however. Moreover, other debts of some PETs are so large that they threaten to drain any intragroup surpluses obtained by these countries. Issues related to stocks of claims in both currencies should preferably be settled outside the framework of a payments union, for otherwise the pressure to divert earnings within the union to settle deficits with other countries would become insuperable.

Moreover, settlements of net imbalances consist of loans and payments within the provisions of an overall quota against which participants can draw. The quota consists of multiple tranches of hardness. Low quota drawings require less currency to be paid by the debtor than received by the creditor to encourage intragroup exports. A time schedule for hardening the tranches needs to be drawn up so that by the end of the facility's existence all payments can be effected in convertible currency (perhaps through a clearing mechanism).

Next, to make such a scheme manageable, as defined, there must be external financial resources to support asymmetric settlements as well as supervisory authority to make maximum use of the available resources to foster the transition. Both tasks should be entrusted to the EC or a European body associated with it. The Surveillance Board should consist of up to a dozen macroeconomists and a few financial diplomats, some of whom must be proficient in the East's affairs. The Surveillance Board should have discretion to temporarily slow down or even to reverse trade and foreign-exchange liberalization, which includes the discretion to do so on a discriminatory basis. But such events should be strictly limited and embraced only to safeguard the more general salutary effects of the transition process toward operational market-based decision making.

In addition, the settlement mechanism should be conceived in such a way that, on balance, the demand for resources from the central fund required for the orderly conduct of flexible trade decreases over time as a steadily rising proportion of cumulative imbalances is being paid in convertible currency to augment the fund's resources. An initial surge in demand for resources because of the one-off shift in trade and payment regimes should be accommodated, however.

Finally, assuming that Western capital support for a payments union is limited, it is important that the greatest bang be obtained out of every dollar or ecu appropriated. To reach this goal, tight supervision is desirable to ensure that the facility promotes market-oriented transformation commitments and includes domestic price liberalization and a significant relaxation of the prevailing trade and foreign-exchange controls all-around. The ecu is the union's currency unit. Microeconomic agents are asked to negotiate contracts in ecu. In the short run, participants manage their exchange rate with respect to the ecu. After some transition, perhaps six to twelve months, an adjustable-peg parity grid will be established and managed by the Surveillance Board.

A critical question is how large the initial capital endowment should be to reach the envisaged objectives of the payments union. Unfortunately, it is all but impossible to predict the imbalances that may arise with the transformation of these economies (Brabant 1991d). Hypothetical estimates, which utilize the trading patterns of 1987–1989 and 1989, suggest that the need for financing would be on the order of at least \$20–700 million and \$6 million to \$1.7 billion, respectively; the lower magnitudes refer to the three Central European countries while the higher ones pertain to all ex-CMEA countries of Europe.[10] Allowing for the unusual imbalances of the late 1980s and the surge in imbalances following upon trade liberalization, the endowment of an initial capital kitty should be about \$2.5 billion. Double that may now be required to accommodate the interrepublican imbalances of the defunct Soviet federation.

This comparatively small amount of temporary outside assistance should be seen against the backdrop of the constructive benefits that such a scheme may yield and indeed the sizable amounts being mooted in the context of the Group of Twenty-four's assistance efforts to the East. Initially the funds may be appropriated from existing commitments to the restructuring efforts of the economies in transition that cannot be quickly disbursed. But once a broader-based Western support program can be devised by the EC in its own name or on behalf of the Group of Twenty-four, the pledged assistance should be replenished, so that the resources available to the payments union would be truly additional.

On the Membership of a Payments Union

Recall that the original proposal for the creation of a Central European Payments Union hinged on pursuing a Central European Economic Union in order to assist in the transformation and especially in bolstering the market orientation of Central Europe. Membership can, therefore, be extended only to those former planned economies bent on moving toward the establishment of the paraphernalia of market-based economic decision making. This initially limited it essentially to Central Europe, but the proposal incorporated an evolving construct: The payments union should allow other Eastern countries, old and new, to join without encroaching upon the resources available to charter participants. The only condition would be a credible commitment to pluralistic decision making, which is a precondition for obtaining Western assistance, and to move decisively forward with the installation of market-based economic systems.

The East encompasses a potential market of some 410 million people. Even if some of the southern Soviet republics were to shun a market transformation for the foreseeable future, the potential size would still be comparable to the present EC's (about 340 million)—very substantial indeed. There is no reason whatsoever why such a potential market should be ignored on economic grounds. In this connection, it is worth facing up to the fact that especially the *de facto* collapse of the Soviet economic and monetary union is bound to lead to spectacular imbalances that cannot be financed; without accommodation, they will compress feasible levels of economic activity very quickly. At the very least, there is now a much broader geographical basis for a payments union and some economic union than I had imagined two years ago. Of course, under the circumstances, it would be politic to assign new names to the two endeavors.

I should stress, though, that even with the rapid installation of a payments and economic unions, however renamed, a sharp compression of the former trade could not have been avoided in the short run as the economically unwarranted trade needs to be weeded out. But matters have gone well beyond the sensible, and the precipitate collapse of intragroup trade has noticeably exacerbated the plight of the truly reforming economies of Central Europe and the former Soviet Union and may have contributed to leading several of these countries into a low-level equilibrium trap from which they find it very hard to extricate themselves by their own efforts.

Certainly the lamentable elimination of intragroup economic relations has many origins. Two are very critical: the profound economic, political, and organizational disarray in the Soviet union and the failure to replace the TR mechanisms with world market conditions. The former has indirectly affected trade among the radically reforming Central European countries. The latter has directly exerted a considerably negative impact on that trade, and the compression of intragroup trade, as a result, has been much more extensive than anyone had envisaged.[11]

A large part is due to the cumulative downward adjustment of effective demand because of domestic austerity policies and the ruthless elimination of unprofitable trade. But some part of the reduction in intragroup trade must be attributed to two factors that could have been taken care of through a payment facility. One has been the overreaction to the desirability of destroying the former CMEA economic links as a vehicle for promoting the chances of EC accession. The other hinges on the institutional vacuum in the transition economies as concerns their ability to clear transactions effectively because the organizational infrastructure for smooth external trade in the East is very primitive.

Thus, these countries find it very difficult to institute export-credit or export-guarantee facilities, to rediscount bills of exchange, to effectively clear reciprocal payments, to extend commercial insurance, and to emulate other normal practices in international trade markets. These observations apply even to the countries that have adopted either formal limited convertibility (Czechoslovakia and Poland) or that have fairly free access to foreign exchange (Hungary); the same prevailed for Yugoslavia in 1990. Moreover, the outlook for an expeditious change in that situation is not good. Note that whereas those conditions prevailed in dealing with the West for many years, for relations with the ex-CMEA countries they are almost completely new.

Conclusion

In my view, the most urgent task in rebuilding the external economic relations of the Eastern Europe and the Soviet Union is twofold. One is gaining access to EC markets and indeed making a credible bid for full accession in not too distant a future. The other is to assist with the institutional infrastructure for conducting all trade. If the latter were to enable microeconomic agents in the more advanced economies to engage in trade links that they find profitable, Western assistance should aim at fostering as wide an access to foreign exchange as is feasible. This would approximate *de facto* convertibility for merchandise trade and related transactions.

It is doubtful that even the Central European countries are now allowing their agents uninhibited access to scarce reserves for intragroup trade, but I may be wrong.[12] If the latter were to be true, I would still advocate the usefulness of having the clearing benefits of some kind of payment facility, but it would no longer be necessary to exercise a considerable degree of surveillance or to extend combinations of loans and payments within a payments union. But if I am right, and the sharp compression in capacity utilization would suggest that I am, then the claimed degree of convertibility is essentially a sham that for now can be adhered to only by the sharp compression in economic activity.

It would be regrettable to have the remaining countries of Eastern Europe, old and new, follow the same costly path toward absorbing the adjustment cost of instantaneous convertibility. A payment mechanism for them, and possibly for Central Europe, would hence be highly desirable. Perhaps most important, it would reinforce the commercial ties of these countries. This would be very helpful in shoring up the rebuilding of trade in conjunction with industrial restructuring, both largely brought about by independent economic actors pursuing profitability within a reasonably well-determined macroeconomic framework. Not only would it support the reform trends from within and strengthen intragroup economic relations, it would also transfer Western assistance in a form that least interferes with the emerging economic incentives for microeconomic actors. Finally, it would stave off either the pressure on Western markets to accommodate significant trade diversion or the contraction in levels of domestic economic activity in the transition economies during the restructuring process because of built-in supply rigidities in these countries.

The transforming countries need all the self-help that can possibly be mustered to make the most effective use of the assistance that the West is willing—and able—to deliver. And the latter's assistance should be better targeted and placed within the context of another large-scale recovery program, this time for the East, with recognition of the awesome tasks of building viable market economies in that part of Europe. But this collaboration cannot be confined to the East-West context. The political will to cooperate within the East *must* be regained to maximum effect, if necessary under prodding of the EC as the *de facto* hegemon on the continent. Only in this way can the adverse implications of large-scale Western assistance to the East for the rest of the world economy, notably the developing countries, be minimized and rectified over a comparatively short period of time.

Notes

Jozef M. van Brabant is Principal Economic Affairs Officer of the Department of Economic and Social Development of the United Nations Secretariat in New York.

The opinions expressed here are my own and do not necessarily reflect those that may be held by the United Nations in general and its Secretariat in particular.

1. The entire East minus Albania, which ceased participation in the CMEA in 1961, and Yugoslavia, which was only an associate member.

2. In what follows, I shall refer only to the European members of the ex-CMEA (Bulgaria, Czechoslovakia, the German Democratic Republic [GDR], Hungary, Poland, Romania, and the Soviet Union). This group is also identified as Eastern Europe, although I shall occasionally use the notion to refer to the six smaller countries; any reference to the period since 3 October 1990 omits the GDR for obvious reasons. But the context makes it then clear that I have this smaller group in mind.

3. Certainly, the decision to abolish the CMEA was not formally taken until 28 June 1991 at the 46th Council Session in Budapest, and the trade and payment mechanisms remained officially in place until the end of 1990. But by then these formal changes were only in recognition of the decay that had already pervasively penetrated the real spheres of trade, payments, and economic cooperation.

4. Article VIII, section 2 states that no member shall, without the approval of the Fund, impose restrictions on the making of payments and transfers for current international transactions (IMF 1978, p. 29). For an interpretation thereof, see Edwards 1985, pp. 390–1 and Gianviti 1989.

5. One cannot deny the potential usefulness of a payments union because of a need for structural finance when there are also temporary payment difficulties, as Rosati (1993) intimates. His references to the EPU are essentially misguided or irrelevant for history does not repeat itself. Whether a payments union could yield benefits to the East similar to those experienced in postwar Western Europe is irrelevant. What matters is the benefits of such a payments union when compared with its cost (of both the financing and the implied discrimination).

6. But this cannot be accomplished chiefly through official multilateral finance as Rosati (1992, p.) posits.

7. This rather spurious argument was skillfully exploited by some critics of the payment proposal, notably Bofinger 1991; Kenen 1991; Polak 1991; Portes

1991; and Williamson 1991a, b, although none of them brought to bear the evidence required to uphold the two propositions. The red herring is still repeated by Rosati (1993) in spite of the overwhelming evidence to the contrary.

8. Total exports had previously been higher than that, of course (up to some 120 million tons). But all that mattered was that at world conditions the Soviet Union would have had sufficient exports to cover Eastern Europe's needs.

9. I cannot go into detail about these and related matters. The interested reader is referred to Brabant 1991a, b, c, d.

10. For details on how these data were derived, see Brabant 1991a, d. Note that the interrepublican imbalances of the old USSR washed out, but will now become international imbalances to be financed. Havrylyshyn and Williamson (1991, p. 60) venture a guess that a capital fund will now have to be on the order of $5 billion.

11. Precisely how large the contraction of trade has been is very hard to determine, due to the convoluted shifts in pricing, exchange rates, foreign-exchange regimes, and statistical accounting. Perhaps the best data available at this stage are those of the Economic Commission for Europe (see EBE 1991, pp. 52ff.). Unfortunately, quantum data for 1991 are not yet available. And value data are almost meaningless in the wake of the above-cited adjustments. Thus, they show a sharp contrast between the magnitudes reported by the Soviet Union with the rest of the European CMEA and the mirror data; part of the problem is undoubtedly the use of a constant TR-dollar exchange rate for all countries, which yield implausible conversions for some countries, notably factoring TR trade too high for Poland and far too low for, say, Bulgaria and the Soviet Union. For example, in current dollar values (but established at uniform crossrates) Soviet exports to the other ex-CMEA countries in Europe contracted by 26.9 and 31.6 percent in 1990 and the first half of 1991; the corresponding magnitudes on the import side were 12.1 and 41.2 percent. Because on the export side a sizable improvement in fuel prices occurred in 1991 and import prices probably declined, there may have been a substantial positive terms-of-trade effect for the Soviet Union (and negative for fuel importers), but no one knows by how much. This suggests that the contraction in export volume must have been even larger than the value magnitude (ECE estimates total export volume to have declined by 35 to 50 per cent, and perhaps slightly more so with former CMEA members; and total imports by 35 to 45 percent, and perhaps slightly more so for former CMEA members), but we simply do not know by how much. The overall terms of trade for the smaller countries in the first half of 1991 worsened by some 15 to 20 percent. Unfortunately, the available data for partner countries simply do not agree with these changes: thus, the ex-CMEA partners report a 16 percent *gain* in import value from the Soviet Union, while the latter reports a 32 percent loss in export value to the same countries(!) but import values correspond better (minus 36 percent as against minus 41 percent).

12. I am far more skeptical than Rosati (1993) is on that score. In this connection, it may be worth pointing out a fundamental contradiction in his argument.

If the collapse of intragroup trade had indeed mostly weeded out unprofitable trade and the Central European countries for all practical purposes had trade convertibility, why would there be short-term financing problems?

Bibliography

Bofinger, Peter, "A multilateral payments union for Eastern Europe?" *Banca Nazionale del Lavoro Quarterly Review*, 1991:1, 69–88.

Brabant, Jozef M. van, *Adjustment, structural change, and economic efficiency—aspects of monetary cooperation in Eastern Europe* (New York and Cambridge: Cambridge University Press, 1987).

_______, "CMEA reform and the formulation of a constitutional framework" (presented at the conference "The radical reform of the CMEA as a precondition of cooperation with the EC—theoretical and practical questions," Sopron, Hungary, 16–20 November 1989a).

_______, *Economic integration in Eastern Europe—a handbook* (Hemel Hempstead: Harvester Wheatsheaf and New York: Routledge, 1989b).

_______, *Remaking Eastern Europe—on the political economy of transition* (Dordrecht-Boston-London: Kluwer Academic Publishers, 1990).

_______, *Integrating Eastern Europe into the global economy—convertibility through a payments union* (Dordrecht-Boston-London: Kluwer Academic Publishers, 1991a).

_______, "Convertibility in Eastern Europe through a payments union," in *Currency convertibility in Eastern Europe*, edited by John Williamson (Washington, DC: Institute for International Economics, 1991b), pp. 63–95.

_______, "Key problems of creating a Central European Payments Union," *Banca Nazionale del Lavoro Quarterly Review*, 1991c:2, 119–49.

_______, *A Central European Payments Union: technical aspects* (New York: Institute for East-West Security Studies, 1991d).

_______, "The demise of the CMEA—the agony of inaction," *Osteuropa-Wirtschaft*, 1991e:3, 234–54.

EBE, United Nations Economic Commission for Europe, *Economic Bulletin for Europe*, Vol. 43 (1991).

Edwards, Richard W., Jr., *International monetary collaboration* (Dobbs Ferry, NY: Transnational Publishers, 1985).

Gianviti, François, "The International Monetary Fund and external debt," *Recueil des Cours*, 1989:3, 213–86.

Havrylyshyn, Oleh and John Williamson, *From Soviet disUnion to Eastern economic community?* (Washington, DC: Institute for International Economics, 1991).

IMF, *Articles of agreement* (Washington, DC: International Monetary Fund, 1978).

Kenen, Peter B., "Transitional arrangements for trade and payments among the CMEA countries," *IMF Staff Papers*, 1991:2, 235–67.

Polak, Jacques J., "Convertibility: an indispensable element in the transition process in Eastern Europe," in *Currency convertibility in Eastern Europe*, edited by John Williamson (Washington, DC: Institute for International Economics, 1991), pp. 21–30.

Portes, Richard, "Introduction," *European Economy*, 1991: Special Edition No. 2, 1–15.

Rosati, Dariusz, "The CMEA Demise, Trade Restructuring, and Trade Destruction in Eastern Europe: Initial Assessment" (mimeo), 1991.

Williamson, John, *The economic opening of Eastern Europe* (Washington, DC: Institute for International Economics, 1991a).

Williamson, John, ed., *Currency convertibility in Eastern Europe* (Washington, DC: Institute for International Economics, 1991b).

6

Liberalizing Foreign Trade in a Socialist Economy: The Problem of Negative Value Added

Ronald I. McKinnon

In their remarkably swift adoption of free trade with full current account convertibility in 1990, both East Germany and Poland experienced rapid industrial decline: the collapse—or threatened bankruptcy—in an astonishingly wide variety of manufacturing and agricultural industries that turned out ex post facto not to be internationally competitive. Are there constraints on how fast currency convertibility, and free arbitrage between domestic and foreign markets for goods and services, is best achieved in a liberalizing socialist economy?

At first glance, the great difficulty of East Germany and Poland in expanding (new) export activities as import substitution industries contract seems to refute the Ricardian law of comparative advantage. Whether under free trade or economic autarky, the Ricardian model of comparative advantage assumed that all goods be, produced according to predetermined production technologies from basic labor. Even if average labor productivity was low, therefore, conventional textbook wisdom had it that the comparative efficiency of at least some major domestic industries soon would assert itself if the real wage could be set sufficiently low, i.e., the real exchange rate was sufficiently devalued. And some reasoning such as this lay behind the willingness of the Polish and German policy makers to move so quickly toward unrestricted foreign trade.

Alternatively, this chapter considers the circular flow of production in a "typical" socialist economy. Goods are produced from intermediate products such as energy and other material inputs as well as from labor and capital, and there are substantial substitution possibilities for combining them. In this substitution model, technological capabilities—including labor productivities—are conditioned by the pre-existing structure of protection before liberalization occurs. By taking this implicit protection in the traditional Stalinist economy properly into account, I will first show that, no matter how the exchange rate is set, most manufacturing and food processing industries need not be viable under free trade at pre-existing combinations of factor inputs: in the short run they might well exhibit negative valued added at world market prices; and, second, propose a more gradual program of trade liberalization based on temporary tariff protection and the repricing of material inputs so as to winnow out those industries that could not survive in the long run under free trade from those that could.[1]

Implicit Protection in the Traditional Stalinist Economy

In the traditional Stalinist economy for which the Soviet Union will be our leading prototype, virtually all domestic production of more or less "finished goods"—those sold directly to consumers or sold back to industry as plant and equipment—was insulated from foreign competition. Because the ruble was inconvertible into foreign exchange on current account, protection for domestic manufacturers—including processed agricultural goods—was absolute: the State trading agency refused to authorize competing imports unless there were pronounced domestic shortages of similar products. Although there were no formal tariffs or quota restrictions in any legal codes, the implicit rate of protection was very high as if quantitative restrictions had eliminated competitive pressure from abroad. At some "equilibrium" exchange rate to be discussed below), domestic prices for finished goods—after discounting for their normally poorer quality in the protected setting—were typically higher than their foreign counterparts. Thus, in its general repercussions on economy-wide resource allocation, this price wedge is similar to the effect of a high tariff on the importation of competing finished goods.

At the same time, exports of energy, raw materials, and limited amounts of manufactures (largely military equipment in the Soviet case) were largely determined centrally by "a vent-for-surplus" doctrine. That is, after domestic "needs" for, say energy, at low domestic prices had been more or less satisfied, the residual (quite a large residual in the Soviet case) was then sold abroad at much higher world market prices. The effect was similar to imposing an export tax on, say, energy that drives the domestic price below that paid by foreign buyers. Energy in all forms—together with nonfood raw materials which were similarly "taxed"—amounted to over 60 percent of Soviet exports in 1989, and over 75 percent if one omits "protected" military sales from the export base.

In order to approximate how these relative prices in the Stalinist economy differ from those prevailing in the world economy, therefore, let us partition the tradable goods produced and consumed into two categories: finished goods, which are largely manufactures and processed foodstuffs; and material inputs, which are largely energy products and nonfood raw materials.

For modeling purposes, assume that all finished goods are largely import substitutes or imports and are not exported; whereas material inputs are either exported or used up in the domestic manufacture of finished goods. Reinterpreting the notation and methodology of Tan (1970),[2] denote the gross output of finished goods industry i by Z_i, where the corresponding production function is

Equation 1

$$Z_i = Z_i\,(L_1, L_2, \ldots L_n; M_1, M_2, \ldots M_r)$$

The L_i's refer to the primary factors such as labor or land, and the M_i's are intermediate material inputs. In considering the production choices facing industry i (Figure 1), however, let us dispense with all but one intermediate input, M, and one domestic factor L. We can then denote value-added in domestic prices of finished goods industry i as

Equation 2

$$V_i = P_i Z_i - P_m M$$

where P_i and P_m are the domestic-currency prices of the finished product and material input, respectively. The value added by the domestic factor(s) is simply gross value minus the cost of intermediate inputs—and the normal presumption is that value added at domestic prices is positive.[3] But what determines the relative prices of Z_i and M in domestic commodity markets, and how is that linked to domestic factor costs?

The Coefficient of Protection for Finished Goods

Consider relative commodity prices first—presuming that one unit of the domestic currency exchanges for one foreign. Because we are dealing with an economy that is a small part of the world economy, foreign currency prices—denoted with asterisks—are fixed. Let t_i represent the implicit tariff protecting domestic production of the finished product—the gap between the foreign and quality-adjusted domestic price—such that

Equation 3

$$P_i = (1 + t_i)\,P_i^*$$

and let t_m represent the similarly calculated implicit export tax on material inputs such that

Equation 4

$$P_m(1+t_m)+P_m^*$$

In order to see the divergence between domestic relative prices and their foreign counterparts, divide Equation 3 by Equation 4 and rearrange to get

Equation 5

$$P_i/P_m = (1+t_i)(1+t_m)(P_i^*/P_m^*)$$

Equation 5 captures the dual aspect of the overall protection to the gross output of finished goods: the effect of restricting competing imports and of subsidizing the use of material inputs. Indeed, from Lerner's Symmetry Theorem (Lerner, 1936), we know that restricting imports or taxing exports have "equivalent" protective effects in long-run equilibrium—as worked out more fully in the presence of intermediate products by McKinnon (1966). For industry *i*, we thus define the overall "coefficient of protection" to be

Equation 6

$$1+r_i=(1+t_i)(1+t_m)$$

On the vertical scale of Figure 1, the coefficient of protection shows the domestic relative price of finished goods in terms of material inputs. To better interpret Figure 1, however, let us first consider domestic value added at world prices.

Equation 7

$$V_i^* = P_i^* Z_i - P_m^* M$$

From Equation 5, we can rewrite V_i^* in terms of domestic prices to get

Equation 8

$$V_i^* = \frac{P_i Z_i - (1+t_m)(1+t_i)P_m M}{(1+t_i)}$$

Although we presume V_i remains positive, there can be no presumption that domestic value added at world prices is positive. Indeed, if either t_m or t_i are sufficiently high, and if the relatively cheap M is substituted for other factors of production, Equation 8 tells us that

$V_i^* < O.$

These relationships are depicted in Figure 1, which is a modified version of that used by Tan (1970). For a "typical" finished goods industry i (which is one of many), the unit isoquants Z_i and Z_i' portray alternative possibilities for substituting the tradable material input for the domestic factor of production in the long run, i.e., not taking transitional adjustment costs into account. The distance *OA* on the vertical axis represents the material inputs which are equivalent to one unit of finished goods at world prices. For example, at the hypothetical free trade equilibrium at point *g*, where the new budget line *AC* (whose slope now reflects the relatively higher world cost of energy in terms of labor) is tangent to the unit isoquant Z_i, one unit of final output could buy *OA* in material inputs.

Going one step further, we can scale our measure of output in Figure 1 so that one unit of the finished good is worth just one dollar of foreign exchange: the unit isoquants Z_i or Z_i' denote just one dollar's worth of finished good i. Similarly, we can scale our measure of material inputs on the vertical axis so the one unit of, say, energy is worth just one dollar: the distance *OA* in Figure 1 is one.

Then, under the preexisting system of implicit protection and using this scaling, Equation 5 tells us that the domestic relative price of the final output in terms of material inputs—the distance *OH* in Figure l—is simply our coefficient of protection $1 + PI_i$. The higher domestic price of

FIGURE 1 **Value Added and Protection in Finished Goods**

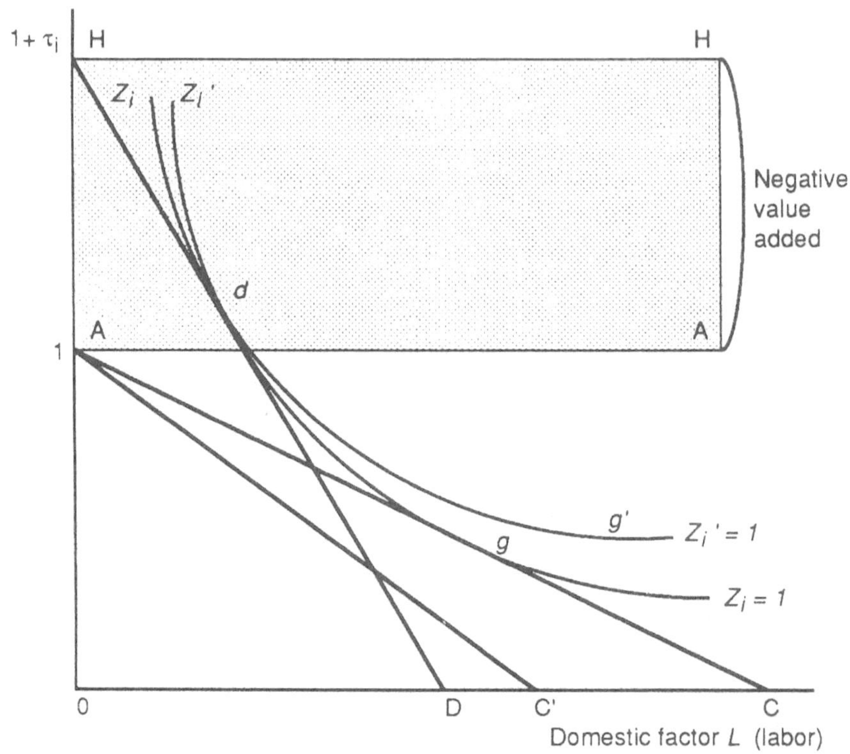

finished goods compared to that prevailing on world markets (and compared to the price of material inputs) reflects both the implicit export tax on material inputs and the implicit tariff on competing imports.

The Overuse of Material Inputs and the Shoddy Product Syndrome

Under protected domestic prices, all feasible input combinations—feasible in the sense of domestic value added being positive in the production of one unit of finished goods—must lie below the horizontal line *HH* in Figure 1. Below *HH,* the domestic value of finished goods output exceeds the domestic cost of the material inputs used in their production.

At world relative prices, on the other hand, all feasible input combinations must lie below *AA* if domestic value added is to be positive. Indeed, all production points in the shaded area lying above *AA* in Figure 1 show negative value added at world prices. For example, the point *d* is profitable under the existing mantle of protection: the budget line *HD* (whose slope shows relatively cheap energy and expensive labor) is just tangent to the unit isoquant Z_i (or its alternative Z_i'). Nevertheless, *d* shows negative value added if the final output had to be sold, and material inputs had to be purchased, in unrestricted world markets.

Why is this phenomenon of negative value added at world prices probably commonplace in Soviet (and Eastern European) industry? First, as drawn in Figure 1, the relative prices of energy and other material inputs to most sectors of the Soviet economy have been kept very low—causing them to be used intensively. In addition, the old Stalinist system of rewarding managers by whether they (over) fulfill gross output targets encourages them to waste material inputs. "According to the calculations of the Soviet Institute of World Economy and International Relations, we use 1.5 times more materials and 2.1 times more energy per unit of national income than the United States . . . Our agricultural production is 15 percent less than the United States but we use 3.5 times more energy." (Shmelev and Popov, 1989, p. 128)

Second, the Stalinist planning system based on gross output targets tends to produce manufactured or processed outputs of uncertain quality. "The quality of Soviet produce appears to have been declining steadily since the 1960s, as a result of permanent excess demand, regardless of technical progress." (Aslund, 1989, p. 76). For example, take a common household product like detergent that is introduced at a certain benchmark standard. The (protected) domestic producer will have continual incentive to degrade product quality if, by so doing, more units can be produced. After complaints roll in, the enterprise might get permission to introduce a new and "improved" benchmark detergent at a higher price and for which it gets more weight in its gross output target.[4] Then the slippage in quality begins all over again. For short, I will call this process the shoddy product syndrome.

In Figure l, the shoddy product syndrome affects the position of the unit isoquant because material inputs at world prices—or, equivalently, units of foreign exchange—is the numeraire by which final output is measured. The shoddier the product or more uncertain the product quality, the further to the northeast will be the unit isoquant, say at Z_i' rather than Z_i–. In the sudden German trade liberalization of 1990, for example, the adverse signaling from simply knowing that a good had been produced in East Germany was sufficient to induce East German consumers to reject it in favor of higher-priced West German goods—thus increasing the distress in East German industry.

In a sudden move to free trade at any exchange rate, therefore, a finished goods industry chosen at random would likely show negative cash flows under the (pre)existing combination of factor inputs and low valuation of the finished product in world markets. A devaluation, coinciding with the (hypothetical) move to free trade, would simply raise material input prices in tandem with the prices of shoddy finished goods. In the short run before input combinations and product quality could be adjusted, negative value added would persist. Because manufacturing absorbs a much higher proportion of the labor force in the Soviet Union than in the United States (Shmelev and Popov, 1989), a wholesale industrial collapse would be intolerable.

The Adjustment Problem

In "long-run" free-trade equilibrium, however, could industry *i*, as depicted in the substitution model of Figure 1, be viable? Suppose our putative reformers observe the "protected" starting point *d*, a combination of output and inputs with negative (or very low) value added at world market prices. Yet they do not know whether industry *i* (and similar finished goods industries) would be sufficiently productive, and capable of ultimately shifting away from its current heavy dependence on material inputs while improving product quality, to become profitable under free trade. In the long run, whether industry *i* was on an "efficient" unit isoquant such as Z_i running through the point *d*, or on an "inefficient" unit isoquant such as Z_i' also running through the point *d*, is uncertain. In the former case, output at world prices would ultimately be sustainable at the point *g*. In the latter case, the best industry *i* could manage in the long run after energy became more expensive was a production point like *g*′: the value of gross output at *g*′ remains less than the total cost of production.

Notice that the long run viability of the industry *i* depends not only on its production efficiency, i.e., whether it is on the unit isoquant Z_i or Z_i', but also on the prevailing costs of the domestic factors of production after a new free-trade equilibrium is established. Suppose labor is the principal domestic factor of production. Then the budget line *AC* shows the real wage (in terms of material inputs) to be sufficiently low under free trade so that the point *g* tangent to Z_i is profitable. However, if the equilibrium real wage is higher, so that *AC*′ is now the relevant budget for producing one unit of the finished good, then industry *i* will not be profitable under free trade. *AC′* lies to the left and below Z_i The real wage in long-term equilibrium facing any particular industry *i* will be the outcome of a complex macroeconomic interaction as all industries liberalize simultaneously.

Given this fundamental uncertainty about substitution in production, product quality, and equilibrium real factor costs when all industries are finally liberalized in the long run, could the reformers devise a system of interim protection at "correct" relative input prices that, first, initially sustains the profitability of most existing production of manufactures and processed goods; and, second, when systematically reduced over the next several years, allows market mechanisms to phase out inefficient finished goods industries while encouraging "learning by doing" in others so that they eventually thrive under free trade?

From Implicit to Explicit-Tariff Protection: The Case of Chile

The trade liberalization in Chile after 1973 was perhaps the most comprehensive and draconian (before the Polish and East German experiences in 1990) of modern times—see Edwards and Edwards (1987) for putting the remarkable empirical details into a solid analytical perspective. Chile's tariff and foreign exchange policies provide useful clues of what to do, or what not to do, in a similarly comprehensive trade liberalization program in a socialist economy like the Soviet Union's.

In 1973, Chile had some very high formal tariffs protecting finished goods, averaging over 90 percent with some, improbably, going as high as 500 percent—as shown in Table 1. However, these numbers conceal the fact that much protection in Chile in 1973 was from nontariff barriers. Quota restrictions or absolute prohibitions on imports of finished goods were commonplace—along with restrictions on the export of food and industrial raw materials. In addition, the government refused to allocate foreign exchange for imports that didn't suit its immediate social objectives, and set multiple exchange rates across different categories of imports and exports so that many tariff rates themselves had become rather meaningless.

Therefore, the first order of business in the Chilean liberalization of foreign trade in 1974 and 1975 was to (1) unify the exchange rate so that all exporters and importers transacted at the same rate, then (2) convert all quota restrictions into some rough tariff equivalent—lumping similar commodities together in the same tariff category, then (3) move to

TABLE 1 Profile of the Chilean Tariff Reform

		Average nominal tariff rate (precentages)	*Maximum nominal tariff rate (percentages)*
1973	July–Dec	94	500+
1974	Jan–June	80	160
	July–Dec	67	140
1975	Jan–June	52	120
	July–Dec	44	90
1976	Jan–June	38	70
	July–Dec	33	60
1977	Jan–June	24	50
	July–Dec	18	35
1978	Jan–June	15	20
	July–Dec	12	15
1979	June 30 onwards	10[2]	10
1980		10	10
1981		10	10
1982		10	10

[1]With a few exceptions for some (but not all) automotive vehicles. Small cars may be imported at the standard tariff rates.

[2]Of the 4,301 commodities or tariff lines that are classified for customs purposes, only 12 are exempt from any duties.

Source: Central Bank of Chile.

unrestricted foreign exchange convertibility on current account. The net effect of these first steps taken in 1974 and 1975 was to convert implicit protection by direct controls into explicit protection by tariffs—albeit still very high tariffs as Table 1 shows. By 1976, this conversion into a system of explicit tariff protection in Chile was virtually complete. Then the government proceeded to phase out the explicit protection slowly over a period of several years by (4) reducing the higher tariffs, in preannounced small steps, to converge to a modest uniform import tariff at a prespecified future date.

In the event, Chile speeded up this process slightly and converged to uniform 10 percent tariff on all imports (for revenue) by July of 1979 (Table 1) with no other significant import restrictions. The uniform tariff was justified on revenue grounds, and from Lerner's Symmetry Theorem, we know such a tariff is equivalent to a 10 percent tax on all exports in long-run equilibrium.

Note that after 1973 Chile also removed all controls and other significant taxes on exports per se. However, in parallel with what should be the case for the natural resource based exports of the Soviet Union, the Chilean government continued to tax the profits and other economic rents associated with natural-resource based industries rather systematically. For example, in Chile's huge copper industry, which dominated Chile's exports much like petroleum now does the Soviet Union's, the government retained ownership and control of a number of major mines; and concessions given to private mining companies—whether international or domestic—were rather carefully taxed. The important point for our purposes, however, is these were "profits" taxes rather than export taxes. Hence, after liberalization, they did not drive a wedge between the price seen by domestic users and by foreign buyers of exportable material inputs—unlike the Soviet energy industry today.

In summary, in difficult political circumstances, Chile in late 1973 eschewed the "cold turkey" approach to free trade adopted by (forced on?) Poland and East Germany in 1990. Instead, Chilean producers of finished goods had some years in which to adjust. The one major mistake was to allow excessive capital inflows that a forced a severe overvaluation of the Chilean peso in 1978–82 and caused widespread bankruptcy in the newly opened tradable goods sectors (McKinnon 1991a, Chapter 6). Despite this early trauma, Chile's trade liberalization itself, and political commitment to free trade, have been successfully sustained into the 1990s.

A Transition Parable for Soviet Foreign Trade

Suppose the spirit of the deliberate Chilean approach to free trade—as summarized in steps 1 to 4 above—can be depicted within the confines of our two-commodity substitution model of the Soviet economy. How might an "idealized" Soviet approach to free trade be worked out? The Soviets got off on the wrong foot in 1989 by decentralizing foreign exchange contracting by domestic enterprises before their budget constraints were hardened so that domestic commodity prices could be decontrolled, and before the regime of multiple exchange rates was unified. In 1990, hundreds of individual exchange rates, ranging from the old official rate of .64 rubles per dollar to more than 20 rubles continue to proliferate. Thus, as a practical matter, the best option for the Soviet government might have been to recentralize foreign exchange allocations until the domestic financial controls necessary for supporting a market economy have been established (McKinnon, 1991) and until the exchange rate is unified as per step 1 above.

But how should this single (unified) nominal exchange rate be set when unrestricted commodity or financial arbitrage with the outside world does not yet exist? We know that the price of exportable material inputs—inclusive of the huge energy sector—must rise sharply relative to domestic factors of production including labor. Moreover the ruble prices of these fairly homogeneous material inputs can be directly compared to those prevailing on world markets, which are typically quoted in dollars. Thus, the exchange rate, in rubles per dollar, can be set according to a limited version of the principle of purchasing power parity as follows.

Take the prevailing domestic wage level in rubles as a starting point. Then estimate the average increase in the relative price of energy (and other material inputs) against wages that would prevail in long-run equilibrium if the economy were to move toward free trade. Accordingly, adjust the domestic ruble price of energy (and other material inputs) sharply upwards—doubling or trebling it in terms of wages at the outset of the trade liberalization process. In Figure 2, the slope of the budget line *BB′*, running through the old production point *d*, now represents this higher price of energy relative to labor; whereas *HD*, also running through *d*, represents the old budget line when energy was previously underpriced.

Simultaneously, to make the new ruble price level for material inputs effective, set the exchange rate in rubles per dollar to equate (average) domestic prices of material inputs to those prevailing in world markets. This new unified exchange rate would now apply to all current account transacting, on either the import or export sides, for material inputs, finished goods, or services. Once established, this nominal ruble/dollar exchange rate would be invariant to further ups and downs of world prices for material inputs. At the fixed exchange rate, continual minor changes in the domestic ruble prices of individual material inputs (and other tradables) would keep them aligned with their counterparts on world markets.

What have we accomplished by this exercise in exchange rate unification? First, the implicit export tax on energy and other material inputs has been eliminated as their ruble prices rise sharply to world levels. (Note, however, that the revenue position of the government would be greatly enhanced if it retained a full claim on the profits or surpluses being generated by natural resource based industries at the higher domestic prices.) In the short run, producers in industry *i* would have immediate incentive to begin economizing on energy and other material inputs.

Second, this nominal exchange rate is now capable of sustaining the real purchasing power of domestic money in terms of material inputs—

FIGURE 2 Interim Tariff Protection in the Transition to Free Trade

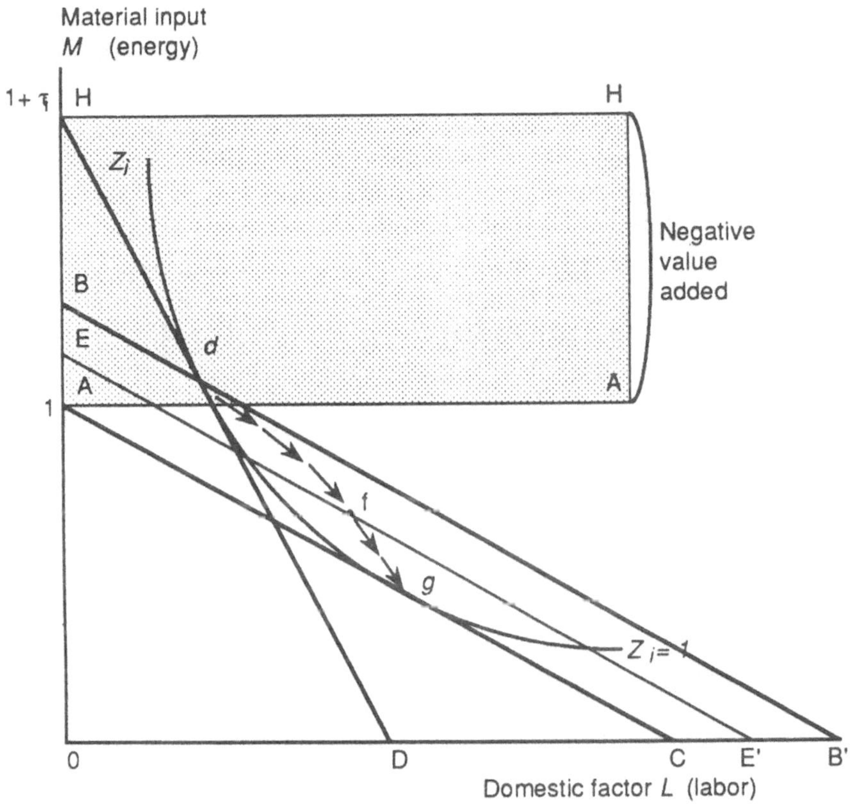

a very broad class of primary commodities produced, traded, and consumed throughout the economy—once full current account convertibility is achieved. This potentially stable "real" exchange rate also provides a benchmark for converting the implicit tariff protection associated with quota restrictions and with the existing system of exchange controls into explicit tariff equivalents. That is, the authorities may now calculate the t_i's sufficient to keep most finished goods manufacturing in existence—a calculation requiring a stable real exchange rate if effective protection by tariffs is, itself, to remain operative at some prespecified level.

For finished goods industry *i* portrayed in Figure 2, the vertical scale at point *H* shows the coefficient of protection, $1 + PI_i$, prior to this elimination of the domestic subsidy to the use of material inputs. This total implicit protection depends on the preexisting implicit tariff on imports of finished goods and on the old input subsidy. As before, the resulting budget line for producing one unit finished good *i* at point *d* is *HD*, whose steep slope reflects the low relative price of energy and other material inputs relative to domestic labor.

After the prices of material inputs increase to world levels, however, explicit tariff protection from competing imports of finished goods would have to be adjusted upwards from its old implicit rate if industry *i* is to survive. Suppose t_i' is the new explicit tariff needed to keep industry *i* in business once exchange controls were removed and current account convertibility was achieved. Then $t_i' > t_i$. To compensate for the increased price of energy and other inputs, the initial explicit tariff would have to be somewhat higher than the previous quality-adjusted differential between the foreign and domestic price of finished good *i*.

The vertical distance *AB* in Figure 2 shows the level of this new (hypothetical) explicit tariff relative to the (newly increased) prices of material inputs. Insofar as the domestic price of material inputs now equals the world level of one dollar, *AB* also represents the actual ad valorem tariff needed to protect the domestic industry. *BB′* is the corresponding new budget line just sufficient to sustain production at point *d* (at the old combination of domestic factors and material inputs). *BB′* is somewhat flatter than the old budget line *HD* in order to reflect the newly increased price of material inputs relative to labor. Because the price of material inputs has also increased relative to that of the finished goods, the distance *AB* is correspondingly less than *AH*.

But this is not the end of the parable. Because the slope of the new budget line *BB′* is flatter (reflecting higher energy costs), *BB′* now cuts the unit isoquant Z_i at point d rather than being tangent to it. This induces the manager of industry *i* to raise profits by increasing the demand for domestic factors and reducing energy dependence, i.e., to start moving along the new budget line from *d* in the direction of *B′* as fast as the reequipment of the enterprise permits. The great advantage of raising material input prices rather sharply at the outset of the trade liberalization is that firms immediately see the "right" relative factor costs for inducing them to economize on material inputs, exports of which will then slowly increase.

Nevertheless, our controlled liberalization differs from a strategy of jumping directly to free trade. Under immediate free trade with no interim protection for domestic finished goods, industry *i* would face the budget line *AC* in Figure 2, which could not support existing production at point *d*. Because the world market would bid them away from domestic uses, exports of material inputs and energy would jump sharply and so cause the collapse of most domestic manufacturing and goods processing activities.

That said, our parable based on interim tariff protection should leave no doubt in the minds of domestic industrialists, merchants, and farmers that the economy will eventually move to free trade—as in step 4 of the Chilean program cited above. Simultaneously with the introduction of explicit tariff protection for finished goods industries, the liberalizing socialist government could announce that the higher tariff rates would be scaled down by small steps until, say 10 years hence, all rates had converged to some low uniform level. Further reductions in this resulting "revenue tariff" would then depend on the government's fiscal position.

Figure 2 nicely illustrates the nature of this declining tariff protection in smoothing the transition to free trade. Starting with the high explicit tariff equal to the vertical distance *AB*, the relevant budget line supporting production at point *d* is *BB′*. Then some years later, formal tariff protection for our representative finished good is reduced to AE so as to support production at point *f* along the new budget line *EE′*. Finally, tariff protection for finished goods industries is phased out altogether; the relevant budget line becomes *AC*: that prevailing under free trade. (For diagrammatic simplicity, Figure 2 does not show the process ending with a low revenue tariff; and I have simply assumed that the initial guess of the authorities in raising the price of material inputs relative to domestic factors turns out to be correct in free-trade equilibrium.)

During this transition, successful in the particular case of industry *i* shown in Figure 2, the combination of factor inputs for producing one unit of the finished good shifts along the locus shown by the arrows from *d* to *f* to *g*. Only at the beginning point *d*, and the end point *g*, are these production combinations actually on the unit isoquant Z_i– That is, the unit isoquant traces out efficient production points in long-run equilibrium after the industry has the necessary time to rebuild its capital stock and restructure its labor force when relative prices change. The other points on the locus *dfg* are above the efficient long-run unit isoquant; and their "excessive" use of material inputs and domestic factors represents the real (social) costs of the transition. These costs are covered by the interim tariff protection and thus are shifted forward to the final user of the finished good in question.

However, the change from implicit quota restrictions and import prohibitions to explicit tariff protection could still benefit users of finished goods. First, even over high tariffs, the new threat of import competition would curb the monopoly power of concentrated domestic manufacturers. Manufacturing industries in the former Soviet Union are indeed highly concentrated. For example, 100 percent of Soviet sewing machines are produced by a single state enterprise; the same is true for such diverse goods as tram rails, locomotive cranes, and coking equipment. All hydraulic turbines produced in the country come from a small number of plants run by a single government ministry; the same can be said for tin plate production and certain consume goods such as color photographic paper and freezers (*The Economist*, 11 August 1990, p. 67). Second, the shoddy product syndrome would be immediately alleviated: The worst domestic products would not survive in the face of even modest competition from abroad. Indeed, the successful transitional production locus in Figure 2, the movement from d to f to g, implicitly incorporates improvements in product quality.

A Generalized Cascading Tariff?

These advantages from the move to explicit tariff protection presume that the government does not precisely tailor individual tariffs to keep each finished goods producer in business at the outset of the liberalization. Rather, the vertical distance AB in Figure 2, is best interpreted as simply a representative initial tariff—a common levy—that applies to imports of all finished goods in a similar category. Following the Chilean experience described earlier and that of other primary products producing countries such as Canada which once had quite high tariffs, one could start off with fairly broad tariff categories: a "cascading" tariff scaled downwards according to the distance from the final consumer and degree of manufacturing complexity.

Ranked from highest to lowest, a single tariff rate could apply to each of the following or similar categories: (1) consumer durables: autos, home appliances, and so forth; (2) consumer nondurables: textiles and highly processed foods; (3) capital goods and manufactured intermediate products; (4) industrial materials and basic foods. The highest tariff in category 1 could be over 100 percent depending on how one computed their average survival capability after the prices of material inputs had been raised sharply; whereas the lowest would be the final uniform tariff of say, 10 percent, on imports of material inputs in category 4. As far as possible, the government would set a simple across-the-board "yardstick" tariff in each category. Not only would this general approach weed out the most inefficient producers (basket cases) at the outset, but "rent seeking" by individual industries petitioning for protection especially geared to their own needs would be minimized.

Then, over, say, a ten year interval similar to that used in the recently concluded Canadian-American free trade agreement, the rates in categories 1, 2, and 3, would be gradually but firmly reduced to those prevailing in category 4—again without accepting special pleading for exceptions. In order to facilitate adjustment in his own mix of inputs and outputs, each producer should know the cumulative tariff reductions[5] at the end of every year until virtual free trade was established.

A cascading tariff schedule, but one that is not adjusted downwards, is often used by LDCs to protect "infant" industries for producing finished goods. In our transition parable, by contrast, the purpose is quite different: to make explicit and then phase out already very high levels of implicit protection for domestic manufacturing. Moreover, with the degree of uncertainty involved as to which firms would ultimately survive and which not, it is simply not feasible for those firms that would be viable in the long run to jump immediately to free trade—and to cover their early losses and transition costs by borrowing. Indeed, such massive borrowing by socialist enterprises would undermine the hard budget constraints, based on limited access to external capital, which were pivotal for achieving domestic financial control (McKinnon, 1991a and 1991b). Instead, temporary tariff protection, which increases the internal cash flows of manufacturing firms, is fully consistent with keeping self finance as the main financial mode for liberalized enterprises in a transitional socialist economy.

Are Foreign Capital Inflows Necessary?

Because a properly orchestrated move to free trade presents no inherent problem of foreign exchange shortages for the ex-Soviet Union, our parable of step-by-step trade liberalization did not discuss the role of capital inflows from abroad. Quite the contrary, the country abounds with energy and other material inputs that are overused at home. Thus the elimination of implicit export taxes should allow exports to increase rather easily. Indeed, flooding the economy with foreign exchange by borrowing abroad could well worsen the adjustment problem. Domestic finished goods industries would face additional competition from "subsidized" manufactured imports that reduced their international competitiveness (McKinnon 1973).

Are there circumstances where one might want to mitigate this seemingly harsh judgment against heavy reliance on foreign capital inflows to "ease" adjustment to free trade? Unlike the ex-Soviet Union, some of the smaller countries of Eastern Europe are not particularly rich in natural resources that are easily traded internationally. Worse, their extensive manufacturing and agricultural industries have also become addicted to cheap material inputs—particularly energy. Before 1990, at least, the close trade links among the countries of Eastern Europe simply extended the ambit of the old Stalinist industrial system. Through the trading apparatus of the CMEA (the Council for Mutual Economic Assistance), the Soviet Union sold relatively cheap energy and other material inputs to smaller Eastern European economies in return for manufactured goods of a lesser quality than those traded in Western markets. In fact, the extensive trade among the CMEA countries (Table 2), albeit largely bilateral because of the absence of a freely convertible trading currency, also included the mutual exchange of (shoddy) manufactured goods through direct bargaining by state trading agencies.

The problem for ex-CMEA countries to then adjust to full-scale trade liberalization with the West is obvious. The smaller ones that have not much in the way of primary products (what we have been calling material 24 inputs) exports would find themselves with an immediate shortage of foreign exchange. First, they stand to lose the subsidies for their Soviet-produced material inputs: the willingness of the Soviet authorities to accept their manufactured products at very favorable terms of trade. Second, the syndrome of negative value-added (at world market prices) means they can't sell their manufactures, without significant improvements in product quality, to the West. In effect, they are currently producing at a point like *d* in Figure l; but where the vertical axis showing material inputs now reflects actual imports—rather than potential exportables as in the Soviet case. Hence, a highly industrialized country like Czechoslovakia, where in 1988 about 80 percent of its exports went to other Socialist economies (Table 2), faced an immediate foreign exchange shortage when the CMEA trading umbrella collapsed.

In a general equilibrium model based on just two highly aggregated commodities, the Stalinist system of protection under the prototypical "Soviet" case can be distinguished from the prototypical "Czech" case. In the Soviet case, exports of primary materials are heavily (albeit implicitly) taxed with the domestic government collecting the tax revenue, whereas potential imports of finished manufactures face very high (implicit) tariffs. In the Czech case, imports of material inputs such as energy are subsidized by an outside agent (the Soviet Union); and so are exports of finished manufactures subsidized[6]: first by the cheap energy inputs, and second insofar as they can be unloaded in other CMEA countries.

The distinction between these two cases is important. In the Soviet case, a natural method of easing the transition to free trade is to impose temporary explicit tariffs on competing imports of finished manufactures—as sketched above—in order to give domestic producers of these goods time to adjust as the price of energy and material inputs increases

TABLE 2 Trade Flows for the CMEA, 1988 (percent of total exports and imports)

	Six[1]	*USSR*	*Dev. market economies*	*Ldcs*	*Rest*[2]
Exports					
Bulgaria	18.1	62.8	6.4	9.1	3.6
Czechoslovakia	29.9	43.1	16.3	4.7	6.0
German Dem. Rep.	26.1	34.8	29.9	3.6	5.6
Hungary	17.0	27.6	39.5	9.9	6.0
Poland	16.2	24.5	43.3	10.2	5.8
Romania	16.8	24.0	33.7	19.0	6.5
USSR	48.9	—	21.9	14.2	15.0
Imports					
Bulgaria	20.1	53.7	15.5	7.8	2.9
Czechoslovakia	32.3	40.3	18.6	3.5	5.3
German Dem. Rep.	25.3	36.8	31.8	2.7	3.4
Hungary	18.7	25.0	43.3	7.7	5.3
Poland	17.2	23.4	45.7	7.1	6.6
Romania	24.6	24.0	13.5	18.8	19.1
USSR	54.1	—	25.1	8.2	17.6

[1]Six: Bulgaria Czechoslovakia, German Democratic Republic, Hungary, Poland, and Romania.

[2]Rest: Rest of the world (predominantly Yugoslavia and China).

Source: Finance and Development, Sept. 1990, p. 29. Based on official statistical yearbooks of the reporting countries and UN estimates.

to world levels. But that would be insufficient in the Czech case. Czech producers of finished goods need some temporary protection in their export markets when their energy subsidies are removed. And, even if such export subsidies to Czech manufactures were allowed under the GATT, they would be a big drain on the Czech government's budget. Perhaps continuing with CMEA trade for some years into the transition would have been a partial solution.

However, converting the CMEA into a full fledged common market with convertible currencies and a common external tariff (in the mode of Western Europe) seemed completely out of the question (Schrenk, 1990). This is much more difficult task than reforming each socialist economy individually. Nevertheless, apart from the schema for tariff based liberalization sketched above, continuing the bilateral exchange of manufactured products through state trading agencies on an interim basis could be helpful for some years before each socialist economy is fully liberalized. Very likely, however, the net debits or credits arising out of bilateral imbalances in such trade would have to be settled in convertible Western monies—rather than inconvertible trade rubles as is presently the case.[7]

In proceeding with the main task of liberalizing its foreign trade with the West, therefore, a smaller Eastern European country might well require carefully crafted bridging finance from some international agency, such as the European Bank for Reconstruction and Development set up in 1990. However, the conditionality imposed by this agency for lending the money might well follow our parable sketched above and reflected in Figure 2: a discrete increase in the domestic price of energy and other material inputs to world levels coupled with conversion from implicit protection through exchange controls to an interim system of explicit protection for finished goods through tariffs or special export subsidies. At the beginning of such a liberalization, with otherwise free convertibility on current account, the agency might well provide the foreign exchange necessary for, say, Czechoslovakia, to continue buying material inputs until its manufactured exports become more competitive in world markets.

But accepting official bridging finance based on strict conditionality is not tantamount to a general relaxation of controls over private capital movements. Only after the domestic capital market is fully liberalized, with unrestricted borrowing and lending at equilibrium domestic interest rates, should the post-socialist economy's currency be made convertible into foreign exchange on capital account. Many years will have to pass before individuals and enterprises—including joint ventures with foreign firms—could be allowed to choose freely between domestic and foreign sources of finance. But this is the last, rather than the first, step in the optimum order of liberalization.[8]

Conclusion

Let us now return to summarize the main results of the chapter.

In a traditional, centrally planned Stalinist economy, protection for domestic manufacturing is almost entirely implicit. Through exchange controls and the apparatus of state trading, disguised subsidies to users of energy and other material inputs are coupled with virtually absolute protection from competing foreign manufactures. Although no formal tariffs appear in any legal codes, the implicit structure of tariff equivalents "cascades" downward from very high levels for the domestic production of finished consumer goods through manufactured intermediate products through industrial raw materials and energy, whose production is negatively protected because of implicit export taxes (or import subsidies).

This highly cascaded structure of implicit tariffs in socialist economies raises effective protection in finished goods to the point where most manufacturing well exhibit negative (or very low) value added at world market prices. In such circumstances, a precipitate move to free trade could provoke the collapse of most domestic manufacturing industries—no matter how the exchange rate is set, and no matter that some of this industry might eventually be viable at world market prices.

Thus, reforms to make commercial policy more explicit should accompany efforts to make the currency convertible on current account. This paper suggested the simultaneous "tarification" of quantitative restrictions on competing imports and the elimination of implicit export taxes on energy and material inputs as the economy moves quickly to a market-based system. Once made explicit, the highest tariffs in the cascade can then be phased down step-by-step to zero (or a low uniform level) over a preannounced five to ten year time horizon. The newly marketized economy would then converge to free foreign trade at a more deliberate pace—one that better recognized the problem of overcoming distortions from the preexisting system of protection.

Notes

Ronald I. McKinnon is in the Department of Economics at Stanford University

This chapter is a shortened, adapted version of Chapter 12 in the author's recent book *The Order of Economic Liberalization: Financial Control in the Transition to a Market Economy,* Baltimore: The Johns Hopkins Press, 1991. I would like to thank John Hussman, David Robinson, John Williamson, and Michael Treadway for their help in preparing this chapter.

1. Behind the scenes in this chapter is the presumption that the liberalizing socialist economy has strong domestic fiscal and credit controls in place that prevent enterprises from overbidding for scarce resources. Thus, the national government need not resort to blocking the cash balance positions of enterprises, i.e., to "commodity inconvertibility" (John Williamson, 1991), in order to prevent domestic inflation. To avoid this syndrome of commodity inconvertibility, however, the whole structure of domestic taxation and money and credit may have to be reformed at the outset of the liberalization—see McKinnon (1991a and 1991b). Here, I simply assume that liberalization has proceeded to the point where enterprise money can be spent freely for domestic purposes.

2. Tan was concerned with the structure of differential tariffs in LDCs where finished goods—largely consumer manufactures—received high tariff protection; but intermediate inputs entered duty free. For our analysis of the Soviet

Union, I treat the taxed export good as the relevant intermediate product. However, for the smaller Eastern European economies where material inputs are imported, one might want to introduce an untaxed importable as a third commodity in the analytical model—as per McKinnon (1966).

3. In any market economy, value added being positive at domestic prices is a necessary condition—although by no means sufficient to assure profitability—for the firm to exist. In a socialist economy, in extreme cases one could imagine a degree of public subsidy that enabled an enterprise to keep going even when it was not covering the costs of its material inputs. But I am ruling out this unlikely possibility.

4. This absence of a market test for valuing final outputs is one important reason why the growth in Soviet GNP may have been significantly overstated in the postwar period. Continual decline in product quality did not reduce measured GNP, while the continual introduction of "new and improved" products was allowed to increase it.

5. The authorities don't have to reveal any exact dates on which tariffs would be discretely adjusted—thereby inviting inventory speculation. Continual adjustment by very small amounts to yield a prespecified cumulative change would be much preferred.

6. I am greatly indebted to Peter Kenen for suggesting this point to me.

7. The possibilities for hardening the trade ruble, making it convertible into Western monies, are discussed in McKinnon (1979, Ch. 3).

8. That the international convertibility of the ruble on capital account comes last rather than first in the optimum order of economic liberalization is well recognized by Academician Abel Aganbegyan (1988) and is discussed at some length in McKinnon (1991).

Bibliography

Aganbegyan, Abel. 1988. The New Stage of Perestroika, Institute for East-West Security Studies, pp. 25–44.

Aslund, Anders. 1989. Gorbachev's Struggle for Economic Reform. Ithaca, New York: Cornell University Press.

Edwards, Sebastian and Alejandra Cox Edwards. 1977. Monetarism and Liberalization: The Chilean Experiment, Ballinger, Cambridge Mass.

Lerner, A.P. 1936. "The Symmetry Between Import and Export Taxes" Econòmica, 111, August, pp. 308–313.

Lipton, David and Jeffrey Sachs, "Creating a Market Economy in Eastern Europe: The Case of Poland," 1990, Brookings Paper on Economic Activity, 1.

McKinnon, Ronald I. 1991. the Order of Economic Liberalization: Financial Control in the transition to Market Economy. Baltimore: The John Hopkins University Press. (forthcoming).

_______. 1991. "Financial Control in the Transition from Classical Socialism to a Market Economy," Journal of Economic Perspectives.

______. 1979. Money in International Exchange: The Convertible Currency System. New York: Oxford University Press.

______. 1973. Money and Capital in Economic Development. Washington, D.C.: Brookings Institution.

______. 1966. "Intermediate Products and Differential Tariffs: A Generalization of Lerner's Symmetry Theorem," Quarterly Journal of Economics, vol. 80, November pp. 584–615.

Schrenk, Martin. 1990. "Whither Comecon?," Finance and Development, Sept.

Shmelev, Nikolai and Vladimir Popov. 1989. The Turning Point: Revitalizing the Soviet Economy. New York: Doubleday.

Tan, Augustine. 1970. "Differential Tariff," Negative Value-Added and the Theory of Effective Protection," American Economic Review vol. 60 (1) March.

The Economist. 1990. "Industrial Concentration in the USSR," August 11–17,p 67.

Williamson, John. 1991. "Convertibility, Trade Policy, and the Payments Constraint," in J. Williamson ed. Currency Convertibility in Eastern Europe, Institute for International Economics.

PART THREE

Privatization of State Capital Assets

7

East European Transformation: The Supply Side

Wojciech W. Charemza

One main reason for the replacement of the centrally planned economies (CPE) by market systems in Eastern Europe is to achieve greater economic efficiency. A series of measures such as financial liberalization (that is, the abolition of price controls), privatization, other forms of deregulation, and generally a tendency towards the creation of a *laissez faire* economic environment is intended to move an economy from a stable but inefficient position into a more efficient one. Since, as has been shown by tracking the economic performance of Eastern Europe in 1990–1992, financial liberalization and the formal introduction of market mechanisms can be achieved reasonably easily, most of the numerous works published recently on Eastern European transformation concentrate on the methods and prescriptions on how to speed up the processes of privatization, demonopolization and restructuring, usually with an emphasis on privatization.

The aim of this chapter is to show that narrow-sense privatization, that is, the mere a transfer of ownership rights from state to private hands of the existing capital, may not even be a necessary condition for an improvement in economic efficiency. In the case where there is substantial allocative inefficiency (or simply a distortion of the supply structure) privatization of existing resources may not have a positive effect on economic performance, even in the long run. Analogously, a demand management policy may, in the absence of forces causing a shift of aggregate supply, lead to the achievement of an inefficient, but stable, equilibrium, which is difficult to improve upon. This calls for a reexamination of the somewhat old-fashioned and widely criticized supply-side economics in an Eastern European context.

While the demand-side anti-inflationary policies undertaken in Eastern Europe in 1990–1992 have been generally effective, little has been done in respect to an improvement of the supply side. In the second section of this chapter I argue that without an active supply-side policy, it may not be possible to leave an inefficient equilibrium and move to a more efficient one. The third section gives an account of the supply-side distortions that existed in Eastern Europe at the beginning of the transformation process while the fourth section briefly summarizes the anti-inflationary efforts of reforming Eastern European countries in 1991 and discusses their supply-side effects. In the fifth section I analyze practical aspects of supply-side policies, in particular deregulation prior to privatization, wide-sense privatization, and taxation and industrial policy.

Demand/Supply Effects of Economic Reform

Suppose that prior to economic reform the economy is centrally planned in an East European style. Aggregate demand and supply curves for such an economy are shown in Figure 1a. Aggregate demand is represented by the curve AD_0 and potential output by Q^*. Due to involuntary employment (or overemployment—see Oxenstierna, 1990) the economy is constantly producing at a level above the potential output (that is above that corresponding to the natural rate of unemployment). The realized level of output is denoted by Q_0. As widely described in the literature, aggregate supply is price-inelastic (see e.g. Portes and Winter, 1977, 1980; Nuti, 1989; Kornai, 1980; Charemza and Gronicki, 1988). The price at which trading takes place, p_0, is below equilibrium, so that a positive excess demand develops, equal to $D - Q_0$. The aggregate demand curve is relatively price-inelastic, due to the fact that persistent shortages develop expectations of future shortages that eventually lead to a distortion in preferences (see Alexeev, 1988; Burkett, 1988).

Next, particular stages of economic reform are gradually introduced. In Eastern European economic reforms it is desirable to distinguish between demand-side and supply-side elements. Since the aggregate supply is initially price-inelastic, price reform is essentially a demand-type policy. Privatization is evidently a supply-side policy. The other types of supply-side policy considered here in an East European context are *transactional liberalization,* that is the abolition of restrictions on labor allocation and an effective bankruptcy law, and *secondary policy,* aimed at increasing competitiveness and efficiency independently from the privatization process but under the condition that transactional liberalization has taken place. Secondary policy includes demonopolization, the

FIGURE 1 **Supply Effects of Economic Reform**

Fig. 1a: Price liberalisation

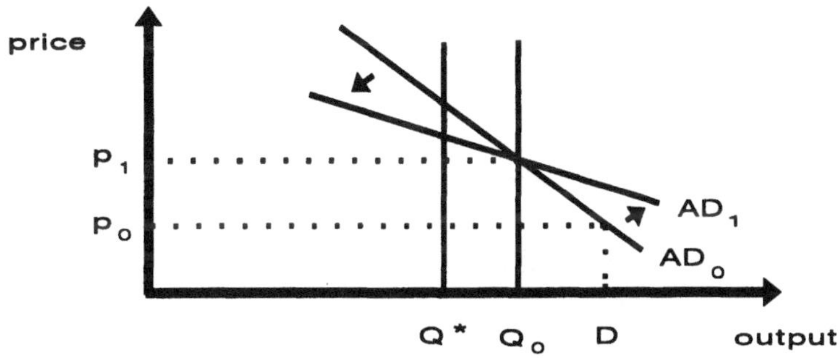

Fig. 1b: Transactional liberalisation

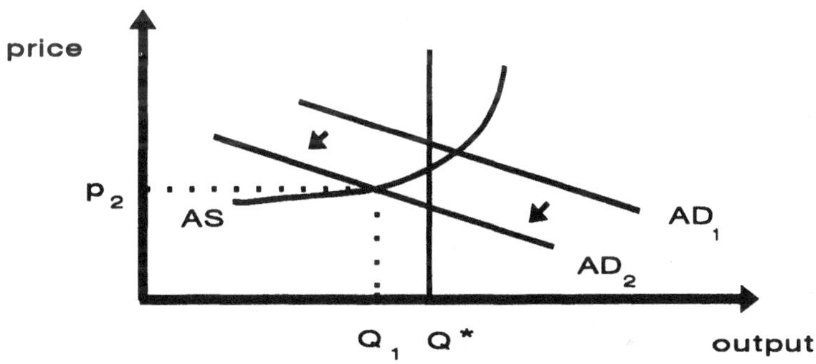

Fig. 1c: WSP and secondary policies

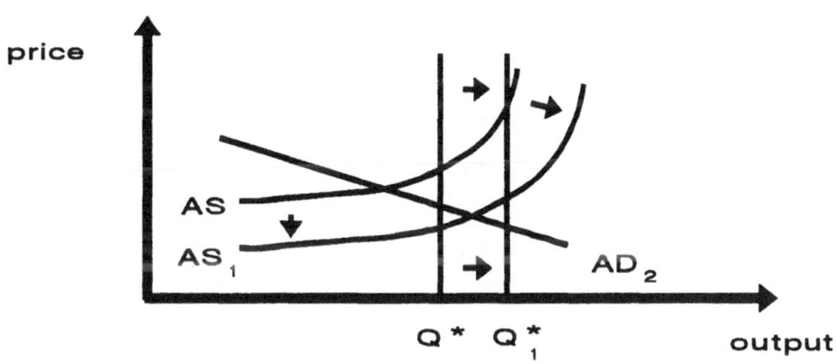

establishment of contestable markets, incentive taxation scheme, industrial policy, *etc.*

Let us start with an analysis of the reform sequence that does not include secondary policy, that is the following sequence: (1) Price liberalization, (2) Transactional liberalization, (3) Privatization. Eastern European economic reforms usually aim to carry out reform in this order, that is price liberalization is to be followed by transactional liberalization followed by privatization. In practice, however (and as discussed further in the text) stages 2 and 3 cannot be clearly separated in time.

As the result of price liberalization, the price level price simply moves upwards towards the equilibrium level. At the same time, the aggregate demand curve becomes more price elastic, due to the disappearance of quantity constraint expectations and moves to position AD_1. Since the supply curve is still price-inelastic, prices and quantities finally find the equilibrium point $(P_1; Q_0)$.

If transactional liberalization is introduced at this stage, the aggregate supply curve (denoted as *AS* in Figure 1b) become price-elastic. Withdrawal of the involuntary employed labor and bankruptcies create a potentially recessive situation, which becomes a reality if an anti-inflationary demand policy is introduced simultaneously. In the Eastern European practice of 1990–1992 monetary and income policies shifted the AD_1 curve down to a position AD_2 (Figure 1b). Given input costs, the position of the aggregate supply curve on the graph depends on the initial allocative and X-inefficiency. The more inefficient the initial allocation is, the higher the *AS* curve is placed. This adds to inflation creating, as a result, a stagflationary situation.

Suppose that at that stage a privatization policy is introduced. It is important to distinguish herein between the narrow-sense privatization, (abbreviated by *NSP)* that is merely the transfer of property rights to private hands of the existing capital and wide sense privatization (*WSP*), which means that *NSP* is accompanied by the development of the private sector by starting new investment projects. This is herewith called *active privatization.* Let us suppose that initially the economic policy concerned is that of *NSP.* It is unlikely that this would have any definite positive supply-side effect (i.e. the movement of Q^* to the right and of *AS* down and/or to the right). Strictly speaking, the initial positive supply-side effect of *NSP* would happen only if it improves allocative and X-efficiency since, given the allocation, the rate of return on the production factors remain unchanged (in the long-run, there would be also a cost-multiplier effect of any efficiency improvement).

Without getting into technicalities, the concept of allocative efficiency if understood as the generation of an optimal structure of output by the most efficient combination of inputs (an advanced introduction and exhaustive references to the subject are given in Reiter, 1987). The concept of X-efficiency is described as a situation in which total costs can be minimized given that inputs are at their maximum feasible level (for a formal definition see Leibenstein, 1966 and the huge literature that followed).[1] It is widely accepted that privatization may stimulate X-efficiency—see e.g., Pera (1989), Vickers and Yarrow (1988). (It is, however shown in later in this chapter that it is questionable whether some privatization programs introduced in Eastern Europe are X-efficient). Nevertheless, it is likely that privatization and transactional liberalization would, under the initial allocative inefficiency, not have a positive impact on the aggregate supply curve. Achieving the optimal output structure under central planning, given the unrevealed and distorted, due to shortages, consumers' preferences requires perfect planning (that is, optimal planning under perfect information) and it is widely known that this was never achieved (see e.g., Ellman, 1989, Charemza and Kiraly, 1990).

Even if planning were perfect in the sense that it reflected consumers' preferences in the best possible way under the repressed inflation regime, it would not generate an allocative efficient structure if preferences changed. Since preferences do change, due to the disappearance of expected quantity constraints, the structure would not be optimal any more. With some exaggeration one may say that consumers after economic reform are not prepared to buy red banners, tanks and barbed wire at any sustainable price even if these were the goods they required previously . With less exaggeration, but assuming that a country is open to competition from abroad, it can be similarly argued that they would not prefer the old-fashioned labor-intensive and expensive domestic technology. Correspondingly on the labor side, the structure of labor skills that had been optimal under the former regime may not be optimal after the regime changes.

Consequently, after financial and transactional liberalization and exposing the industry to competition, a substantial part of potential output would not find buyers and has to be scrapped, whether the *NSP* takes place or not. This would shift Q^* to the left and move the *AS* curve accordingly. Also, this would offset any positive effect of possible X-efficiency improvement. For the sake of clarity, it is assumed that *NSP* would not alter potential output and that its supply-side effect is, at best, neutral.

Suppose now that a policy of *WSP* is implemented rather than *NSP*, that is, that a "dead-start" development of the new private sector alongside the existing one has been successfully encouraged. Alternatively, it can be assumed that the *NSP* policy has been accompanied by a secondary supply-side policy. It can be safely asserted that the newly built private sector is more X-efficient than the old one. If there is also an improvement in the information flow due to increased market efficiency, the allocation has to be more efficient. This would shift Q^* to the right (Figure 1c) to the position Q^*_1. Consequently, the *AS* curve should also move to AS_1 . An equilibrium can be found at a lower price, which would increase the effectiveness of any subsequent demand policy.

A practical conclusion from this is that after a long period of central planning, a simple policy of the handling over of what is left to private hands is unlikely to have a positive effect on the economy. A positive effect can be made either be implementing *WSP* rather than *NSP,* that is by building a new industrial structure alongside (or in place of) the old one, or by actively implementing a secondary supply-side policy. Stopping or reversing the privatization process in order to avoid a chronic recession would also not be effective. It may move the economy into another inefficient equilibrium with a low level of privatization (see Roland and Verdier, 1991).

Supply-Side Distortions

The assertion that the supply side of Eastern European economies has been a distorted structure is strongly supported by numerous empirical studies. Especially important seem to be the results of Hughes and Hare (1991, 1992) concerning the industrial efficiency of existing industries in Eastern Europe. They have computed estimates of value added for industrial branches for Bulgaria, Czechoslovakia, Hungary, Poland, and the USSR for the years 1986–1989. They found that, at quality-adjusted world prices, more than 50 percent of industrial output in Bulgaria has a negative value added. For Czechoslovakia and Hungary the share is about 35 percent and for Poland below 10 percent. This illustrates the significant uncompetitiveness of the industries in these countries and implies a huge allocative inefficiency (for a discussion of further consequences of these findings see Dhar, 1992; for a thorough evaluation of industrial distortions in Czechoslovakia, Hungary, and Poland see Landesman and Szekely, 1991).

Distortion of the industrial structure is also confirmed by an analysis of the distribution of the enterprise and plant size in Czechoslovakia, Hungary, and Poland (Newbery, 199lb; also Charemza, 1991). This shows a huge concentration of employment in big enterprises, with an average plant size in most industries higher than in developed countries. Concentration and average plant size varies significantly between countries, with the largest concentration in Czechoslovakia, followed by Hungary and Poland. Such a large concentration is usually explained by features of central planning and evidently has nothing in common with increasing returns to scale. Without further deliberation it can be asserted that such a distorted industrial structure is an additional cause for the allocative inefficiency of Eastern European economies.

In addition to industrial type inefficiency on the supply side, as a consequence of abolishing central planning another type of distortion appears, namely informational inefficiency. Central planning, however inefficient, did in fact provide some type of information signals to and from enterprises. Price liberalization would not immediately fill the gap left by central planning. Information that helps the estimation of future prices and supplies must, in order to be efficient (that is, to create an efficient market environment) be accompanied by a relatively small variation in their future (believed) distribution. This is, in the process of price liberalization, usually not the case. First, price liberalization creates an inflationary situation and it is to be expected that inflationary expectations are not accompanied by an increase in future market uncertainty. Second, the dispersion of the believed price and quantity distribution is further stimulated by the fact that a market learning process has just started.

If one believes in any type of a learning process leading to an expectational equilibrium, such an equilibrium must take some time to develop. Hence, the uncertainty that accompanies the price liberalization inflationary process is likely to be greater than would result from mean/variance regularity. As shown by Charemza (1992), such significant uncertainty creates market failure and can be interpreted as another factor that deepens the allocative inefficiency and flattening of the supply curve. Trivializing, one may say that if there is huge uncertainty concerning future prices and demand then the best strategy could be not to produce. Further uncertainties on the supply side can be created by a successful monetary and income policies .

Demand-Side Policies in 1991 and their Supply-Side Effects

After price liberalization had taken place in Eastern Europe, inflationary pressures prompted governments to undertake some type of stabilization policy. Since, at the starting point of economic reform, employment was concentrated in the state sector and an efficient tax system was virtually nonexistent, options were limited to income and monetary policies. With a substantial degree of industrial concentration, direct income policies seemed to be especially attractive. These were undertaken primarily by Czechoslovakia and Poland and to a lesser extent by Hungary, which applied income tax policy rather than direct income policy. However, the 1991 Hungarian income tax system was very inefficient. With a low tax-exempt income and strong progression it gave, under annual inflation higher than expected, only 6 percent of total budget revenues (compared to an average of 18 percent for the European Community countries). Hence, its macroeconomic effect could be similar to that of a direct income policy. Direct income policies took various forms: from a wage fund freeze (used also by some of the late communist governments) through imposing statutory norms to indexation. These policies were limited to the state sector, with an additional aim of encouraging private economic activities. With the introduction of limited transactional liberalization, monetary policy started to gain some importance and was usually combined with a policy of statutory norms or wage indexation.

As far as reducing inflation is concerned, these policies were remarkably effective. Figure 2 shows time paths of monthly inflation, unemployment ratio, and index of industrial output (with the base defined as "corresponding month of 1990") in Czechoslovakia, Hungary, and Poland in 1991. The dynamics of the changes are similar in all these countries. At the beginning of 1991, when inflation was significant, income policy worked very effectively, at a relatively low cost in output and unemployment. This is hardly surprising, since it happened after price liberalization, but before transactional liberalization had fully developed. Economies were operated at the steep part of the supply curve (Figure la); hence the effectiveness of an income policy. From the beginning of the second quarter of 1991, with the progress of transactional liberalization, negative real effects of an income policy started to appear. Since the supply curve becomes flat with the introduction of transactional liberalization, even a small decrease in inflation generates a substantial drop in industrial output. This is especially visible for Czechoslovakia, where inflation was most radically reduced. In the second half of 1991, where the disequilibrium-type direct income policies were relaxed, there are some signs of stabilization of output decrease, at the expense of raising inflation.

For all these countries the decrease in output (and also the increase in unemployment) was in 1991 greater than had been expected. These expectations made at the end of 1990 and used as a base for budget estimations decline of GDP in 1991 were the following (with the real decline in GDP given in parentheses): Czechoslovakia: 5–10 percent (15.9 percent), Hungary: 3–4 percent (7–9 percent), Poland: 3–6 percent

FIGURE 2 Economic Performance in 1991

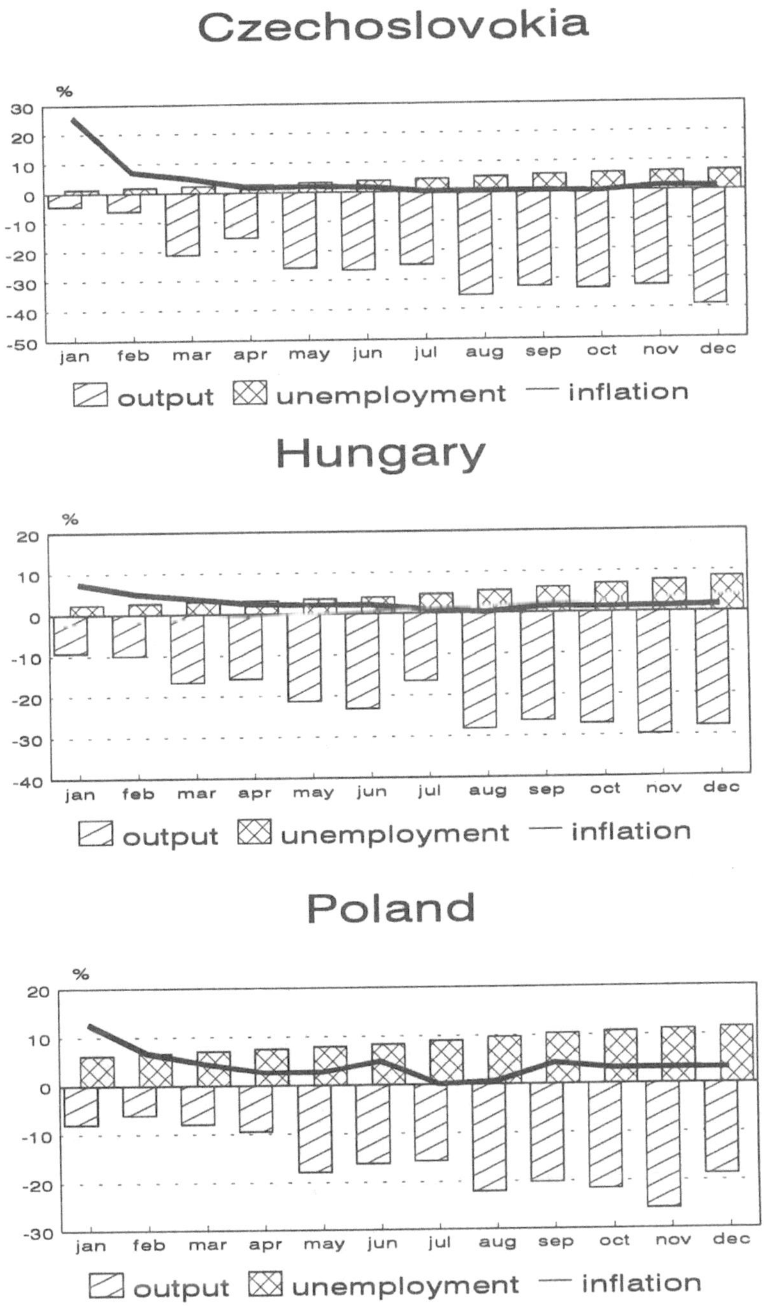

(8–10 percent). Usually, a (hardly unexpected) decline in trade with Soviet Union was blamed for this. It seems, however, that these policies also have less evident, but equally serious, supply-side effects. Incomes policy would have a similar effect on incentives to work as the more widely discussed fiscal policy. However, unlike tax policies, wage fund freeze and wage indexation create distortions in labor markets. They act like a disequilibrium-type quantity constraint, not allowing demand and supply to adjust through a real wage change (see Lane, 1991). Hence, they delay rather than cure inflation.

Directly on the supply side, such constraints prevent an adjustment in the capital/labor allocation. They cause a production process to be more capital-intensive than it otherwise should be. Also, excess demand for labor may result in some state employed workers undertaking private, legal or illegal, activity. If such activity in the private sector is more efficient than in the state sector, this could act towards an improvement on the supply side. If, however, there is a delayed flow of capital and expertise to the private sector and informational uncertainty, this would not lead to an efficient allocation. It would artificially increase the cost of capital and hence reduce investment. It may also be accompanied by a huge social cost of illegal and unreported activity, and increased market inefficiency due to fragmentary information and risk costs. Another serious consequence of an income policy is that, unlike manipulation with a marginal tax rate, it affects average rather than marginal income and hence creates a disincentive to aiming at an X-efficiency increase. Finally, all these policies have a negative labor/leisure substitution effect. With a decrease in income, either due to a direct income policy or through an increase in taxation, leisure becomes relatively more expensive and, with an introduction of transactional liberalization, may lead to the increased substitution of labor by leisure.

Monetary policy would have a similar negative effect on the supply side. A tight anti-inflationary monetary policy would deflate commodity prices and, at the same time, appreciate the domestic currency. This, on the supply side, is perceived as an uncontrollable change in relative prices (supply shock). With an import-intensive industry, this would shift the supply curve upwards. Another aspect of a supply-side effect of a monetary policy is through an increase of informational inefficiency. Under inflationary pressure, costs of holding money are high. Monetary policy would reduce this cost but, since it would not increase real output, uncertainty as how to interpret the price changes would arise. In other words, it would not be clear whether it is better to hold on to money or to invest. Holding on to money would be more advantageous if the opportunity cost of investment increase.

Supply-Side Policies

For 1991, all Eastern European countries reported greater than expected difficulties with privatization. In Czechoslovakia, Hungary, and Poland efforts were primarily concentrated on narrow-sense privatization, that is the transference of property rights of the existing state sector into private hands. This took various forms and was carried out with different intensity but with little success (for a detailed comparison of different privatization policies in Czechoslovakia, Hungary, and Poland see Grosfeld and Hare, 1991; and Bolton and Roland, 1992). In Czechoslovakia, there were difficulties is selling the so-called voucher books (which will entitle the buyer to acquire shares of the privatized enterprises in the future) to the public. This was eventually done in the very last month of the selling period, after a rather optimistic promise of a quick and huge profit on all shares purchased, regardless or their market value. In Hungary, in 1991, 9 percent of state enterprises were privatized, and in Poland 2.7 percent. Such pace of privatization, apart presumably for Hungary, is slower than had been expected a year before.

The main reason for this seems to be the difficulties with transactional liberalization. As shown by Hughes and Hare (1991, 1992), substantial proportions of industry, especially in Czechoslovakia and Hungary, would not have survived if exposed to free competition. Hughes and Hare (1992) have also shown that recent changes to Eastern European economies have not improved their competitiveness. Similarly, Prasnikar, Svejnar, and Klinedinst (1992) rejected the claim that an export reorientation of a state enterprise could increase its efficiency. Hence, it can be conjectured that the transactional liberalization of an allocative inefficient industry would bring huge redundancies of labor (often by 100 percent, through bankruptcies and scrapping), in order to improve the allocation. Such deep structural changes in labor do not seem to be admissible for socio-political reasons.

Spatial concentration of industries and acute housing problems in Eastern Europe means that geographical reallocation of labor would be extremely difficult and expensive. Also, the distortions in skill structure of labor are a serious obstacle to its effective reallocation. Consequently, the number of bankruptcies and laid-up firms has been trivial in 1991, despite the substantial drop in output (this had been correctly foreseen by Mitchell (1990) and explained by Schaffer (1991) as labor-managed monopolistic behavior). Hence, it is not surprising that the strategy of survival for Eastern European governments is to slow down the privatization process and hence avoid (or rather delay) its negative socioeconomic repercussions (for a similar conclusions in this respect see Svejnar, 1991).

The extent of this passive supply-side policy can be assessed by comparing the percentage fall in industrial production in 1991 in comparison with the fall in employment in the industrial sectors of the economy. Such analysis indicates that the greatest industrial output decline took place in Czechoslovakia, followed by Hungary, then by Poland. However, this order is reversed for the decline in employment: the greatest is for Poland, then for Hungary, and then for Czechoslovakia. In the era of central planning Czechoslovakia had the most industrialized economy and the smallest (virtually nonexistent) private sector. It can be conjectured that the potential effect of transactional liberalization would have been more damaging for Czechoslovakia than for Hungary and Poland.

After concluding that narrow-sense privatization can be regarded as neither an efficient nor a feasible supply-side policy it would be interesting to discuss its alternatives. An immediate alternative is the other component of wide-sense privatization, that is active privatization. Among various possible secondary policies three are regarded below as particularly relevant: informational policy, incentive taxation and deregulation, and contestability.

Active Privatization

I have defined active privatization as a policy of starting new investment projects within the private sector. Evidently, investment projects require capital and this is generally not available in Eastern Europe. It will be possible to attract some capital from abroad through a policy of profit reinvestment and repatriation attractive for foreign investors and increased informational efficiency (see below). However, if an active privatization policy is going to be the main industrial policy rather than *NSP*, funds must also come from internal sources. Apart from self-financing from savings, this would imply the generation of subsidized investment credit, probably at the expense of a budget deficit and, in the long-run, inflation. It should take the form of a targeted investment credit policy with subsidized target credit rather than offering a generally subsidized low interest rate.

The latter would likely lead to a negative MacKinnon-Shaw effect observed in some developing countries, that is to the creation of disincentives to save and hence reduction in the ability of an economy to invest through self-finance. In the case of capital scarcity self-finance can be at least an equally important source of investment accumulation as borrowing (see Ghatak, 1981, pp. 62–65 and, in the Eastern European context, Charemza and Ghatak, 1990). The targeted subsidized credit would not directly affect the borrowing rate. Part of the investment credit would be allocated at an unrestricted, free market interest rate. This would be topped-up by the government by subsidized credit, offered at a preferential interest rate. The necessity of subsidizing credit is stimulated by the fact that, under the substantial informational inefficiency in Eastern Europe, the problem of adverse selection is likely to be especially acute.

The usual assertion of asymmetry of information between lenders and borrowers, which leads to the settlement of a free market interest rate at a level inaccessible to high risk borrowers (see Stiglitz and Weiss, 1981; Stiglitz, 1985) is, in the Eastern European context, accompanied by the fact that probability distributions of expected returns are subject to relatively high dispersion, due to the informational inefficiency. This would push the reservation value up and add to the tendency to eliminate low-risk borrowers from the market. Also, because the loans issued within this policy have to be relatively large and, as is widely accepted, the propensity to default increases with the increase of a loan size, the moral hazard problem would also be important. This again could be tackled through a secondary policy on increased informational efficiency but also through the allocation of preferential credit to self-controlled risk-sharing investment pools rather than to individual companies.

Informational Policy

As I indicated above, informational inefficiency can be regarded as an important supply-type distortion affecting the entire process of economic reform. The need for an improvement in information is going to be more urgent if active privatization through credit targeting is implemented. Apart from reducing the risk of adverse selection in the process of credit allocation, better informational efficiency may reduce one of the negative impacts of inflation, namely price uncertainty (variation of the distribution of future prices, regarded as a random variable) and supply risk. As shown by Charemza (1992), a reduction in the future price dispersion would act as a stimulant for the lessening in market imperfection through a reduction in market failure and, in some cases, in recovering missing markets.

The most important factor in achieving informational improvements seems to be the development of proper legalization of economic activities. At present, legal regulations concerning the economy are, especially in Czechoslovakia and in Poland, unclear, inconsistent, and often not practically implemented. This presumably results, to a large extent, from the widespread conviction that there is a simultaneous feedback between any economic policy and economic legislation. If there are difficulties in establishing a clearly defined and efficient economic policy, legislation has to suffer.

This opinion seems to be only partially justified. It seems that a large part of economic legislation like rules of business responsibility, laws on bankruptcies, foreign trade activities, and especially commercial banking practices and techniques are largely independent of whatever economic policy is going to be implemented. Other means of improving informational efficiency are those concerned with the flow of information on current prices and quantities, such as all types of statistical information services, trading bulletins, *etc.*

Incentive Taxation

In a traditional supply-side economy the problem of incentive taxation is usually the central one and tax policy is in most cases the focus of both theoreticians and practitioners (see e.g., Canto, Joines, and Laffer, 1983; Bartlett and Roth, 1983). It is undoubtedly important also in the Eastern European context since, on the one hand, taxes creates a primary source of a revenue needed, among other things, to subsidize credit in the active privatization policy and, on the other, to provide an incentive on the supply side. Traditionally, the problem of incentive taxation illustrated by the so-called *Laffer curve,* which shows the relation between government revenue and the taxation rate. This is shown by Figure 3, where the middle curve represents the typical Laffer curve, with a maximum revenue at point *A*. An increase of the tax rate above the point *A* would generate a decrease in revenue, due to a disincentive effect.

According to Gutmann (1983), if there is an propensity to cheat on taxes by hiding a part of income, this propensity will increase with the increase of the tax rate. Consequently, the Laffer curve is positively skewed, with a maximum at point *B,* which indicates that the government, in order to maximize revenue and create an incentive effect, should be prepared to tolerate part of an underground economy. In an Eastern European situation, however, an effect of inefficiency of the tax collecting system due to a lack of income information (informational

FIGURE 3 Laffer Curve and Tax Inefficiency

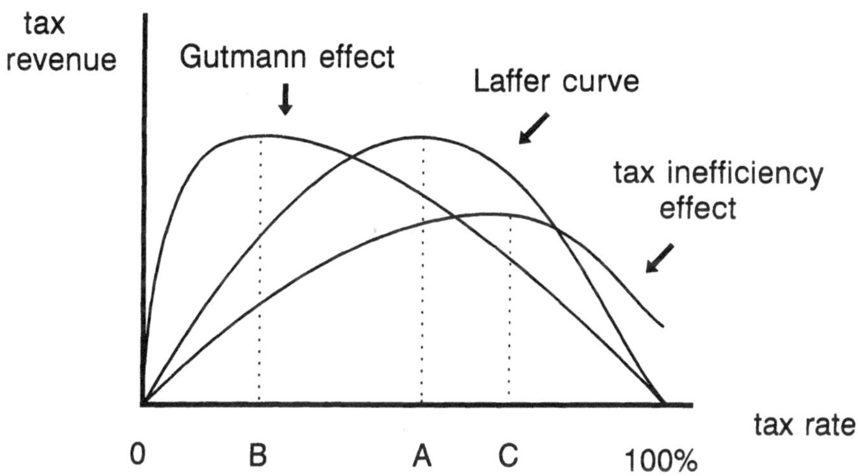

failure) can be more relevant. It is assumed that, instead of the Gutmann effect of tax cheating, the tax collectors fail to identify $g \cdot 100$ percent of income. Consequently, the tax is imposed not on the entire income but on $(1 - g) \cdot 100$ percent of it.

Suppose also that the incentive effect is as in the Laffer curve without the Gutmann effect, that is the maximum revenue would be a tax rate equal to A if g were equal to 0. Actually, for $g > 0$, at a tax rate A taxpayers have still a positive incentive, since their actual income is taxed at the rate $A' = A \cdot (1/(1 + g))$, which is less than A. Tax revenue will start to fall after the point $C = A \cdot (1 + g)$ is passed. Due to the failure in the tax collection system, the total revenue would never be as high as under the perfect scheme, with or without the Gutmann effect. Also, the maximum revenue will be achieved at a higher tax rate.

Hence, if the authorities decide first to fix an "incentive" tax rate and next to improve on the tax collection system (that is, to move to the original Laffer curve), the tax rate would be too high and the total tax revenue would be too low. This would be even more drastic if the Laffer curve is subject to the Gutmann effect, since in this case the tax rate corresponding to the maximum tax revenue would be even lower. The above analysis suggest that in Eastern Europe, where the tax collection systems are by no means perfect, there can be a tendency to impose a tax rate at a too high level, if this is done prior to the imposition of an effective tax collection system.

Demonopolization and Contestability

One of the main symptoms of supply-side distortions to the centrally planned economy was the huge concentration of industry, which led to a substantial monopolization of the economy. During the process of price liberalization this would add to inflation, since monopolies would try to establish monopoly pricing system. During transactional liberalization, monopolization could result in increased unemployment since the maximization of monopolistic rent may likely be done through a reduction in employment.

The danger of monopolization has been recognized in early stages of the economic reform, although not a lot has been done. Various demonopolization commissions have been established in Czechoslovakia, Hungary, and Poland, and some demonopolization legislation has been imposed. This, however, has had little success. In 1991 industrial concentration in Eastern Europe still remained substantial, in comparison with Western Europe. Although the average size of an enterprise has diminished, this was mainly due to an increase in the number of small scale enterprises in the already established private sector rather than to a demonopolization policy. In industry, only for Hungary was the average number of employees in an enterprise, equal to 81, comparable to that in Western Europe (i.e., about 50 for the United Kingdom). For Poland the average number of employees was 230 and for Czechoslovakia 250 (these figures are not exactly comparable, due to differences in definition of an enterprise).

There seem to be three main reasons for these difficulties in demonopolization. First, it is organizationally very difficult to break up highly organized enterprises consisting of big plants that dominate the industrial structure of Czechoslovakia and Poland into smaller more effective units. Second, if transactional liberalization is going to be halted due the unemployment threat, it is easier (although presumably more costly) to maintain an artificially high level of employment in big enterprises rather than in small. The third reason is related to the fact that so far the most effective way of privatizing industrial enterprises has proved to be selling the most profitable enterprises to foreign buyers. Very often, maintaining the monopolistic position of an enterprise was in the essential interest of the buyer and an unspoken condition for a transaction to be completed.

Since deregulation through demonopolization seems often to be unrealistic, there is a need to establish a policy that would prevent monopolies from charging a monopolistic price. One such policy is to make monopolistic markets contestable, that is making a market vulnerable to a "hit-and-run" outsider, if the sunk cost of entry is low and there are no barriers to exit (see Baumol, 1982; Baumol, Panzar, and Willig, 1982; in the privatization context see Vickers and Yarrow, 1988, pp. 54–57; in an application to Eastern European privatization see Charemza, 1990). Generally speaking, if markets are contestable, monopolies cannot charge a monopolistic price since this would likely be undercut by an entrant. They may prevent entry by maintaining a relatively low price at which an entrant cannot make a profit by undercutting the incumbents' price.

Since the "hit-and-run" entrant would, at least before the active privatization is fully developed, come from abroad, the policy of maintaining the contestable environment would consists of a targeted tariff policy. Apart from being anti-inflationary, such tariffs combined with other export stimulating policies, could help to overcome some problems connected with the question discussed above of negative value added at world prices (see McKinnon, 1991). This, in turn, requires a sufficient level of informational efficiency concerning the degree of monopolization and of pricing policies.

Conclusion

In general, conclusions regarding the speed of privatization and its efficiency are, at least in relation to the existing state sector, rather pessimistic. It seems that it is simply sociologically and politically not possible to sustain such a significant level of unemployment, which would be brought about by the large scale privatization of the state sector. It would not have any significant positive supply-side effects and, in the current political realities of Eastern Europe, would probably bring an abrupt end to a government that would dare to be serious about it.

If huge structural unemployment is not an alternative, it seems that an economy would be relatively (or rather conditionally) better off by keeping the inefficient state sector running rather by scrapping it. This reflection is, generally, in the rather pessimistic mood of Hare (1991), Kornai (1990a, b), Svejnar (1991), and especially Roland (1991), who stressed the relevance of political constraints for the speed of privatization. It seems to contradict to some extent the optimistic views of the possibility of a rapid privatization process (Lipton and Sachs, 1990). The threat of recession means that, if the privatization is done in a "cold turkey" manner (see Kolodko et al., 1992, p. 110) the cold turkey will be served with a hot potato.

It does not, however, mean that the government has only to watch how the state sector is going to rot. On the contrary, the supply curve is going to move is the desired direction and hence reduce the pain of the rotting process only through a sensible supply-side policy. This especially means changing the government's attitude from promoting narrow privatization to supporting active privatization. Since this inevitably means inflation, an effort should be made to increase the informational inefficiency, which would likely lead to reducing price uncertainty and supply risk. In other words, it would be much easier to cope with an expected inflation rather than with the unexpected one.

Particular Eastern European countries are likely to react to the eventual supply shock with different intensity. Among Czechoslovakia, Hungary, and Poland, Hungary seems to be the best prepared. Informational inefficiency seems to be the smallest in Hungary (in particular the legalization of the economic reform is the most advanced), its tax system is relatively well developed, and already a tax-incentive policy has been undertaken (although not without difficulties—see Newbery, 1991a; Pudney, 1991), and the industrial structure is not as centralized. Next is Poland, mainly because it had a private sector already well established under the centrally planned economy, which should speed up the learning process and generally reduce the uncertainties. The worst prepared for the shock seems to be Czechoslovakia. Its industry has the most centralized and therefore the most distorted structure, and it started the reform process with a virtually nonexistent private sector, which may delay the learning process to increase the informational efficiency. Finally, a privatization voucher-based scheme such as implemented in Czechoslovakia does not seem to have an incentive mechanism included that would help in increasing the *X* efficiency.

Notes

Wojciech W. Charemza is in the Department of Economics at the University of Leicester.

I am indebted to Derek Deadman and George Norman for their helpful comments on an earlier draft of this chapter. I am solely responsible for remaining deficiencies. Financial support of ESRC Research Grant No. R000231827 is gratefully acknowledged.

1. Leibenstein (1987) quoted an example of the *X*-efficiency from the *New York Times* of two identical car plants in the U.K. and Germany, where the German plant produced 50 percent more cars with 22 percent less labor.

Bibliography

Alexeev, M. (1988), "Are Soviet consumers forced to save?" *Comparative Economic Studies 30*, pp. 17–23.

Bartlett, B. and T.P. Roth, eds. (1983) *The supply-side solution*, Macmillan, London.

Baumol, W.J. (1982), "Contestable markets: an uprising on the theory of industrial structure," *American Economic Review* 72, pp. 1–15.

Baumol W.J., J. Panzar and R.D. Willig (1982), *Contestable markets and the theory of industry Structure*, Harcourt Brace Jovanovic, New York.

Bolton, P. and G. Roland (1992), "The economics of mass privatization," Universite Libre de Bruxelles (mimeo).

Burkett, J., (1988), "Slack, shortage and discouraged consumers in Eastern Europe: estimates based on smoothing by aggregation," *Review of Economic Studies* 19, pp. 483–506.

Canto, V.A., D.H. Joines and A.B. Laffer (1983), *Foundation of Supply-side economics*, Academic Press, New York.

Charemza, W.W. (1991), "Alternative paths to macroeconomic stability in Czechoslovakia," *European Economy*, Special Issue No. 2, pp. 41–56.

Charemza, W.W. (1992), "Market failure and Stagflation: Some aspects of privatization in Poland," *Economics of Planning* 25.

Charemza, W.W. and S. Ghatak (1990), "Demand for money in a dual-currency, quantity-constrained economy: Hungary and Poland, 1956–1985," *Economic Journal* 100, pp. 1159–1172.

Charemza, W.W. and M. Gronicki (1988), *Plans and disequilibria in centrally planned economies: empirical investigation for Poland*, North-Holland, Amsterdam.

Charemza, W.W. and J. Kiraly (1990), "Plans and exogeneity: the genetic-teleological dispute revisited," *Oxford Economic Papers* 42, pp. 562–573.

Dhar, S. (1992), "Enterprise viability and the transition to a market economy," World Bank, ECVAP (mimeo).

Ellman, M. (1989), *Socialist planning* (2nd edition), Cambridge University Press, Cambridge.

Ghatak, S. (1981), *Monetary economics in developing countries*, Macmillan, London.

Grosfeld, I. and P. Hare (1991), "Privatization in Hungary, Poland and Czechoslovakia," Discussion Paper No. 31, Centre for Economic Performance, London School of Economics.

Gutman, P.M. (1983), "Taxes and supply of national output," in: Bartlett, B. and T.P. Roth, eds. *The Supply side solution*, Macmillan, London.

Hare, P. (1991), "Privatization in Eastern Europe: some theoretical issues," Discussion Paper No. 3, Department of Economics, Heriot-Watt University.

Hughes, G. and P. Hare "Competitiveness and industrial restructuring in Czechoslovakia, Hungary and Poland," *European Economy*, Special Edition No. 2, pp. 83–110.

Hughes, G. and P. Hare (1992), "Industrial policy and restructuring in Eastern Europe," Discussion Paper No. 653, Centre for Economic Policy Research, London.

Kolodko, G.W., D. Gotz-Kozierkiewicz and E. Skrzeczewska-Paczek (1992), *Hyperinflation and stabilization in post-socialist economies*, Kluwer, Dordrecht.

Kornai, J. (1980), *Economics of Shortage*, North-Holland, Amsterdam.

Kornai, J. (1990a), "The affinity between ownership and coordination mechanisms," WIDER, United Nations University, Helsinki.

Kornai, J. (1990b), *The road to a free economy*, Norton Press, New York.

Landesman, M. and I. Szekely (1991), "Industrial restructuring and the reorientation of trade in Czechoslovakia, Hungary and Poland," paper presented at the CEPR workshop *Economic Transformation in Eastern Europe*, London.

Lane, T.D. (1991), "Wage controls and employment in a socialist economy," International Monetary Fund, mimeo.

Leibenstein, H. (1966), "Allocative efficiency versus X-efficiency," *American Economic Review 72*, pp. 392–415.

Leibenstein, H. (1987), "X-efficiency theory," in: J. Eatwell, M. Milgate and P. Newman, eds., *The new Palgrave: a dictionary of economics*, Macmillan, London.

Lipton, D. and J. Sachs (1990), "Privatization in Eastern Europe: the case of Poland," *Brookings Papers on Economic Activity 2*, pp. 293–341.

McKinnon, R.I. (1991), "Liberalising foreign trade in socialist economy: the problem of negative value added," paper presented at the conference *Currency Convertibility in Eastern Europe*, Vienna.

Mitchell, J. (1990), "The economics of bankruptcy in reforming socialist economies," Cornell University, mimeo.

Newbery, D.M. (1991a), "An analysis of the Hungarian tax reform," paper presented at the conference *The Eastern European Transformation*, Princeton.

Newbery, D.M. (199lb), "Competition policy in Eastern Europe," paper presented at the conference *Deregulation in Eastern Europe*, University of Nottingham.

Nuti, D.M. (1989), "Hidden and repressed inflation in Soviet-type economies," in: C. Davis and W. Charemza, eds. *Models of disequilibrium and shortage in centrally planned economies*, Chapman and Hall, London.

Oxenstierna, S. (1990), *From labor shortage to unemployment? The Soviet labor market in the 1980s*. Almquist and Wicksell, Stockholm.

Pera, A. (1989), "Deregulation and privatization in an economy-wide context," *OECD Economic Studies 12*, pp. 159–204.

Portes, R. and D. Winter (1977), "The supply of consumption goods in centrally planned economies," Journal *of Comparative Economics 1*, pp. 351–365.

Portes, R. and D. Winter (1980), "Disequilibrium estimates for consumption goods markets in centrally planned economies', *Review of Economic Studies 47*, pp. 137–159.

Prasnikar, J., J. Svejnar and M. Klinedinst (1992), "Structural adjustment policies and productive efficiency of socialist enterprises', *European Economic Review 36*, pp. 179–199.

Svejnar, J. (1991), "Microeconomic issues in the transition to a market economy," *Journal of Economic Perspectives 5*, pp. 123–138.

Reiter, S. (1987), "Efficient allocation," in: J. Eatwell, m. Milgate and P. Newman, eds., *The new Palgrave: a dictionary of economics*, Macmillan, London.

Roland, G. (1990), "Political economy of sequencing tactics in the transition period," Discussion Paper No. 9008, CEME, Universite Libre de Bruxelles.

Roland, G. and T. Verdier (1991), "Privatisation in Eastern Europe: irreversibility and critical mass effect," CEME., Universite Libre de Bruxelles, mimeo.

Schaffer, M.E. (1991), "A note on the Polish state-owned enterprise sector in 1990," Centre for Economic Performance, London School of Economics.

Stiglitz, J. (1985), "Credit markets and the control of capital," *Journal of Money, credit and Banking 17*, pp. 133–153.

Stiglitz, J. and A. Weiss (1981), "Credit rationing in markets with imperfect information," *American Economic Review 71*, pp. 393–410.

Vickers, J. and G. Yarrow (1988), *Privatization: an economic analysis*, The MIT Press, London.

8

Inflation Tax, Household Wealth, and Privatization in Poland

Przemyslaw T. Gajdeczka

Since 1989, countries of central and eastern Europe have undertaken major reforms aimed at the transformation of their economic system from one characterized by central planning to one based on market mechanisms. An essential part of the transition to a market economy involves far-reaching structural reforms, and in particular privatization. The scope of required privatization is unprecedented. In the majority of these countries, nearly all productive assets are still owned by the state; private sector contribution to GDP has been modest by international standards, and state-owned industries have dominated industrial output.[1] In Poland, for example, it is estimated that some 8,000 firms will need to be privatized over the medium term.[2]

The discussion of privatization has concentrated on the design of the privatization process and the issues of governance, including the management model and the extent to which the new class of owners has effective control over the management of the privatized enterprises.[3] This chapter discusses the issue of private sector's inability to purchase state-owned assets in Poland.[4] The chapter shows that private sector's resources that can be used to purchase the enterprises are small because their real value has been significantly eroded by inflation. This loss of wealth stemmed from the fact that in Poland the private sector (including the household sector) was restricted to accumulating largely monetary assets which were continuously taxed through inflation, while fixed assets were accumulated by the broadly defined public sector. The private sector was a structural net creditor while the state sector was a structural net debtor.

Households accumulated the monetary assets and became structural creditors voluntarily because under the unwritten social contract that prevailed until 1990 they expected that a significant part if not all of the future supplies of goods at controlled prices is assured by the "social" ownership of means of production. However, because of high inflation and strongly negative real interest rates private sector wealth was implicitly taxed, what in turn benefited the state enterprise sector. As a result, the household sector was unable to accumulate any considerable wealth and its ability to purchase state-owned assets was severely undermined.

This chapter is organized as follows. In the second section I discuss specific features of the centrally planned economy (CPE) with regard to wealth accumulation, as well as the nature of asset holdings of the household sector. In the third section, sectoral balance sheets are analyzed in order to determine the flow of resources and the accumulation of assets in various sectors of the economy and their overall impact on the net worth of individual sectors. In the fourth section, consolidated banking data are used to estimate the transfer of resources effected through the inflation tax from the private to the public sector. The effects of the inflation tax on the distribution of wealth and the choice of privatization scheme are discussed in the fifth section. Concluding remarks discuss the impact of privatization on private sector's saving behavior.

Wealth Accumulation in a Centrally Planned Economy

Several of the features differentiating a centrally planned economy (CPE) from a market economy put the household (private) sector at a disadvantage from the point of view of wealth accumulation, while allowing the public sector to accumulate most of the wealth of a country in the form of physical assets.[5] In Poland, as was typical of a CPE, the government owned most capital assets, including those in the hands of the enterprises,[6] and determined most prices, including interest rates, wages, and the official exchange rate; it was also in full control of the banking system.[7]

Restrictions imposed in CPEs on private sector activity and on the ownership of physical assets were far more severe than in most developing countries, where property rights have generally been recognized. In the absence of capital or financial markets, savings could be invested only in physical assets or held in the form of monetary assets. The household sector placed its savings largely in monetary assets, including foreign currencies,[8] because its ability to acquire physical assets was restricted by tight regulations.[9] By contrast, most of the public sector's saving, including the enterprise sector, was in the form of physical assets.

The accumulation of a large stock of monetary assets by the household sector has been frequently attributed to involuntary saving decisions. It has been argued that a large portion of household monetary holdings had been acquired involuntarily and thus constituted "monetary" or "saving overhang."[10] The overhang would emerge when shortfalls in supplies of goods are not accompanied by price increases to restore equilibrium in goods markets. One of the important implications of this hypothesis would be that household monetary assets have little if any real value.

The monetary overhang hypothesis has been disputed on various grounds, with the implication that these assets do have some positive value. Several hypotheses have been put forward to explain why, under repressed inflation—that is, when at existing prices and wages aggregate demand exceeds aggregate supply—households accumulated monetary assets voluntarily.[11] Some hypotheses highlight the fact that there are always alternatives to (forced) saving. Households can always increase leisure (as in Barro and Grossman, 1974) or opt for queuing or buying goods on parallel markets (Hartwig, 1983). Alexeev (1988) stressed the voluntary nature of saving and pointed out that savings must be high because of high prices of durables and the lack of consumer credit. The need for large holdings of monetary assets can also be explained by a large transactions demand necessary under conditions of chronic shortages—households need to continuously hold large money balances to be able to purchase goods when they are available. According to similar hypotheses (Acharaya and Spagat, 1990 and Osband, 1991), money is a "lottery ticket" that allows consumers to purchase goods in the controlled market. Others disputed the "overhang" hypothesis by pointing out the measurement problem. Hartwig (1983) and Nuti (1986) argued that the value of money stock is rather small when parallel market prices are taken into account. Finally, the existence of monetary overhang has been also questioned on empirical grounds by Portes, Quandt and Yeo (1988) and in Portes and Winter (1980).[12]

The argument for the voluntary character of household saving can be strengthened further by pointing out certain features of the implicit social contract prevailing in the CPEs. This social contract involved an understanding that monetary assets were used to invest in the capital stock that will yield the expected level of consumption in the future. That, in turn, gave the households a basis to believe that the value of their monetary holdings was backed by the real assets (capital stock) of the country.[13] In this sense these assets represented claims on the stock of state-owned productive assets. Households placed their savings in monetary assets in the belief that under the prevailing social contract at least a significant fraction of consumer goods would be available in the future at controlled prices.

In broad terms, assets holdings in a CPE can be interpreted as a scheme whereby the state-owned banking system was a financial intermediary between the households as savers and the state as the entrepreneur, and the banking systems' liabilities vis-à-vis the household sector were backed by loans to firms that invested in physical assets managed on behalf of the state. Households were a structural creditor who held claims on the net debtor enterprise sector, while the central government's fiscal position was balanced (except for external debt). The household sector accumulated monetary claims that reflected voluntary saving decisions, even though these holdings were probably placed in an undesirable menu of instruments, and the value of households' monetary assets corresponded to the net worth of the broadly defined state sector, i.e., the present value of the enterprise sector's after-tax profits. If the government subsidized the enterprise sector via money creation that contributed to inflation, it was effectively taxing the household sector, as interest rates on monetary assets did not compensate for inflation. Moreover, to the extent that the resources were used inefficiently, the real value of the household sector's assets was also being eroded via this channel.[14]

Asset Holdings and Net Worth

The following subsections analyze the flow of resources and patterns of changes in the net worth of individual sectors in Poland during 1981–91, with a special focus on the past two years. In order to trace the accumulation of wealth, the government sector is disaggregated into the government, the enterprise sector, and the banking sector. The private sector consists primarily of households, with only a small private business component. In each case, the net worth is determined as a difference between the stock of assets and liabilities, and for simplicity the net present value of revenues and expenditures is omitted.[15] Because of the lack of other than monetary data the discussion is largely confined to the conceptual framework.

The Government

The government is defined here to include central and regional level authorities and various extra-budgetary funds that are under the government's control. Net worth of the broadly defined public sector depends on the net worth of the government, the enterprise sector, and the banking sector. However, the factors affecting the government's net worth are discussed separately. The government's net worth (NWg) can be defined as follows:

Equation 1

$$NWg = Ag - Dg + NWe - EB^*$$

where assets ($Ag = R+Mg+Kg$) include foreign exchange reserves (R), deposits with domestic banking system (Mg), and fixed assets (Kg). Net worth of the enterprise sector (NWe) is included to represent the government's "equity" stake in the state-owned enterprises and therefore is the government's asset. In this context, the enterprise sector's net worth would appear on the liability side of its balance sheet. Dg denotes government's bank debt, and EB^* denotes external debt converted into domestic currency at the exchange rate E.

The government's net worth is positive if the sum of the net worth of the enterprise sector and other net assets ($Ag - Dg$) exceeds the level of external debt.[16] The government could increase its net worth through saving or by investing the resources at its disposal more productively. The government's net worth will increase if the present value of future revenues exceeds the present value of total future government expenditures, excluding capital expenditures in the enterprise sector. Because the government budget was in balance until 1989 and net borrowing from the domestic banking system was negligible, the only gains in its net worth could arise from investing external resources in the enterprise sector.[17]

In Poland, the government fiscal position was balanced until 1989, when tax revenues fell by some 8 percent of GDP. Government revenue was collected primarily from the enterprise sector, although the turnover tax which amounted to roughly 10 percent of GDP, or one-third of the total, was levied primarily on consumer goods. The revenues were spent largely on subsidies to the enterprises and households and on capital expenditures. Because borrowing from the domestic banking system was negligible until 1989, external debt constituted the largest government liability.[18]

The Enterprise Sector

The net worth of the enterprise sector was affected by its profits, tax payments and transfers to and from the government, and the net value of its assets and liabilities. Assets of the enterprise sector consisted of fixed capital and liquid assets and reserves (*K*), and bank deposits (*Me*). Liabilities consisted of bank debt (*De*) and various liabilities vis-à-vis the government. Net worth of the enterprise sector is conceptually akin to an "equity" stake of the government. *NWe* denotes net worth of the enterprise sector and corresponds to the net present value of the future stream of net after-tax profits.

Equation 2

$$NWe = K + Me - De$$

The Government was able to influence the flow of resources between enterprises and across branches and sectors by setting prices and interest rates in the domestic markets. Capital accumulation in desired sectors was achieved by fixing the prices of outputs and inputs or by imposing taxes or providing subsidies, or in the case of large investment projects, by direct government financing. In addition, the enterprise sector had direct access to credit from banks. Because interest rates charged on domestic credit were generally negative in real terms, and the enterprise sector's liabilities considerably exceeded its deposits with the banks, this sector enjoyed a continuous reduction in the real value of its net liabilities and an increase in its net worth.

The impact of negative real interest rates was growing over time as internally generated funds and subsidies were increasingly replaced by borrowing from the banking system. In the first half of the 1980s, after-tax profits constituted roughly 60 to 65 percent of all sources of funds used by the enterprises for investment, stock-building, and social programs. In the second half of the 1980s, the share of profits fluctuated considerably, and fell to 16 percent in 1989. By contrast, the share of net borrowing from banks soared from around 20 percent at the beginning of the 1980s to over 70 percent of the funds available to the enterprises in 1989.[19] Up to 1988, roughly 45 percent of these funds were used for fixed capital investment. Over time, with growing shortages of key inputs, the role of stock-building grew in importance. Over the same period, the share of gross capital formation in GDP in Poland increased from around 23 percent to nearly 30 percent, in part reflecting the increase in stocks and capital gains on foreign exchange accounts of state enterprises.[20]

The Private Sector

The private sector's net worth has been affected primarily by saving and the return on its holdings of monetary assets. In turn, saving depended on the level of money incomes, including wages and other income, and on the desired level of consumption. The accumulated savings were placed largely in liquid assets in the form of domestic and foreign currency cash and deposits (*Mp*). Other assets (*Kp*) included agricultural land, housing stock, and the capital stock of privately owned industry.[21] Liabilities were small and were mostly in the form of debt owed to commercial banks (*Dp*). Household sector net worth can thus be defined as follows:

Equation 3

$$NWp = Kp + Mp - Dp$$

Throughout most of the 1980s, disposable money income of the household sector was within a range of 50 to 60 percent of GDP. Wages alone constituted around 50 percent of personal money incomes of the household sector. Other income included social money benefits, incomes from agriculture and other private sector activities, and implicitly also subsidies to goods and services purchased by the household and private sectors. The income of the household sector was also enhanced by interest subsidies for housing credits provided by the state. However, their impact was rather modest as the private ownership of the housing stock was limited.[22] Roughly 10 to 20 percent of household monetary income was saved, and up to 90 percent of such saving was in the form of monetary assets. The build-up of monetary assets continued between 1982 to 1988, from around 40 percent of GDP to over 90 percent of GDP, even though the real value of monetary assets was continuously eroded by inflation.[23] (See Figure 1.)

The Banking System

Given that the accumulation of physical assets was largely confined to the enterprise sector, the consolidated balance sheet of the banking system can provide a useful tool to examine the flow of resources between the public and the private sectors. The banking system's balance sheet rearranged in terms of net asset and net liability positions of individual sectors can be presented as follows:[24]

Equation 4

$$(Dg - Mg) + (De - Me) = (Mp - Dp)$$

Two net debtor sectors—the government and the enterprise sectors—are placed on the left-hand side of the equation. Their combined net liability position is equal to net asset position of the private sector.[25]

FIGURE 1 Monetary Income and Assets in Poland (in percent)

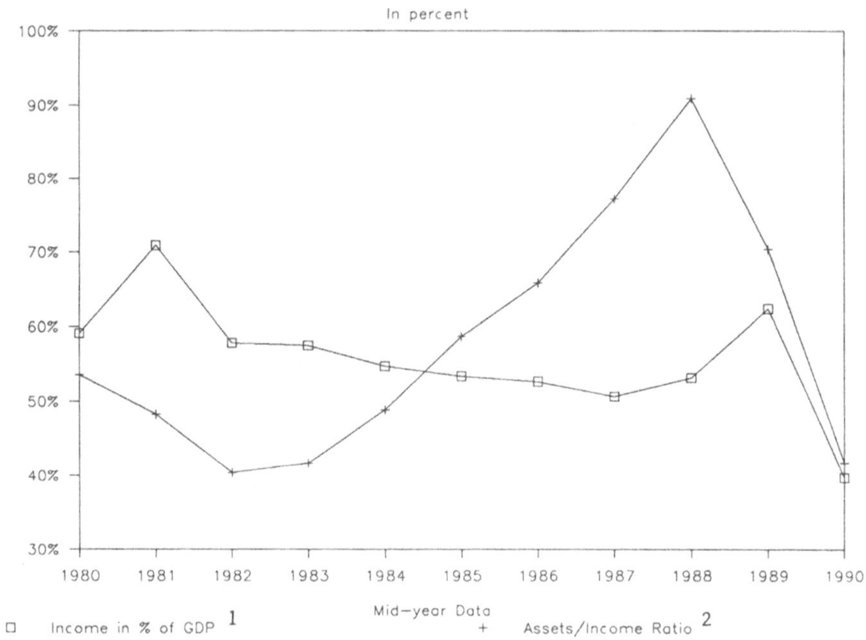

[1]Household disposable money income in percent of GDP.
[2]Total monetary assets to disposable money income.
Source: Author's estimates based on Rocznik Statystyczny 1990.

As shown in Table 1, the private sector's monetary assets constituted a very large segment of banking sector domestic liabilities. On the asset side, however, credit to the private sector amounted to a small proportion of total domestic claims. As in most countries, the private sector was a structural creditor. Under inflationary conditions with negative real interest rates, the implicit inflation tax acted as a capital levy on private sector's monetary assets. Given the balanced budget position of the government and very modest holdings of monetary assets, most of the implicit resource transfer benefited the enterprise sector.

The Inflation Tax and Household Wealth

The inflation tax can be defined as the loss in the real value of monetary assets that usually occurs in a situation where the public sector finances its expenditures by expanding the money supply that leads to an

TABLE 1 Composition of the consolidated Balance Sheet of the Banking System (in percent)

	1980	*1985*	*1988*	*1989*	*1990*
Assets					
Claims on general government	—	13.6	15.2	14.7	10.4
Claims on the enterprise sector	95.1	74.1	59.9	45.1	54.7
Claims on the private sector	4.9	6.5	6.6-	2.9	9.3
Other assets	—	5.8	18.2	37.2	25.6
Liabilities					
General government deposits	24.2	11.9	5.2	3.1	9.5
To the enterprise sector	23.8	20.4	15.6	17.2	17.8
To the private sector	34.4	55.4	65.1	49.2	42.4
Other liabilities	17.6	12.4	14.1	30.5	30.2

Source: Author's calculation based on Rocznik Statystyczny 1990.

increase in the overall price level. The increase in prices reduces real money balances, and with fixed nominal interest rates, it reduces the purchasing power of bank deposits. Similarly, if due to institutional rigidities or deliberate policy nominal interest rates fail to compensate creditors for the impact of inflation on the real value of their claims, the debtors benefit from the inflation subsidy. As noted above, in Poland and in other CPEs, the private sector was particularly exposed to the inflation tax because of the lack of alternative investment outlets that might protect the real value of assets against rising prices. However, because of open inflation private sector wealth in Poland was affected to a far greater degree than in any other country in the region.

The tax base for the inflation tax consisted of monetary assets held in domestic currency. Throughout the 1980s, households allocated some 70 to 90 percent of annual savings to increase their holdings of monetary assets (see Table 2). Because of the erosion in the real value of domestic currency monetary assets, their nominal value declined to 8 percent of GDP in 1990, one-fourth of the 1981 level. Over the same time, the domestic currency value of foreign currency holdings soared from negligible amounts to over 31 percent of GDP in 1988 and 1989 and then collapsed to below 9 percent of GDP during the last part of 1989 through 1990. This pattern reflected the shift away from domestic currency into foreign currency deposits and a continued increase in black market rates (see Figure 2).[26] The most dramatic change in the real value of broad money took place after the liberalization of food (and later also other) prices in 1989 and in January 1990.

TABLE 2 Household Savings in Poland (in percent)

	1980	1981	1982	1983*	1984*
Change in gross holdings of monetary assets (in percent of savings)**	70.5	85.5	80.6	75.8	73.5
Savings rate (in percent of disposable money incomes)	8.6	16.8	14.3	10.3	8.8
	1985*	1986	1987	1988	1989
Change in gross holdings of monetary assets (in percent of savings)**	75.7	77.0	70.3	86.0	90.0
Savings rate (in percent of disposable money incomes)	9.9	10.0	7.9	16.5	20.5

*Including the impact of 1982 bond issue.
**Small amounts of net borrowing from banks is included in gross savings.
Source: Author's calculation based on Rocznik Statystyczny 1990.

The inflation tax levied on the private sector is computed on the basis of estimated midyear stocks of domestic currency monetary assets and according to the following simplified formula:[27]

Equation 5

$$IT = m\left(1 - \frac{1}{1+p}\right) + d\left(1 - \frac{1+i}{1+p}\right)$$

where *IT* denotes inflation tax, *m* is currency, *d* bank deposits, *p* denotes inflation rate and *i* is the arithmetic average of interest rates offered on sight and time deposits during a given year.[28] The inflation subsidy to the enterprise sector was calculated according to a similar formula.[29]

The impact of inflation on monetary assets and liabilities was particularly pronounced in 1982 and during two recent waves of price liberalization, in the second half of 1989 and in early 1990, and affected primarily the private and the enterprise sectors.[30] The inflation tax reached the highest annual proportion of nominal GDP in 1982 (11 percent), even though the inflation rate, although high (101 percent), was nowhere close to the levels reached in the last two years. (See Figure 3.) This can be explained by the fact that during 1981 the ratio of domestic currency monetary assets to GDP was very high, and in combination with a large

FIGURE 2 Trends in Household Monetary Assets (in percent of GDP)

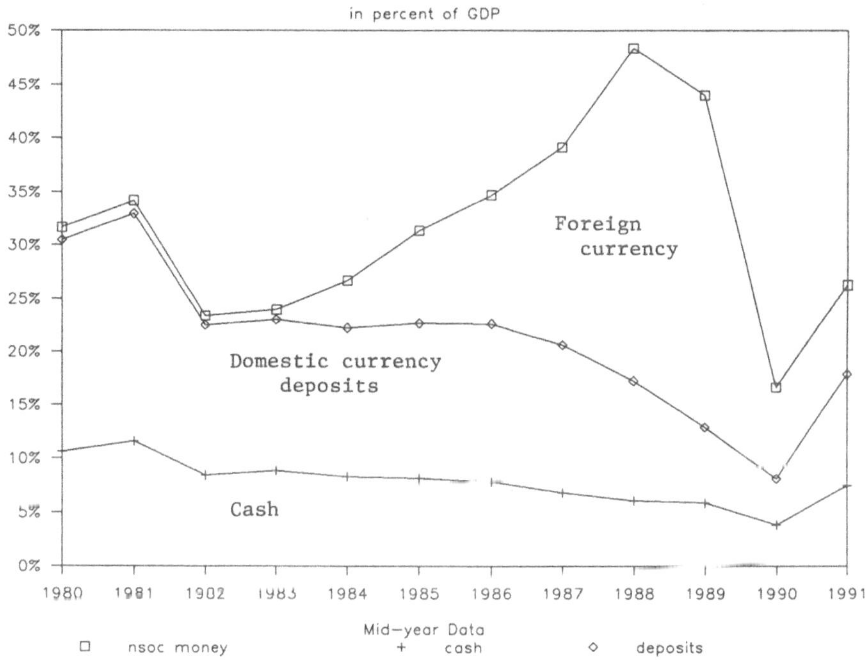

Source: Author's estimates based on Rocznik Statystyczny 1990.

price adjustment and a sharp fall in real GDP the inflation tax ratio reached a very high level. By contrast, during 1989–90 the ratio of monetary assets to GDP was fairly low, and only because of a rapidly accelerating inflation the inflation tax reached 8.5 percent and 7 percent of GDP, respectively.[31] During the 1980s, the net inflation subsidy obtained by the enterprise sector ranged from 2 percent to 21 percent of GDP.

During 1989–90, the private sector's wealth was also adversely affected by a significant erosion of the value of foreign currency holdings. (See Figure 4.) Up to the first half of 1989 the domestic currency value of the outstanding dollar holdings was rising not only due to continuously increasing foreign currency holdings by the private sector but also because of the increasing premium of the parallel exchange rate over the official rate. Rapid progress in price liberalization that had been initiated in the second half of 1989 and continued in 1990 brought about substantial changes in relative prices, including the real appreciation of

FIGURE 3 Inflation Tax and Subsidy in Poland (in percent of GDP)

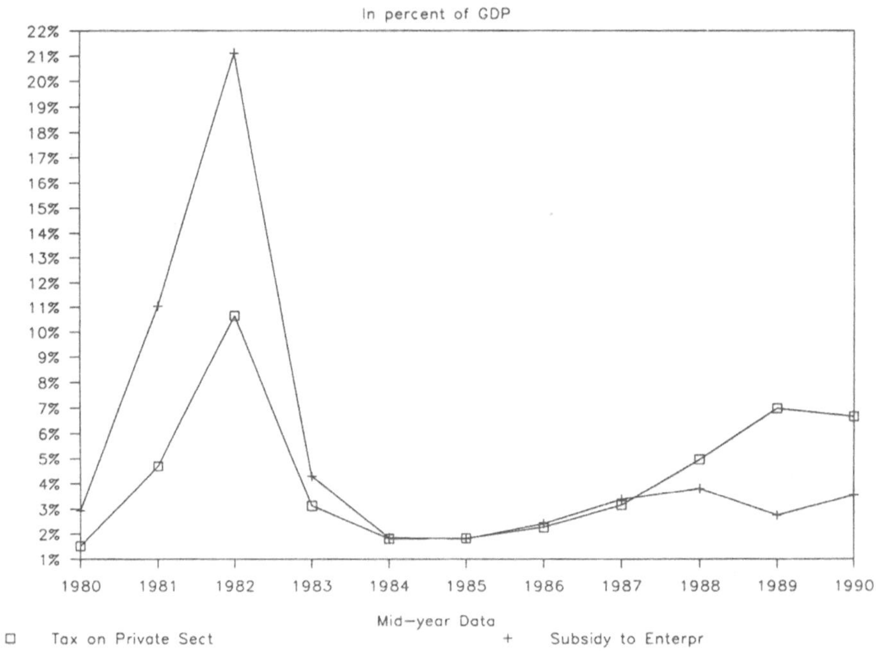

Source: Author's estimates based on Rocznik Statystyczny 1990.

the zloty.[32] This phenomenon was reflected, for example, in the steep increase in the dollar value (at free market exchange rates) of average monthly wage from around $20 through most of the 1980s to $150–$200 in 1990.

The most important effect of the inflation tax was the underlying redistribution of wealth from the household to the enterprise sector. This implicit transfer of wealth has undermined the feasibility of privatization schemes based on sale of state assets to domestic investors and is likely to influence the saving behavior of the private sector in the near term. As shown above, the most pronounced impact of inflation on the real value of household monetary assets was in the second half of 1989 and early 1990.

The redistributive effects of inflation can be examined by substituting *NWe* and net liability position of the government and the enterprise sectors by equations 2 and 4, and by rearranging equation 1.

FIGURE 4 Black Market Rates and Consumer Prices (index in log terms)

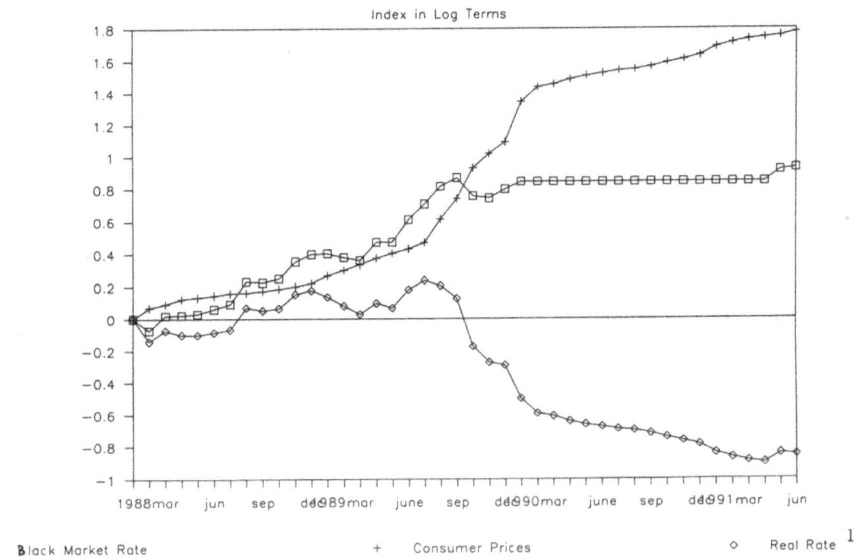

[1]Deflated by consumer price index.
Source: Author's estimates based on Rocznik Statystyczny 1990.

Equation 6

$$R + Kg + Ke = NWg + (Mp - Dp) + EB^*$$

Equation 6 presents the balance of key assets and liabilities of a nation, in nominal terms. The left-hand side includes foreign assets and the capital stock, and the right-hand side includes net claims of the domestic private sector, foreign creditors, and the net worth of the government. As discussed above, only the real value of net monetary claims of the private sector was substantially affected by inflation. By contrast, the real value of all other assets and liabilities did not change, and the government's net worth was, in fact, positively affected by the erosion in the real value of the private sector monetary claims. By the same token, the real value of net financial liabilities of the broadly defined public sector declined.

The impact of inflation tax on private sector's wealth and its ability to participate in the privatization of state-owned assets can be measured by the cumulative loss of value of the monetary assets.[33] For example, if households saved the same proportion of their income and placed them in the instruments yielding zero real rate of return but fully protecting against inflation, the real value of such assets that would have accumulated during 1980–90 would have exceeded the total value of the 1990 GDP.[34] This compares with the same year's actual ratio of private sector monetary assets to GDP of around 17 percent. Because the reduction in the real value of the private sector's net claims on the banking system constituted a decline in the real value of net liabilities of the indebted sectors, this also represented the increase in the net worth of the enterprise sector.

The significant reduction in the net worth of the household sector substantially changed the distribution of national wealth in favor of the broadly defined state sector. In terms of accumulated wealth, the state sector became even richer by shedding much of its liabilities, while the private sector's net worth declined in absolute and relative terms. Within the household sector the most adversely affected were the most thrifty and industrious individuals, and those that were in a privileged position under the communist regime. Among the enterprises, in the most advantageous position were units that financed a large share of their activities with bank credit.

Household Wealth and Privatization

The published proposals for privatization envisaged three possibilities: (1) a swap of monetary assets for shares in the privatized enterprises, (2) an outright sale, and (3) a free distribution of shares.[35] However, the considerable erosion in the real value of household savings accumulated in the form of monetary assets and the lack of political acceptance for massive sales to foreign investors limited the choice of feasible options in implementing the intended privatization program to some form of free or nearly free distribution of shares.[36]

Currently, the private sector has very little resources to participate in the privatization of state-owned enterprises.[37] In fact, the lack of large resources in the hands of households has so far effectively limited the scope of privatization to small enterprises, mainly in the services sector. This problem could be overcome by issuing credit to finance the purchase of enterprises. It is unlikely, however, that the broad public would be willing to assume additional large liabilities in order to acquire firms. Even in the case of experienced investors, this would be difficult because the value of privatized assets and the expected rate of return is extremely difficult to estimate. Furthermore, in light of the recent experience with inflation, households have little reason to place much confidence in the assurances given by the state.

The feasibility of asset sales is further circumscribed by the lack of public's readiness to invest in equities and assume risk, and the likely restrictions placed on participation by foreigners. Based on international experience it can be expected that households would voluntarily place only a fraction of their total wealth in shares of the newly privatized enterprises.[38] Objections to wide ranging foreign acquisitions of state-owned firms can easily arise in countries where foreign business presence has been very small, and the accusations of the "sell-out" of national patrimony can provide an effective barrier to foreign investment. If foreign investment is allowed, and given the uncertainty and high risk, foreign investors are likely to offer only modest prices for privatized assets. Low asset prices are one of the ways to assure high rates of return under conditions of high risk and uncertainty. But even if in domestic residents' view these assets were underpriced, they wouldn't be able to outbid the foreign investors because of the recent large reduction in household wealth.

A swap of monetary assets for shares was originally conceived as a way of absorbing the monetary overhang. Such a swap could be alternatively interpreted as a forced conversion of monetary assets into shares at prices determined by the state. It is unlikely, however, that such a move would achieve a desired effect if the monetary overhang hypothesis holds. If, as the hypothesis assumes, most of the monetary assets are held involuntarily, their mere conversion into another financial asset is not likely to change the private sector's desire to use them at the nearest possibility to buy consumer goods. Therefore, the likely outcome would be a sale of assets at very low prices, with the resulting effect similar to a large inflation tax through price liberalization.

The conversion of the monetary assets into equities could restrain their use to purchase goods only if private agents view their savings as voluntary but placed in an undesired portfolio. A similar effect could be achieved by simultaneously liberalizing goods and asset markets and prices. When offered the opportunity, private agents would presumably convert some of their monetary assets into alternative financial (as opposed to monetary) assets. This option would allow the private agents to reclaim their rights stemming from the original social contract, as the private sector would be able to convert its indirect (monetary) claims into direct (ownership) claims on state-owned assets.

The privatization of state-owned assets through a free distribution of shares to households is likely to involve wealth transfers of a magnitude similar to the implicit transfers effected through inflation that took place in the opposite direction during the 1980s and in 1990. In fact, under the "social contract" hypothesis, households would view a free distribution of shares as a restitution of their wealth. However, because the privatization through a free distribution of shares would also result in a substantial redistribution of wealth within the private sector, the restitution of wealth would be only global; from the individual household point of view the link between past holdings of monetary assets and the newly distributed equities could be tenuous.

Conclusion

This chapter has discussed the effect of inflation on household wealth and its impact on the feasibility of various privatization schemes. In a CPE, household voluntary savings were accumulated mostly in the form of monetary assets held in the banks, and households were a structural net creditor vis-à-vis other sectors in the economy. Under the unwritten social contract, the net claims on the banking system represented household sector claims on the future flow of consumer goods at largely controlled prices. Future consumption was understood to be assured by the "social" ownership of the means of production. In that sense, the private sector's claims on the banking system represented claims on state-owned enterprises. High inflation of the 1980s and particularly of late 1989 and in early 1990 sharply reduced the real value of the enterprise sector's liabilities and of private sector's assets, thereby seriously undermining the private sector's ability to purchase state-owned assets. Because of the lack of large resources in the private sector and low political acceptability of massive asset sales to foreigners, the privatization options are therefore largely limited to some form of free or nearly free distribution of shares. This process would reverse the large implicit transfer of wealth from the private to the public sector.

The analysis presented above affects the interpretation of the impact of privatization through a free distribution on the private sector's saving behavior.[39] The impact of privatization on saving depends on whether households interpret the underlying transaction as an increase in net wealth, and whether their current wealth level was in equilibrium. Consider first the situation where prior to the privatization the household wealth/income ratio is at the desired level, and assume that government consumption will not change and will be financed by the same tax revenue.[40] Households that would not perceive the free distribution of shares as an increase in their net wealth, on the assumption that government consumption will not decline and it will be financed with the unchanged tax revenues, would view the transfer of shares as an increase in their net wealth only to the extent that they expect to share in the benefits of the more efficient use of resources in the privatized enterprises.[41] The anticipated increase in net wealth would tend to increase consumption and reduce private savings out of current income until such gains materialize. By then, their disposable income would increase and result in a higher saving rate. Other households would not change their saving behavior until the actual distribution of shares, which they would perceive as an increase in net wealth, and then increase their consumption accordingly. Their saving rate would fall in the end, because they would tend to overestimate the increase in net wealth to the extent that they do not account properly for tax liabilities they incur during the privatization process.

The effect of privatization on private saving would be different, however, if households viewed their current wealth/income ratio as below the desired level. In fact, unless the privatization scheme is announced, households would be likely to save more because they would irrationally assume that they could restore the desired wealth/income ratio.[42] At the time the privatization is announced, the saving behavior of the first group of households would return to the historical (pre-reform) pattern as they might treat such a transfer of wealth as a mere restitution of their lost wealth, until the privatization actually takes place because they would regard the process as a return to equilibrium. However, as in previous examples, when privatization begins to yield productivity gains that result in higher income their saving rate would rise.

This analysis has also relevance for cases where concerns are particularly strong that planned price liberalization may ignite hyperinflation. As discussed above, aside from the scope of the required price adjustment, there appears to be little difference between the aggregate macroeconomic effects of monetary reform combined with privatization and the goods markets liberalization followed by privatization through a free distribution of shares. However, such a privatization scheme may affect the aggregate saving behavior because of the redistribution of wealth within the private sector as the individual effects will depend on whether households view privatization as the windfall gain or as the restitution of their wealth.

Notes

Przemyslaw T. Gajdeczka is affiliated with the International Monetary Fund in Washington, D.C.

An earlier version of this paper was presented at First U.S.-Polish Economic Roundtable in Seattle, Washington, June 7–9, 1991. The author has benefited from comments on earlier versions of the paper from Peter Clark, Tim Lane, Mark Stone, Ken Warwick and various participants of the Roundtable. The views expressed are those of the author and do not necessarily represent those of the Fund.

1. In Hungary, state enterprises accounted for 90 percent of annual output in 1988. See, Hare (1990), p.40.

2. See, International Monetary Fund (1991b), p. 32.

3. For a discussion of factors hampering the privatization process, see, for example Blanchard et al (1990), Frydman and Rapaczynski (1990), Borensztein and Kumar (1991), and Sachs (1991).

4. The total value of state-owned assets available for privatization may be as high as $120 billion. This estimate is based on the capital-output ratio of 4.2 published in the official statistical yearbook and assuming that the socialized sector contributes 80 percent of GDP ($70 billion) and half of the capital stock is effectively worthless under the new conditions. See, Rocznik Statystyczny (1990), p.123. Sachs (1991) estimated the capital value of the largest 500 firms at around $25 billion, on the basis of the after-tax profits of $5 billion and a price-earning ratio of 5.

5. Unless explicitly differentiated, the terms household and private sector will be used interchangeably. For a discussion of distinctive features of CPE, see Wolf (1985).

6. From the legal viewpoint, the government "administered" national assets on behalf of the population. However, because the population had little, if any, influence on government policies this "administration" was tantamount to ownership.

7. In a typical CPE the banking system was a "monobank," i.e., a monolithic system in which "commercial" bank branches belonged to the central bank. In Poland, this monobank was supplemented with several specialized banking institutions. For a discussion of issues involved in transforming banking systems, see, for example, Sundararajan (1990).

8. In Poland, the possession and later also trading of foreign currencies by household sector has gradually been liberalized since the early 1970s. Over the last 20 years state-owned banks have been accepting foreign currency deposits.

9. All transactions outside the public sector involving the transfer of ownership were as strictly controlled as transactions between public sector entities, and the authorization was required to enter a contract involving the transfer of land or physical assets of considerable value. Also, restrictions on employment by the private sector and high taxes severely restricted private sector activity. Nevertheless, the private sector's contribution to GDP reached 20 percent in 1989, half of which was accounted for by agriculture.

10. The concept of monetary overhang refers to the difference in the level of money holdings under and without rationing. Saving, or wealth overhang denotes the cumulative value of involuntary saving. Further discussion of these concepts and estimates for the Soviet Union can be found in iMF et al. (1991b) and Cottarelli and Blejer (1991). For a review of theoretical and empirical issues related to monetary overhang see, for example, van Brabant (1991), Nuti (1986) and Portes (1989).

11. For a recent summary critique of the monetary and the savings overhang hypotheses, see, for example, Cochrane and Ickes (1991).

12. These studies reject the hypothesis of perpetual excess demand in Poland during 1955–80, and the existence of suppressed inflation in Czechoslovakia, East Germany, Hungary and Poland in 1955–75. For a critique of the validity of these studies on methodological and theoretical grounds see, for example Podkaminer (1989) and Winiecki (1985). In another study, Charemza, Gronicki and Quandt (1988) test the assumption of permanent excess demand in the automobile market in Poland and conclude that there may exist permanent excess demand for particular durable goods.

13. This refers only to a portion of total saving, investment and consumption, as the government and the socialized sector were also saving and investing. The income of the socialized sector was in turn providing revenues to the government which thus financed various social expenditures such as education, health care etc.

14. Other government liabilities (and household sector claims) included free health care, national education, effective unemployment insurance and a national pension system.

15. This approach uses the present value measure of all assets and liabilities of each sector. For the application of the forward-looking balance sheet approach to assess a government's solvency, see e.g., Guidotti and Kumar (1991).

16. This refers to contractual values. When the government's net worth falls below zero, the market value of its debt would decline; the government cannot pay more than it collects in taxes and owns in assets.

17. This refers to the general government, that is, including various extra-budgetary funds under government's control. The central government itself was in deficit throughout most of the 1980s. The total government's liabilities were continuously increasing even though general government budgets were balanced because budgetary accounts are constructed on a cash basis and debt service payments in arrears are not included in fiscal data, even though they added to the stock of debt. See, Rocznik Statystyczny (1990).

18. See, Rocznik Statystyczny (1990). Here external debt is defined to include also foreign exchange liabilities vis-à-vis the domestic banking system. Domestic banks held substantial amounts of foreign exchange deposits of the household sector which were re-lent to the government.

19. The residual includes various subsidies and investment financing from state budget. Author's estimates based on Rocznik Statystyczny 1990.

20. Author's calculation based on Rocznik Statystyczny (1990).

21. In Poland, private assets included mostly agricultural land, a relatively small stock of privately owned housing, and the capital stock of small private enterprises in services and industry. The net worth of the private sector was relatively small and changed little over time as most of the private farms and enterprises, including in the services sector, were undercapitalized and required substantial new investment. Housing stock was largely owned by the state and the overwhelming majority of the newly built housing units was distributed on a tenancy basis.

22. For a discussion of interest subsidies for housing in Eastern Europe, see, e.g., Holzmann (1991).

23. The value of foreign currency deposits was estimated at parallel market rates.

24. The distinction between currency and other monetary assets is made for calculating the inflation tax in the section below.

25. The external debt which is excluded here will be taken into account in the section devoted to inflation tax and household wealth.

26. Lane (1991) reviews this issue in the context of monetary overhang and the implementation of stabilization policies.

27. Computation of the inflation tax is subject to many methodological difficulties, especially in countries with high and variable inflation rates. Not only does the key parameter in these calculations—the inflation rate—fluctuate considerably, but also there are usually frequent changes in interest rates and there is a continuous erosion in the tax base. For example, the inflation tax calculated on the basis of monthly data during 1990 amounted to 5.1 percent of GDP, compared with 6.9 percent obtained on the basis of annual (midyear) data. For a good discussion of methodological problems in calculating the inflation tax see, Oks (1989).

28. The simple mean of the lowest rates for sight deposits and the highest rates for time deposits.

29. It was assumed that lending rates were equal to deposit rates offered to the private sector. The inflation tax was calculated on the basis of net claims on the enterprise sector, i.e., net of deposits.

30. The government benefited from inflation mostly in 1989, when the budget deficit was financed through interest free credit from the central bank.

31. The inflation tax estimated for Poland is in line with the experience of other high-inflation developing countries. For example, Dinh and Guigale (1991) estimated that in Egypt the inflation tax reached 10.6 percent of GDP in 1987. See also Edwards and Tabellini (1991) for the estimates of the inflation tax for a sample of 52 developing countries.

32. Price liberalization led to the increase in the aggregate nominal price level but a reduction in parallel market prices and thus eliminated the very high scarcity premium that had been embodied in the parallel market price for foreign exchange.

33. The implied transfer of wealth between the private and the enterprise sector measured by the inflation tax is likely to be exaggerated in an environment where some prices are controlled and shortages are widespread. In such circumstances the stock of monetary assets deflated by the price level (M/P) overestimates the purchasing power of monetary assets.

34. The nominal value of household saving was adjusted to the 1990 prices by applying the consumer price index.

35. For a recent review of proposals for privatization in Eastern Europe see, for example, Borensztein and Kumar (1991). Vuylsteke (1988) lists seven basic methods of privatization: 1) public offering of shares, 2) private sale of shares, 3) private sale of government or enterprise assets, 4) fragmentation, 5) new

private investment in state-owned enterprises, 6) management/employee buy-out, and 7) leases and management contracts.

36. Examples of successful privatization by means of free distribution of shares in Canada and Chile are cited in Hinds (1991) p. 133.

37. By the end of 1990, the total stock of monetary assets of the private sector amounted to around $14 billion, as compared to the quoted above estimates of the gross value of capital stock ranging from $25 billion to $120 billion.

38. There are significant differences across countries in terms of distribution of household wealth between real and financial assets and investment in equities. Among the seven major industrial nations only in the United States and Canada did the households hold more wealth in financial than in real assets. Also, the share of equities in total financial assets varied considerably, and in 1989 was the largest in France (nearly half) and the lowest in Germany (below 5 percent). See, OECD (1991).

39. See, e.g., Borensztein and Montiel (1991). Their analysis of the impact of privatization on the saving behavior after the free distribution of shares overlooks the impact of changes in household wealth, and thus implicitly assumes that the households' wealth/income ratio after the stabilization reflected equilibrium. At the same time, they oppose the "monetary overhang" hypothesis and argue that households voluntarily maintained large monetary assets.

40. The discussion of this situation draws on Borensztein and Montiel (1991) pp. 19–20.

41. Unless government consumption is expected to decline, privatization in itself does not increase net wealth of the household sector, as the ownership title is transferred together with the tax liability.

42. When they realize the loss of their wealth, including a loss of job security and other benefits provided by the state, precautionary motive may boost their saving rate because they would rationally assume they would have to provide more for their own welfare out of their personal income stream.

Bibliography

Alexeev M. (1988), "Are Soviet Consumers Forced to Save?" *Comparative Economic Studies*, Vol. 30, No. 4, Winter 1988, pp. 17–23.

Acharya A, and M. Spagat (1990), "Individual Savings and Monetary Overhang: A Model with Empty Shelves and a Second Economy," mimeo.

Barro, R.J. and Herschel I. Grossman (1974), "Suppressed Inflation and the Supply Multiplier," *Review of Economics and Statistics*, Vol. 41, No. 1, January, pp. 87–104.

Blanchard, Olivier, Rudiger Dornbusch, Paul Krugman, Richard Layard and Lawrence Summers (1990), "Reform in Eastern Europe," 1990 Report of the WIDER World Economy Group.

Borensztein E. and Peter Montiel (1991), "Saving, Investment and Growth in Eastern Europe," IMF Working Paper WP/91/61.

Borensztein E. and Manmohan Kumar (1991), "Proposals for Privatization in Eastern Europe," IMF Working Paper WP/91/36.

Charemza W., M. Gronicki and R.E. Quandt (1988), "Modelling Parallel Markets in Centrally Planned Economies. The Case of the Automobile Market in Poland," *European Economic Review*, Vol. 32 (1988), pp. 861–883.

Cochrane J. and Barry Ickes, "Inflation Stabilization in Reforming Economies: The Myth of the Monetary Overhang," *Comparative Economic Studies*, Vol. 33, No. 2, (Summer 1991), pp. 91–122.

Cottarelli C. and Mario Blejer, "Forced Saving and Repressed Inflation in the Soviet Union: Some Empirical Results," IMF Working Paper WP/91/55.

Dinh H.T., and M. Giugale (1991), "Inflation Tax and Deficit Financing in Egypt," PRE Working Paper WPS 668, the World Bank, May 1991.

Edwards S., and G. Tabellini (1991), "Explaining Fiscal Policies and Inflation in Developing Countries," *Journal of International Money and Finance*, Vol. 10, S16–48.

Frydman R. and Andrzej Rapaczynski (1990), "Markets and Institutions in Large Scale Privatization," paper presented at the Conference on Adjustment and Growth: Lessons for Eastern Europe," Pultusk, Poland, October.

Guidotti P. and Manmohan Kumar (1991), "Domestic Public Debt of Externally Indebted Developing Countries," IMF Occasional Paper, IMF Washington D.C. 1991.

Hare, P. (1990), "Reform of Enterprise Regulation in Hungary—from Tutelage to Market," *European Economy*, No. 43, March 1990.

Hartwig, K.H. (1983), "Involuntary Liquid Assets in Eastern Europe: Some Critical Remarks," *Soviet Studies*, Vol. XXXV, No. 1, January, pp. 103–105.

Hinds, M. (1991), "Issues in the Introduction of Market Forces in Eastern European Socialist Economies," in *Managing Inflation in Socialist Economies in Transition*, edited by Simon Commander, Economic Development Institute of the World Bank, Washington D.C., 1991.

Holzmann R. (1991), "Budgetary Subsidies in Centrally Planned Economies in Transition," IMF Working Paper WP/91/11.

International Monetary Fund et al. (1991a), A Study of the Soviet Economy, Washington D.C.

International Monetary Fund (1991b), World Economic Outlook, Washington D.C. May 1991.

Lane T. (1991), "Inflation Stabilization and Economic Transformation in Poland: The First Year," paper presented at Carnegie-Rochester Public Policy Conference, Rochester, New York, April 1991.

OECD Economic Outlook (1991), No. 50, OECD, Paris.

Oks D. (1989), "Inflation Tax, Theoretical Derivation and Calculation for 80–87." Annex II in "Peru: Policies to Stop Hyperinflation and Initiate Economic Recovery," Country Economic Memorandum, the World Bank, 1989.

Osband K. (1991), "Can the Notion of Forced Savings be Salvaged?" September 1991, mimeo.

Nuti, Mario (1986), "Hidden and Repressed Inflation in Soviet-Type Economies: Definitions, Measurement, and Stabilization," *Contributions to Political Economy*, Vol. 5, March 1986, pp. 37–82.

Podkaminer L. (1989), "Macroeconomic Disequilibria in Centrally Planned

Economies: Identifiability of Econometric Models Based on the Theory of Household Behavior under Quantity Constraints," *Journal of Comparative Economics*, 13, pp. 47–60.

Portes, R. (1989), "The Theory and Measurement of Macroeconomic Disequilibrium in Centrally Planned Economies," in International Studies in Economic Modelling Series, *Models of Disequilibrium and Shortage in Centrally Planned Economies*, ed. by Ch. Davis and W. Charemza, Chapman and Hall, London.

Portes R., Richard Quandt, Stephen Yeo (1988), "Tests of Chronic Shortage Hypothesis: The Case of Poland," *Review of Economics and Statistics*, Vol. 70, No. 2, pp. 288–295.

Portes R. and David Winter (1980), "Disequilibrium Estimates for Consumption Goods Markets in Centrally Planned Economies," *Review of Economics and Statistics*, Vol. XLVII, pp. 137–159.

Rocznik Statystyczny (1990), Central Statistical Office, Warszawa, October 1990.

Sachs J. (1991), "Accelerating Privatization in Eastern Europe," paper presented at the World Bank Annual Conference on Development Economics 1991.

Sundararajan, V., "Financial Sector Reform and Central Banking in Centrally Planned Economies," IMF Working Paper WP/90/120, Washington D.C., December 1990.

Van Brabant J. (1990), "Socialist Economics: The Disequilibrium School and the Shortage Economy," *Journal of Economic Perspectives*, Vol. 4, No. 2, Spring 1990, pp. 157–175.

Vuylsteke Ch. (1988), "Techniques of Privatization of State-Owned Enterprises," Vol. 1, World Bank Technical Paper No. 88, the World Bank, Washington D.C., 1988

Wolf T. (1985), "Economic Stabilization in Planned Economies," IMF Staff Papers, vol. 32, No. 1 (March 1985), International Monetary Fund, Washington D.C.

Winiecki J. (1985), "Portes ante Portas: A Critique of the Revisionist Interpretation of Inflation under Central Planning," *Comparative Economic Studies*, Summer 1985, pp. 25–51.

9

The Economic Transformation of Eastern Europe: The Case of Poland

Jeffrey Sachs

In virtually every aspect of economic life, the communist legacy is adverse. Normal market institutions were destroyed by the communist rulers in the early post-war period, so that even the most basic categories of economic life in a market economy—corporations, bankruptcy law, securities trading, collective bargaining—must be painfully reconstructed. For four decades, capital spending was dictated by political fiat, in a system that valued heavy industry to the neglect of basic consumer needs, and that ruthlessly reoriented trade from Western Europe to the Soviet Union.

The economic effects of the communist period are just now coming into clear view among analysts in the East and West, and the picture is even worse than expected. Living standards in Czechoslovakia, Hungary, and Poland are now estimated to be at the levels of the middle-income developing countries of Latin America, and far below the levels of even the poorer countries of the European Community.[2] At the same time, the industrial structure seems even less suited to the requirements of competition in world markets than was hoped, and the environmental degradation caused by decades of disregard for the environment constitutes another urgent and costly legacy of the previous regime.

The Economic Reform Program in Poland

The deficiencies of Poland's economic structure are evident across the economy: an overgrown and inefficient heavy industrial sector completely protected from international competition; an underdeveloped light industrial sector; a neglected and undersized service and distribution sector; a particularly inefficient and underdeveloped financial sector; and a technologically backward agricultural sector, in which millions of poor farmer households work tiny plots of land.

Poland's economic reform strategy does not aim to address these problems mainly by direct intervention in these sectors, but rather through the generalized introduction of market forces that will guide most of the needed restructuring. For this reason, we have to think about Poland's economic transformation from two perspectives. The first is the timing and content of the reforms; the second is the timing and content of the actual restructuring that will take place as the result of the reforms. The reforms themselves can and should be introduced quickly, in three to five years. The restructuring, on the other hand, will necessarily last for a much longer period, presumably a decade or more, since there must be time enough for a substantial buildup of investments in new sectors of the economy in response to the newly introduced market signals.

Poland's comprehensive economic reform program has three main types of policies. Economic liberalization is the broad rubric for all of the legal administrative changes needed to create the institutions of private property, and to introduce market competition. Macroeconomic stabilization involves measures to limit budget deficits, reduce the growth of the money supply, and establish a realistic and uniform exchange rate for the currency, in order to create a working monetary system based on a convertible currency and stable prices. Privatization includes the wide range of measures needed to transfer ownership of state property to the private sector. Note that there are two ways that the private sector will develop: through the formation of new firms made possible through economic liberalization, and through the privatization of existing state property.

I should also stress that the steps of liberalization, stabilization, and privatization do not exhaust the range of key governmental actions over the economy. In addition, the government must make certain that there is a strong social safety net in place at the time of reforms in order to prevent the reform actions from gravely affecting the most vulnerable parts of the society. This was in fact fairly readily accomplished in Poland, since the old regime had already in place many of the needed social measures. New measures, such as unemployment insurance were introduced at the outset of the program. Also, the government must oversee a public investment program, mainly for needed infrastructure, as a complement to the restructuring of the economy.

Poland's strategy has been to introduce the three main pillars of reform as rapidly as possible, an approach that is being emulated widely throughout Eastern Europe. The motivation for comprehensiveness and speed in introducing the reforms is clear cut. Such an approach vastly cuts the uncertainties facing the public with regard to the new "rules of the game" in the economy. Rather than creating a lot of turmoil, uncertainty, internal inconsistencies, and political resistance, through a gradual introduction of new measures, the goal is to set in place clear incentives for the new economic system as rapidly as possible. As one wit has put it, if the British were to shift from left-hand-side drive to right-hand-side drive, should they do it gradually . . . say, by just shifting the trucks over to the other side in the first round?

If we examine the timing of reform actions more carefully, we note that many of the key steps of economic liberalization can be introduced very quickly, indeed virtually overnight by a well-prepared government. The crucial steps of establishing free trade, market pricing according to the forces of supply and demand, key aspects of commercial law and private property rights, and the end of state orders and central planning, were introduced in Poland in the space of a few weeks at the end of 1989 and the beginning of 1990.[3]

Macroeconomic stabilization can also be achieved relatively quickly, with key steps of eliminating the budget deficit and tightening monetary policy in Poland taken at the time of the "big bang." The need for quick macroeconomic action in Poland was particularly acute, since the weakness of the last communist government and the final breakdown of the old regime had led to an extraordinary financial destabilization that was capped by a brief period of hyperinflation at the end of 1989. The hyperinflation would surely have intensified save for the decisive actions of the new Solidarity-led government, which came to office at the end of 1989.

On January 1, 1990, the new government took stringent macroeconomic measures, including large cuts in budget subsidies (which meant higher prices passed on to consumers), higher tax collections, wage controls, and a sharp devaluation of the currency. These measures, together with the elimination of most price controls as part of the economic liberalization, led to a large one-time jump in the price level, of nearly 100 percent in the month of January, 1990! But soon after this extraordinary one-shot jump in prices, the new economic environment brought a rapid end to the high inflation of the previous year, and even more remarkably, a rapid end to decades of chronic shortages and lines.

Without question, privatization is the most challenging and time-consuming of all of the steps of the reform program. Many countries around the world have sold state enterprises to private investors in recent years, but none has faced the magnitude of the challenge in Poland and the rest of Eastern Europe. Under the communist regime in Poland, more than 90 percent of industry, in roughly 3,000 industrial enterprises, was in state hands, and the share of state ownership was also very high in other parts of the non-agricultural economy.

To put the issue into perspective, consider the fact that under the aggressive privatization campaign of the Thatcher era, the U.K. succeeded in privatizing approximately 50 enterprises during the 1980s, roughly 5 firms per year. At the Thatcherite rate (which benefited from a sophisticated capital market and a large private sector to absorb the state firms), the Polish task of privatization would take several hundred years. "British-style privatizations" cannot be the main answer for Eastern Europe.[4]

The basic framework law for privatization was put in place in mid-1990. Under this law, privatization has proceeded remarkably rapidly for small firms, such as retail shops, for which privatizations are mostly controlled by local and regional governments. Poland has succeeded in leasing or selling more than 40,000 shops to private operators by mid-1991. It is estimated that as a result of this "small-scale privatization," as well as the rapid growth of new private firms in the service sector, roughly 80 percent of retail trade is now carried out by the private sector. Privatization has also been very rapid in trucking, construction, and small industrial units, where privatization has occurred in part by auctions, and in part by leasing the enterprises to the work force.

Methods of Rapid Privatization

The original intention among many senior officials in the Privatization Ministry in Poland was to carry out the process of privatization mainly through initial public offerings (IPOs).[5] The attempt to rely mainly on IPOs was predictably flawed, even though it was urged upon the government by dozens of investment banks used to that method of privatization. IPOs are always time consuming, and local circumstances suggested that they would be especially difficult in Poland, where there are no capital markets; no domestic investment banks; a stock exchange only beginning operations in April 1991; no reliable basis for the valuation of enterprises; low levels of household financial assets with which to purchase shares; and thousands of enterprises to privatize.[6]

In the summer of 1990, the government had the intention to privatize around 20 enterprises by IPOs during the second half of 1990. In the fall, this was scaled back to 5 enterprises. These enterprises were offered for privatization via IPOs in December. When the shares were undersubscribed for some of the firms, the closing date was extended to early January. In the event, only three of the five enterprises were fully subscribed by the general public; the shares of the other two were purchased by a new state development bank in order to complete the IPO.

Ownership to Insiders

A far simpler method of privatization is to transfer the ownership of the enterprises to the insiders, that is, the management and workers in the firms. This can be done rapidly through direct giveaways, leverage buyouts, or some combination (leveraged buyouts at concessionary prices). Indeed, it would be possible, were it desired, to give away the entire enterprise sector to the current insiders in a very short period of time. Transfers or sales of shares to insiders should be widely employed—and more widely than is now the case—but should be subject to clear standards and limitations.

One key problem here is fairness. While insiders should surely receive some explicit property rights in their enterprises to compensate them for their current implicit property rights, a complete transfer of enterprises to the insiders at very low prices would unfairly benefit the insiders relative to the rest of society. The work force in state industrial enterprises totals about 3.6 million workers in a labor force of 18 million, and a population of 38 million. Some workers are in highly profitable enterprises while others are in bankrupt enterprises.

Another problem with insider privatization is efficiency. In general, worker ownership is desirable neither for the workers, who should diversify their capital not concentrate it, nor for the capital structure of the firm, which should have outside owners as well as inside owners. A firm owned mainly by its workers tends to be isolated from the capital markets, since potential outside investors are concerned that inside owners (who control the firm) will appropriate the profit stream. Worker owners, for example, will have the incentive to push for excessive wage increases at the expense of the outside investors.

The public's outrage against spontaneous privatizations by managers, and the economic team's worry about worker ownership in the large enterprises, led the government in 1990 to resist insider privatization in favor of outsider privatization via public offerings. But the reactions probably went too far. The simplest methods of privatization—direct sales or transfers to the insiders—have been underutilized, while the harder methods (such as IPOs) have been overemphasized.

The Polish Privatization Law passed in July 1990 attempted to allow for, but to strictly limit, insider privatizations. The law allows for a limited concessionary sale of shares to workers. Specifically, workers are entitled to buy up to 20 percent of the shares of the enterprise at half price, subject to the proviso that the total value of the concessions to the workers (the half price times the number of shares purchased) must not exceed one year's wage bill of the enterprise.

The concessionary transfer of shares to the workers has so far played no role in speeding the process of privatization. If the law had simply granted the workers ten percent of the shares for free, then the direct transfer of shares to workers could have been used to speed the privatization process without the agony of determining the "price" of the shares. And even if the government sticks with the plan to make concessionary sales to the workers at half price, it could still choose to use the book value of the enterprise, rather than a market price, as the basis for the sale of shares to the workers.

Since the start of 1991, there has been a promising advance in insider privatization for medium-size firms, generally of about 500 employees or less. The government has approved about 100 leveraged buyouts by worker-management groups of these relatively small firms. The worker-manager group seeking the enterprise buys the enterprise with an up-front payment of about 20 percent of value (based on a quick outside valuation that in fact relies heavily on the book value). The rest of the enterprise is purchased with a loan from the government, that is to be amortized over several years.

Outsider Privatization

The government has operated on the premise that outsider privatization (sales or transfers of shares other than to workers and managers in the enterprises) will be the key method for privatization of large industrial firms. There are four different groups of outsiders who can own shares: small investors in the general public; foreign investors; financial intermediaries (banks, pension funds, mutual funds), whose shares in turn would be owned by the general public; and other industrial enterprises.

Of those, the most promising seems to be the reliance on financial intermediaries, as suggested by the practices of the most advanced market economies. Here, more than half of the equity is owned by financial institutions, including banks, pension funds, and investment trusts (or mutual funds). The capitalization of financial intermediaries offers an enormously promising way to proceed with rapid privatization, though this method is almost wholly unexploited to date. (See Lipton and Sachs, 1990, for a more detailed discussion of the proposals in this section).

The most important opportunity lies in share ownership by commercial banks, as in Germany and Japan. Poland has nine state-owned commercial banks that dominate the commercial banking market (around 50 new private commercial banks have been licensed, but most of these banks are still very small). These state banks are in the process of being converted into joint stock companies for subsequent privatization, and the government is aiming to privatize two or three of the banks this year.

The case for giving shares to the banks is very strong. Since the banks are the one existing financial institution in Poland capable of holding and managing corporate equities, it would be natural to use them for this purpose. Moreover, a growing body of international evidence and theoretical reasoning points to the conclusion that banks are excellent candidates for share ownership in that they provide particularly effective corporate governance.[7]

A second way to privatize shares via financial institutions is to capitalize pension funds using the Treasury's shares. Under current arrangements, pensions in Poland are paid entirely by the government on a pay-as-you-go basis financed by a payroll tax. This system could be partially privatized along the lines successfully carried out in Chile in the early 1980s. The Government would deposit a proportion of its equity ownership into several new portfolios, each of which would be managed as a private pension fund by a portfolio management group licensed by the government.

The specific design of the PMFs has been heatedly debated. There are several practical areas of disagreement.[8] Should individuals have the choice whether to receive individual shares of enterprises or shares of a PMF, and should individuals be able to choose their PMF? Should the funds be mostly passive investors, or should the funds be allocated to the controlling interests in individual enterprises? Should households be able to trade their shares of the PMFs without restriction, or should there be a period of time (say, one year) in which they must hold on to their claims? How should the PMF managers be compensated?

The predilection among Polish officials is to create a system of maximal choice for households and the funds. For example, one popular notion is that households would not receive investment trust shares directly, but instead would receive voucher coupons that could be used either to buy equities in individual enterprises or to buy a share in an investment fund. In that scheme, the investment funds would receive vouchers, which they would then use to bid for shares from the government, so that the PMFs would have a key role in building its own initial portfolio of shares.

It is also popular among many Polish officials to envision that the investment funds would have controlling interests of industrial enterprises—in some proposals a PMF could hold up to 100 percent of the equity of an enterprise. There is naturally a desire among Polish officials to create powerful ownership groups, modeled on venture capital funds, that could play a key role in restructuring the state enterprises. The investment funds are widely looked upon as the institutions to carry out such a function.

I would strongly opt for a far simpler system, with much less choice at the outset, and with weaker funds, in order to minimize risks and to save enormous administrative complexities. The process of creating investment funds will require the prompt distribution of shares to 25 million adult Poles in a situation in which there do not now exist any tested institutions of share ownership, brokerage houses, or even established investment funds.

In the interest of simplicity, individuals can be randomly assigned to investment trusts without any choice (e.g. based on the number of their national identity card). In turn, the Treasury's shares would be randomly allocated to the investment trusts, again with no choice. There would seem to be little gain to expending great efforts in auctioning the shares to the investment funds when these funds will be free to trade their initial allocations after they are received. The initial allocation of shares should be designed administratively to meet two criteria: equality across fund portfolios in the reported post-tax earnings in 1990 and equality of the book values of the enterprise shares held in each fund. Subsequent to this initial distribution, the investment funds would be allowed to trade their shares.

I would also strongly argue against allowing the investment funds to gain a majority stake in individual enterprises. In fact, in my view, the ownership of any enterprise by any PMF should be limited to 10–15 percent of the shares of the enterprise. Even though it might seem attractive to create powerful active investors, this should not be done artificially with newly established investment funds that have no management track record and that do not even have the fund managers' own money at stake.

The Early Effects of Poland's Reforms

Even in the first two years of economic reform, the combination of liberalization, stabilization, and privatization measures has had a profound and beneficial effect on the Polish economy. In the first few weeks of Poland's "big bang," Poles were startled to see the end of the shortages that had wracked Poland for decades, as well as the appearance of many new imported consumer goods on the market. Hundreds of thousands of new small businesses started operations in 1990, creating in a matter of months an incredible network of new shops and service establishments, and firms engaged in international trade, construction, and trucking. The development of the service and trade sectors was particularly dramatic in an economy that had long been starved of these sectors.

The economy also quickly adjusted to the opening of markets to international trade. Polish exports to the West surged in 1990, as currency and the newly attractive exchange rate following the devaluation and unification of the exchange rate at the start of 1990. The surge in exports continued in 1991, and has helped to pay for a sharp rise in imports as well. The import boom reflects, in part, the eager purchases by Polish households of Western durables goods that were long unavailable, and in part, a substantial increase in machinery imports.

The overall effect in the first two years of the economic changes on the average Polish households is hard to assess. Despite the new availability of goods since the start of 1990, many Poles have complained bitterly about the new higher prices. The evidence suggests that on average, Poles are now consuming somewhat more meats, fruits, and consumer durables than they were before the reforms, so that greater availability of goods has, on average, more than compensated for higher prices. And without doubt, Poles are now saving millions of hours of time per week that used to be wasted in long queues for consumer goods in scarce supply.

But, of course, average levels of consumption tell only one part of the story. There are surely important groups in the population that have lost ground in the first two years of the reforms. These groups include, for example, the hundreds of thousands of farmers working on tiny and inefficient farms, who have lost the production subsidies that used to help them stay in operation. Similarly, there are hundreds of industrial enterprises, with hundreds of thousands of workers, that are unable to compete under the new market conditions. As a result, there has been a sharp loss of jobs in industrial firms, which has contributed to a sharp increase of the unemployment rate, which has risen to nearly 10 percent in mid-1991.

Not all of the rise of unemployment is due to the reforms, however. Some was always present, but was simply unrecorded by the previous regime, under which unemployment was a crime and not a circumstance meriting compensation. Also, the collapse of the Soviet economy, and the breakdown of trade relations with the Soviet Union, has led to an enormous and rapid decline in exports from Eastern Europe to the Soviet Union. Hundreds of enterprises in Poland and the rest of Eastern Europe are being forced to close their doors, or at least to cut back dramatically on production, as a direct result of the Soviet crisis. The economic reforms in Poland have in fact helped to ease this shock, by creating conditions in which enterprises can shift their exports from the Soviet Union to Western markets. Nonetheless, the loss of national income and employment due to the Soviet crisis is widely attributed by the Polish public to the economic reforms themselves.

The dominant mood in Poland may be described as a grudging acceptance of the need for the reforms, and an appreciation for the achievements to date in ending inflation and shortages, and in promoting the private sector. At the same time, however, there is a deep anxiety over rising unemployment and a profound uncertainty about the future. In a recent opinion survey, more than 60 percent of the Poles said that they feared losing their jobs in the near future. While such fears are almost surely exaggerated, the fears themselves are real, and they contribute to a pall that hangs over the country.

The Need for a Breakthrough on Privatization

Poland has made it more than half-way through the reform process needed to transform itself into a market economy. The price system now works according to supply and demand; international trade is free, and as hoped, both exports and imports are rising; new private firms are forming and growing at a rapid rate. Indeed, Poland already can be considered to have a market economy, but one that still has an overwhelming state-ownership of large industrial firms. Poland has so far achieved a form of "market socialism."

This is surely not where Poland wants to remain. Market socialism is not only inefficient, but if continued would almost surely lead to a return of profound macroeconomic instability. The problem is that in the absence of real owners of the industrial assets, the enterprises lack clear goals, and are not subject to any effective corporate governance. In the West, enterprise managers are governed by a board of directors that is legally obliged to govern the firm on behalf of the owners, with the goal of maximizing the firm's value. While this system poses serious problems of how to make sure that managers and board directors in fact operate on behalf of the owners, at least the legal responsibilities and basic incentives of corporate enterprises are clear.

Under the communist regime, governance was provided by a system of commands from the state administration and the Communist Party, backed up by terror or its threat. With the merciful collapse of communist terror, governance of the industrial sector has also collapsed, with striking and pathological effects. Now, enterprise managers operate on their own behalf, or under the control of a workers' council within the firm. In a small minority of firms, a Supervisory Board has been appointed by the government to represent the interests of the Treasury as the legal owner of the enterprises. In this cases the workers' council role is eliminated, and the enterprise is made subject to normal commercial law for corporations, a process known in Poland as "commercialization."

Throughout the state sector, and particularly in the vast majority of firms that have not been commercialized, there are incessant wage pressures that are not kept in check by managers who represent real owners of the firms. Managers are in fact all to ready to pay out enterprise profits in the form of higher wages. In the absence of centralized wage controls, therefore, there is the tendency towards a wage explosion, of the sort that has occurred in East Germany (where wage controls were not imposed).[8] Therefore, wages are now kept somewhat under control in Poland by economically inefficient and politically debilitating for the government.

Also, in the non-commercialized enterprises, there are reports of widespread self-dealing and conflict of interest by state managers. Managers have been reported to engage in the following kinds of activities: intentionally bankrupting firms to buy them back cheaply; establishing private firms to do business, in sweetheart deals, with the state enterprises that they manage; accepting unfavorable joint venture and takeover offers that provide personal benefits for the manager, while rejecting favorable offers that put the manager's personal position at risk.[9]

Finally, there are "zombie" enterprises, in which incompetent managers simply run down the bank balances and other capital of the new market conditions. In the case of many Polish firms that were hit by the collapse of the Soviet market, enterprises simply continued to produce the normal output levels and build up inventories, waiting for a miracle of some sort. Finally, in mid-1991, the bank balances have run out, and a politically and economically troubling spate of insolvencies has hit the country. Once again, the absence of a capital market (in which a takeover might occur), and the lack of corporate governance, has contributed to these profound managerial failures.

The proper long-term solution for the industrial sector problems is clear. The enterprises should be privatized, and then restructured or liquidated once under private control. The case for privatizing the firms quickly is overwhelming. The onus on the government for restructuring will be greatly reduced; the pressures from the firms for subsidies and protection will be easier to resist; and, presumably, the private owners will do a better job of saving the viable parts of industry and sloughing off the unviable parts. As mentioned earlier, novel approaches to privatization—based on a free-distribution of shares of industrial enterprises—are probably vital to speeding the privatization process. Nonetheless, these novel methods remain controversial and subject to criticisms by various groups, such as managers intent on keeping control over their enterprises.

Before privatization is complete, there is an urgent need to widen the use of commercialization, to bring the enterprises under the governance of Supervisory Boards. While this step does not establish private owners, it does help to establish some modicum of oversight of managerial behavior, and it does subject the enterprise to normal corporate law. Even this step, however, is controversial and slow to be applied in Poland. Some policymakers underestimate the importance of establishing a clear legal framework for the enterprises, while others point to the real, but surmountable, logistical difficulties of finding qualified individuals to sit on the supervisory boards. Still other critics of commercialization worry that if the process is abused, it could lead to a recentralization of governmental power over the enterprises.

Economic Restructuring in the Medium Term

The economic reforms will set in motion a sustained process of economic restructuring. Of particular importance will be the pressures of international competition on Polish industrial enterprises. While we cannot make accurate predictions about the precise long-term consequences of this restructuring, especially as regards which industrial sectors will survive and flourish, and which will decline, we can make some useful predictions about the basic trends that are likely to emerge.

Under communist rule, Poland's economy was heavily skewed towards industry and away from services. This bias was cruelly felt in everyday life, in the form of a shortage of shops and restaurants, miserably inefficient banks, and virtually unobtainable personal services. Once market forces are unleashed, there should be a strong pull of resources into the previously neglected sectors, and out of the overextended industrial sectors. Even in the first year-and-one-half of the reforms, such trends have been clearly evident. Industrial employment has fallen sharply, perhaps by around one-fourth in the state-owned industrial enterprises. At the same time, hundreds of thousands of new private businesses have emerged in trade, services, and residential construction. While Poland is sometimes described as being in a sharp recession, this characterization in fact applies only to the industrial sector. The economy is actually booming in many of the previously neglected sectors, especially through the formation of new small businesses.

Agriculture is another area where we should expect major restructuring. Poland has a large and inefficient agricultural sector made up of hundreds of thousands of tiny farms. As mentioned earlier, these small farms were sustained despite very low productivity by large subsidies granted by the communist regime to keep social peace in the countryside. Poland therefore has not yet completed the great demographic shift of employment from agriculture to industry and services that has been traversed by nearly every advanced industrial country. As a result of the sharp cuts in subsidies to agriculture in the past two years, many small-scale farmers are now under financial pressure. It should be expected that many small farmer households will sell their farms in the coming decade or two, so that farmlands will be consolidated over time into a much smaller number of larger farms.

The third major trend that we should expect is a complete restructuring within the industrial sector, from energy-intensive heavy industry to more labor-intensive and skill-intensive industries that can compete on world markets. Poland enjoys low-cost skilled labor, particularly in engineering, that should make Poland an attractive place to produce industrial goods for exports to Western Europe. Over time, Western firms, mainly from Western Europe, are likely to set up operations in Poland for the sake of export production, in the same way that European firms are investing in Spain, or American firms are investing in Mexico, or Japanese firms are investing in Korea, Taiwan, and the rest of Southeast Asia. So far, foreign direct investment has been modest, since foreign investors remain concerned about the lack of clarity in property rights, and about the political sustainability of Poland's reforms. Assuming that the reforms are in fact sustained, the rate of foreign direct investment should increase markedly in the coming years.

Conclusion

Unfortunately, privatization of large industrial enterprises has proceeded much more slowly, indeed far too slowly. It seems clear that new methods of privatization beyond those that have been used in the West will be needed to speed the process. After much debate and analysis, there are plans in Poland to privatize several hundred large enterprises by giving away their shares to the Polish population. Specifically, the plan is to freely distribute a portion of the shares of these large industrial enterprises into mutual funds, whose shares in turn will be distributed to the adult Polish citizens. There is also some discussion of distributing shares into new private pension funds that would take over some of the burden of the state social security system.

The greatest risk in Poland is that populism, confusion of property rights, and a splintering of political power in the parliament, will lead to weak governments unable to take the last decisive step to private ownership. In that case, the economic situation will almost surely deteriorate, macroeconomic instability will rise, and as in Latin America, democracy itself could be put at risk. The risk is heightened by the fact that Poland has adopted proportional representation as the basis for parliamentary representation. This voting system surely increases the likelihood of weak, splintered political parties, and a government that is dependent on fragile, multiparty coalitions. Twenty seven political parties are putting forward nationwide slates, and no less than 62 parties are fielding at least one candidate, in the parliamentary elections in October 1991.

The key fact about economic reform is that several years must pass before the fruits of reform are widely evident. The intervening period has been called a "valley of tears," and it may be observed in nearly every country that has undergone a radical economic transformation, from post-War Germany and Japan, to Chile and Mexico in the 1980s. The time in the valley depends on the consistency and boldness of the reforms. If there is wavering or inconsistency in economic measures, it is easy to get lost in the valley. Argentina has been lost for forty-five years.

The glue holding together the reforms is the basic social consensus that success will be achieved by "returning to Europe." But if Western Europe shows that it doesn't really want Poland (and the rest of Eastern

Europe) to "return," then the consensus will break apart, and the intense pressures already facing the governments of the region are likely to undermine the reforms. Worse yet, given the stingy attitude of the West to date, and the undoubted cases of rapacious Western investors intent on profiteering from the gaps in adequate legal structure in Eastern Europe, there is already evident a risk of xenophobic backlash among part of the Eastern European population.

Notes

Jeffrey Sachs is in the Department of Economics at Harvard University.

This article is based on a talk delivered for the Sideman Award in International Political Economy for 1991.

1. According to World Bank estimates of dollar GNP for the year 1989, we find: Czechoslovakia, $3,450; Hungary, $2,590; Poland, $1,790. This compares with Portugal, $4,250; Greece, $5,350; Ireland, $8,710; and Spain, $9,330; and in Latin America, with Brazil, $2,540; Uruguay, $2,620; and Venezuela, $2,450. (World Bank, 1991, *World Development Report. 1991*. Appendix Table 1, p. 205).

2. Before Poland's big bang, there had been great concerns about liberalizing prices in the face of a highly monopolized industrial structure. Many economists had insisted that price liberalization could only be accomplished after a substantial, and time-consuming demonopolization of the economy. But this view was basically mistaken, since the immediate introduction of free trade was a quicker and more effective means of instilling competition in Poland's markets than an attempt at administratively guided demonopolization.

3. The British privatizations typically followed a pattern in which the firm was "prepared" for privatization through an internal restructuring; the firm was "valued" by one or more investment banks, to get a base price for an initial public offering (IPO); the IPO was widely advertised and promoted; and then the IPO was carried out several months later. The whole process could take a year or more.

4. This section is based on J. Sachs, 1991, "Accelerating Privatization in Eastern Europe: the Case of Poland," prepared for the World Bank Annual Conference on Development Economics (May).

5. Consider merely the question of the public's financial holdings, for comparison with the capital value of the industrial enterprises. The post-tax profits of the largest 500 state-owned firms are approximately $5 billion. With a price-earnings ratio of 5, the capital value of the largest 500 firms is around $25 billion. The public's financial holdings in the banking system total approximately $10 billion, only forty percent of the capital value of the largest firms at the modest P-E of 5. And taking into account that other property in addition to the 500 large enterprises is also to be privatized, it is clear that in order to privatize through IPOs, the share prices would have to be at very low price-earnings ratios, which in turn would risk a socially unacceptable concentration

of share ownership. The alternatives are to transfer the shares to the public freely by some means (as recommended below); or to sell the shares on a leveraged basis, which would pose its own risks and complications. For a detailed discussion of the concept and motivations for a free distribution of shares, see D. Lipton and J. Sachs, 1990, "Privatization in Eastern Europe: the Case of Poland," *Brookings Papers on Economic Activity*. 1990, No. 2.

6. The finance studies stress that bank ownership of corporate equities tends to foster a healthy long-term relationship between the banks and the industrial enterprises, a relationship that contributes especially to a long planning horizon of the industrial enterprises.

7. The wage explosion in East Germany has had devastating consequences, for it has led to the virtual bankruptcy of the entire East German industrial sector. Most enterprises continue to operate only by virtue of large-scale subsidies from the government. Wages have risen to around 50 to 60 percent of West German levels, even though productivity is perhaps only 20 to 30 percent of West German levels. The wage explosion resulted from a variety of factors: the lack of wage controls; the East German public's belief that they "deserved" West German wage levels; the unwillingness of politicians in West Germany to speak out on behalf of rational wage policies; and the pressure of West German unions to help raise East German wages, lest the lower wages in the East undermine the wages in the West.

8. By favorable or unfavorable I refer to the value of the offer compared to the value of the capital that is being sold to the foreign bidder. Of course, the issue of self-dealing by managers in the face of hostile takeover bids is familiar in American capitalism as well, but the managers are limited in egregious behavior by the board of directors, which is itself bound by corporate law to consider the interests of the shareholders as paramount in the event of a takeover bid.

9. Protectionist pressures will also be easier to resist if the Eastern European countries are successful in signing Association Agreements with the European Community. These agreements should presumably guarantee open markets on both sides, and therefore bind the Eastern European countries to free-trade policies.

Bibliography

Sachs, J. and Lipton, 1990, "Privatization in Eastern Europe: The Case of Poland," Brookings Papers on Economic Activity, No. 2.

Sachs, J., 1991, "Accelerating Privatization in Eastern Europe: The Case of Poland" (mimeo).

World Bank, 1991, World Development Report.

PART FOUR

Alternative Approaches to Economic Transition

10

Evolutionary and Radical Approaches to Economic Reform

Peter Murrell

The Radical Reform Model Begins to Break Down

During 1989, as the East European revolutions proceeded in succession and the economics profession became increasingly engaged in the reform process, there was almost a consensus amongst economists about the way in which reform should proceed. First, there would have to be liberalization—the freeing of all economic actors from central government controls, especially in the setting of prices. That liberalization would necessarily be accompanied by a drastic, market-style stabilization based on tight money and the hardening of budget constraints. The guiding light in the first steps of reform would be that all economic agents, whether state or private, would participate in the market under the same set of conditions. Given the immediate reliance on the market mechanism, the old institutions of traditional control—especially the planners and the supply organizations—would be destroyed. The existing structure of property rights in the state sector would be eradicated in order to give the government complete control over state assets. This measure would occur as preparation for privatization, which would be pursued as soon and as fast as possible.

The 1989 consensus view of economic reform, I will call the radical approach. It emphasizes speed, the destruction of the old, and the quick conversion of organizations to the arrangements of developed capitalist economies. The train of events over the last two years in Eastern Europe has not been kind to the radical model. There are now signs that the former consensus is breaking down. One constantly hears pronouncements from officials and academics that reform is more difficult than expected, more costly than expected, and slower than expected. But disappointed expectations are not the prime factor in cracking the academic consensus. Rather, the radical model is coming into question because of the manner in which expectations have been disappointed. In this introduction, I list a few facts that seem pertinent in this respect. As I do so, I hint at the way in which these facts undermine the radical program of reform and serve to justify a different approach. This paper then outlines this alternative approach.

No normative model is ever implemented cleanly, but in East Germany the radical model came as close to complete implementation as one is likely to see. East Germany seemed to have everything—a big brother to hold the currency firm and to ensure credibility of the reform process, a structure of laws and institutions that were accepted immediately, and immediate entry into the world's largest trading bloc. In addition, the whole package could be implemented overnight. That implementation resulted in the largest economic disaster in Europe in the postwar period.

The economic reform that conformed least to the radical pattern was that of China. In that country, there were the worst initial conditions, including communist leaders who would not let go and a large urban, state-owned industrial sector with much influence. From the radical perspective, the reform was implemented in the most chaotic manner, with distortions of immense magnitude, with opaque property rights, and with large barriers to competition. Nevertheless, there can be no doubt that the reforms in China are as successful as have been seen. The contrast between the Chinese experience and the East German experience should surely give pause to those confident in the radical model.

It is now clear that the radical reform model faces large implementation problems in the East European countries. These problems damage the coherence that is the most important economic property of the model. Consider the following statement by that most radical of all reformers, Vaclav Klaus, the Minister of Finance of Czechoslovakia: "I agree that the opinion claiming that cooperatives will cease to be a significant entity in our agriculture within my lifetime is nonsense and stupid ideological propaganda."

Similarly, Polish government officials have made in the past grand statements about radical implementation of a capitalist economy by swift privatization, refusing to countenance the third way of employee ownership. Nonetheless, the major step toward privatization in Poland so far has been employee buyouts—a method that had been greatly denigrated by the radicals. Moreover, the Western economist most prominent in Eastern European reforms, Jeffrey Sachs, has now accepted that giving the enterprises to workers might be the best available alternative in Poland, despite repeated warnings about this option in the past. The inability to implement major aspects of the radical reform program surely argues that there are problems in its conception, particularly the supposed coherence that is at its heart.

The tenacity of the old appears not only in the inability to destroy existing institutions. The organizations that were expected to change their behavior in response to the new conditions have failed to do so. This is particularly the case for the large state enterprises that still dominate the Eastern European economies. The press reports, the observations of politicians, and the performance of enterprises now speak in one voice on this issue. The lack of organizational response calls into question the notion that austerity and liberalization will rapidly change the behavior of existing organizations. It is now clear that the hope for Eastern Europe lies primarily in the new organizations that are created in the private sector and then selected and shaped by market forces.

Where destruction of the old framework of institutions has been accomplished, the results have hardly been fortunate. The single best example of this is the demise of the CMEA in early 1991. The precipitate dropping of the old CMEA arrangements is now widely recognized to have caused enormous problems in Eastern European trade, which in turn caused large domestic economic crises. Many fewer economists now than one year ago subscribe to the notion that a long-established bureaucratic procedure can be quickly replaced by the market.

While most economists agree that bureaucratic procedure must be replaced by normal monetary transactions in the long run, there is increasing sympathy with the idea that the phasing out of old institutions must be smooth and gradual, in companion with the rise of the new institutions of the private sector. This realization, prompted by the effects of the destruction of the CMEA, is now becoming an important factor in present discussions concerning prospects for the economic composition of the Soviet Union. There are many advocates of the notion that elements of the old system must be protected for a while in order to prevent economic collapse. This is hardly the type of analysis that one would have expected from economists only one or two years ago. It is certainly not consistent with the radical models of reform that were promulgated in those blissful early days of 1990.

Beyond a rise in sympathy for policies that temporarily protect the old system, there is in some instances a movement toward re-creation of previously destroyed parts of that system. Barter deals are now being forged between countries that suffered greatly from the precipitate destruction of the old CMEA barter system. Consider also the fact that the Polish government is now reactivating its interventionist policies of the past, for example as a credit manager for the state sector. "After so many years of a state-steered economy, it is impossible to have no intervention at all.

In summary, little in the economic record of the past two years suggests that the radical program of reform can be successful. The old cannot be simply destroyed and therefore the radical reform plans have serious problems of coherency. Furthermore, it is now becoming increasingly accepted that sudden destruction of the old can be economically inadvisable. The economic pressures associated with this realization are so great that some of the past institutions are being re-created—a re-creation that is far more costly than keeping the old institutions in grudging acceptance of the fact that they cannot be replaced overnight.

Lurking in the literature there have always been elements of an alternative program of reform. Kornai's (1990) emphasis on organic economic processes and his skepticism about reforming the state sector are inconsistent with the radical approach. Similarly, McKinnon's (1991) analysis concentrates on the details of the existing situation and does not assume that functioning markets can be produced overnight. He therefore advocates temporary nonliberal arrangements in the transition. There are also a series of works of my own (Murrell 1991, 1992a, 1992b), which have criticized the radical point of view and offered a different approach that one might label evolutionary. Such an approach places little emphasis on reforming old organizations, but instead pins its hopes on the growth of a nascent private sector.

An evolutionary policy, therefore, combines a policy of the gradual phasing out of the old institutional framework, an active program to promote new private sector activity and the institutions that this sector requires, and gradual privatization using market processes. In this chapter, I summarize some of the strands of thought that provide underpinnings for the evolutionary approach to reform, review the general philosophy underlying that approach, and compare evolutionary and radical schemes.

The Intellectual Underpinnings of an Evolutionary Approach to Reform

There are two conceptually distinct sets of theories that provide underpinnings for an evolutionary approach to economic reform. First, there is the body of theory that falls under the rubric of evolutionary economics. The modern representation of this theory begins with Schumpeter (1950); the most detailed current exposition is that of Nelson and Winter (1982). The informational issues that are at the heart of evolutionary economics are now also a central concern in mainstream theoretical economics. Indeed, the information-theoretic paradigm is challenging the standard neoclassical view (Stiglitz 1991). That paradigm will eventually provide additional elements for a broader conceptual basis for evolutionary reforms.

I label the second set of theories "conservative political philosophy." The leading works in this genre are Burke (1790), Popper (1971), and Oakeshott (1962). Whereas evolutionary economics concentrates on positive economic analysis, conservative political philosophy is more concerned with normative political issues, particularly the ways in which societies change. As we will see, the assumptions of these two sets of theories are surprisingly similar, as are their lessons for economic reform.

Murrell (1992a, 1991, 1992b) examines these two theoretical viewpoints separately but draws similar conclusions for reform from each analysis. This is unlikely to be pure coincidence, given that the two theories concentrate on very distinct aspects of socioeconomic processes. Thus, not surprisingly, one can find many similarities in the assumptions underlying the two sets of theories and the problems that they place at the center of study. Simply put, the worldview of these two basic approaches has much in common.

Since previous papers have discussed in detail each of the individual theories, I concentrate here on establishing a more general overview and on building the rudiments of a single philosophy of evolutionary reform. In the following subsections, I will lay out the central vision of socioeconomic processes that underlies evolutionary theory; examine assumptions of the two sets of theories; and use them to derive some general features of an evolutionary reform process.

Commonalities—Visions of Socioeconomic Processes

Perhaps the central vision underlying conservative political philosophy and evolutionary economics is the notion that socioeconomic mechanisms are information-processing devices. Both theories emphasize the limits on individual intellectual capacities and the complexity of social arrangements. They focus on how societies can efficiently use the knowledge available to them and how socioeconomic processes preserve and enhance the knowledge that exists in society. The conception of socioeconomic mechanisms as information-processing devices might be profitably contrasted with the view of economies as resource-allocating devices.

The second important feature common to conservative political philosophy and evolutionary economics is best illustrated by analogy. Societies can be compared to climbers trying to find the top of hill enveloped in cloud. With limited information on the local topography, the best they can do is to take the path of steepest ascent and to move forward in small steps, reevaluating their information at each stage. If they had a map, they could devise a better procedure. But no accurate map is available.

Similarly, societies proceed using only local information. In understanding economic processes, according to evolutionary economics, we must acknowledge the fact that organizations and individuals are engaged in choices that are sharply limited in scope by finite information sets. In making political choices, according to conservative political philosophy, we must confront the fact that it is simply beyond our capacities to map out a process of complete social change. Societies are never in a full-information world; it is a misleading and dangerous abstraction to assume that they are. The view of societies as hill climbers is in direct contrast with the assumption that the choice of laws and policy can be cast in a first-best framework.

Commonalities—Assumptions and Deductions

Having introduced the two central elements of weltanschauung, we now turn to the underlying assumptions. There are two essential assumptions about human knowledge—one concerns its limits and the other concerns its nature. The first assumption is that there are bounds on individual intellectual capacities, and these bounds place severe constraints on the structure and functioning of institutions and organizations. In the economic dimension, this means that one cannot view organizations as simply larger versions of rational economic man, reacting swiftly and accurately to the winds of fortune. Rigidities in economic behavior must be largely understood in terms of the limits on individual knowledge and the effects of these limits on organizational behavior. In particular, old organizations, created in a past environment, will behave very differently from new organizations. In the political dimension, this means that individuals cannot be expected to understand the effects of schemes for large-scale social renovation, especially when this renovation involves a thoroughgoing replacement of all the institutions of society.

The other pivotal assumption about human knowledge is that important insights are gained by distinguishing between two types of knowledge. The first is technical knowledge, the set of explicit rules and procedures that can be conveyed by lecturers and systematized in textbooks. The other is practical, or personal, knowledge—the inarticulate knowledge that is required in the effective performance of any activity and that can be acquired only by direct acquaintance with the activity. Personal knowledge includes information about individuals and organizations in the economic and political systems with which a person interacts.

Because personal knowledge is acquired through activity, it is specific to particular social contexts. A society's stock of personal knowledge is acquired through a long historical process and is shaped by the institutions and organizations of that particular society. It is useful mainly in the context of those organizations and institutions. Since radical schemes of reform advocate measures that destroy much of society's social knowledge capital, judgments on the relative merits of radical and evolutionary schemes for reform will hinge to a large extent on the relative importance that one attributes to technical and personal knowledge.

Both conservative political philosophy and evolutionary economics place processes of change at the very center of inquiry. Conservative political philosophers maintain that the great disasters of history have been fostered by utopian schemes of change. This emphasis on change interacts strongly with the assumptions regarding the nature of knowledge. It is exactly when a new world is sought that it is most important to recognize the limits placed by the fact that current knowledge has been produced by the old order.

An evolutionary view of economic processes holds that the relative success of different societies is largely a function of their effectiveness in reacting to exogenous events and in generating productive social change. For economic systems, innovation and adaptability are the crucial ingredients for success. Again, the assumptions on knowledge are crucial. Those assumptions largely determine the way in which we should understand the nature of organizations and their reactions to change. In particular, successful societies do not rely on change within existing organizations to undertake fundamentally new activities. Change is accomplished to some great degree by the replacement of the old and by experimentation with, and selection among, new structures:

the process of entry and exit. In the reforming countries, this can only be accomplished within the new private sector.

Commonalities—General Reflections on Reform

Economic and political decisions are circumscribed by limits in social knowledge, especially those limits that result from the fact that this knowledge is inherited from the past. Hence, there will be much persistence in the behavior of the individual organizations and institutions of society. It is quixotic to assume that organizations can escape their past and adopt a thoroughly new mode of behavior. Policy-makers cannot design a fixed and flawless blueprint for change to a new order because socioeconomic processes are highly complex and society's information stock is conditioned by the old order. Such limits are stressed by the evolutionary approach to reform. The radical approach focuses on desires for the future.

Reforms must work with what inheres in any given social situation. The behavior of existing organizations and institutions is not likely to change rapidly, at least not in functional ways. Unless destruction is the goal, many characteristics of existing organizations must be accepted. If one attempts to eradicate all such characteristics immediately, then one invites economic collapse. In the long run, the existing organizations can be replaced by the growing private sector and its associated institutions. But if one ignores such the existing character of organizations when designing economic reforms for the short run, then one risks setting in motion a reform that has properties far from those desired.

In their separate ways, both conservative political philosophy and evolutionary economics lead to what might be called the law of the diminishing marginal productivity of change. From the economic perspective, large changes in the legal and policy framework produce highly dysfunctional outcomes, because the capacities of existing organizations are greatly dependent upon their existing environment. Knowledge of how to behave in the new situation is missing, and much effort must be expended initially in developing a new modus operandi. Moreover, as existing economic relationships are disrupted, much knowledge capital is destroyed. Similarly, from the policy perspective, the effectiveness of policy-measures decreases sharply with the magnitude of the break from the past because the knowledge used to design those measures is reflective of initial conditions.

Distinct elements of the two sets of theories combine to produce the final conclusion, which is specific to the transition from socialism. Conservative political philosophy emphasizes the need to identify the most pressing problems within society and to produce change by attacking those problems rather than by attempting to implement a redesign of the whole system. An evolutionary perspective allows us to identify the central problem of socialist economies—these systems had no capacity for change and renewal (Murrell 1990a). This capacity in capitalist societies is provided to some large extent by entry and exit—the process of demise of the old organizations and their replacement by the new.

The first step in an evolutionary reform is therefore to expose existing institutions to challenge by the new. This can only be accomplished by encouraging the nascent private sector. Such encouragement is so vital that it must be an element in all aspects of policy for the transition and it must help to determine policy towards the old state sector. It is in fact an understanding of the processes of change under capitalism that tells us that socialist reform will be a failure unless that new private sector is the main instrument of producing change within the Eastern European economies.

Dichotomies: Features of Evolutionary and Radical Schemes

The evolutionary and radical strategies for reform are not clearly specified lists of procedures to be followed in specific circumstances. Rather they are philosophies, or worldviews, on general approaches to reform. They are paradigms concerning how to identify the issues that should be addressed and how one should address them. In the following comparison, it is therefore not possible to focus on detailed measures. It is possible, however, to review the most general features of the two worldviews. This is accomplished by highlighting the chief conceptual differences between the two philosophies of reform and illustrating them with examples. Throughout the following, one should remember the most important distinction between the evolutionary and radical views. This is the contrast between viewing society as an information-processing device and viewing society as a resource-allocation device.

Identifying Worst Problems or Implementing the End State

The radical reform program is defined in terms of its intended endpoint. It focuses on immediately implementing the features of a mature market economy. The order for implementation of the parts is determined by feasibility as much as by strategy, since the emphasis is on doing as much as possible, as soon as possible. More importantly, no actions are taken unless they directly relate to attainment of the envisioned endpoint. Existing arrangements are suffered if they cannot be removed, but they are seldom kept by strategic choice. For example, the instruments of macroeconomic control of the old system are eschewed, despite their potentially greater effectiveness than market-based stabilization schemes in the very early stages of reform.

In contrast, the evolutionary approach asks first what features of the old system need to be changed most urgently. The answer is based on a pragmatic assessment of present requirements, rather than a vision of an end-state that is far into the future. The strengthening of certain types of property rights, for example, might be an appropriate response to organizational inefficiency, even if these particular property rights might not be deemed suitable for the long run. An illustration of this is the case for strengthening workers' management rights in certain enterprises when elements of such rights are deeply embedded from the past. Such a move may allow existing information to be used in its most productive way, given the structure of existing organizations.

Under an evolutionary approach, the policy of not destroying workers' management rights is thoroughly consistent with the expectation that workers' management will not be a feature of the end state of the reform process. So long as the workers' enterprises are exposed to competition from the new private sector, the place of workers' management in the economy can be decided by the market. Meanwhile, in the short run, keeping in place an existing system of workers' management rights avoids the destruction of a large part of society's organizational capital. In contrast, adopting a radical approach would most likely entail revoking workers' rights immediately, if they were regarded as inconsistent with the end-state.

Destruction Versus Gradual Replacement

The radical approach emphasizes destruction of old institutions because they are believed to have no value in the end-state and hinder implementation of that end-state. For example, rapid privatization is often advocated as a means of destroying the existing system rather than for any creative purposes. The evolutionary approach, in contrast, would recognize the information that is held in the continuing operations of existing organizations and in the continuing interactions of economic agents in their existing capacities. Rapid change in existing arrangements destroys much of the information that society has built up over time. Even though this information might not be useful in the long run, it could be very productive during the beginning stages of reform, when alternative market arrangements are only beginning to form.

As the new private sector institutions grow, hopefully spurred by state encouragement, the old can be gradually replaced. The destruction of the CMEA illustrates this dichotomy. Those who advocated the CMEA's quick demise are now being forced to acknowledge the short-run costs of replacing it. A policy of gradual replacement would have surely lessened the economic problems of 1991 and would have prevented the need for the Eastern European countries to scramble to construct barter deals to replace the CMEA.

Reversibility Versus Commitment

No concept has been more prevalent in the reform debates than that of commitment—the notion that unless policymakers are able to back themselves into a corner, their policies will have no credibility. Given that the radical approach aims unstintingly at the end-state, commitment to implement this state is obviously an unalloyed good. When the process of reaching the end-state is considered, however, the value of commitment diminishes. The evolutionary approach stresses that there will be an immense amount of learning in the process of reform and that the initial policy stance will depend very much on knowledge obtained under the old regime. Therefore, commitment can well be counterproductive. Initially chosen policies will be unsatisfactory and the ability to change them will be important. Reversibility is especially valuable when changing large socioeconomic systems, since the knowledge of such systems is always terribly incomplete and the costs of poor decisions can be immense.

In fact, the credibility of a reform process (as opposed to particular reform policies) might be enhanced by advocating policies that are more easily reversible. Policy that commits itself to particular features at a time when there is much learning to be accomplished and when large mistakes are inevitable is not likely to be considered sustainable. For example, the commitment to a particular exchange rate early in reform actually lessens policy credibility; it is obvious that policymakers cannot identify an appropriate rate before gaining knowledge of the new system.

Fast Versus Slow

All of the above points reflect to some degree differences of opinion on the optimal speed of reform for the existing institutions and organizations within society. The law of the diminishing marginal productivity of change captures this issue in a general way. Radical reforms pursue speed as a means of destroying the old, on the assumption that the old has no value. The evolutionary approach emphasizes that rapid reforms that disrupt existing relationships also destroy the existing information stock. Such is one interpretation of the collapse of enterprise performance in Eastern Europe after the implementation of shock tactics in several countries.

Additionally, fast reforms do not have the potential for reversibility possessed by more gradual reform processes. Since there is a lag between implementation and effect, fast reforms offer no mechanism for stopping a measure during implementation, in the event that its effect be found less benign than was anticipated at the beginning of reform. It must be emphasized here that the issue of speed only reflects upon the changes in the operating conditions of existing organizations. No similar argument applies to encouragement of the new private sector. Thus, reform should certainly aim at creating, as soon as possible, conditions conducive to the rapid growth of a new private sector

Small Versus Large Experiments

Many experiments will be tried as countries attempt the transition from socialism to capitalism. Such schemes will rely primarily on theoretical design rather than on simple extrapolation of present experience or on the importing of lessons from other nations. The issue of the size of an experiment during reform and the issue of the speed of reform are somewhat similar. A fast reform exposes the society to great risks that cannot be hedged by reversibility; so does a reform that contains a single element that is of very large scope.

Because of the incompleteness of our knowledge of how socioeconomic processes work, the evolutionary perspective holds that society must restrict the scope of any single experiment. For example, the grand voucher schemes of privatization can be viewed as a way of exposing a large segment of society to what is essentially the implementation of a theoretical idea. Implementation of the voucher scheme is anticipated in Poland, Czechoslovakia, and Mongolia. From the evolutionary perspective, these schemes are better to the extent that they rely on existing experience drawn from elsewhere, to the extent that the changes that they render are transparent and simple, and to the extent that they are reversible. In these senses then, the Polish scheme is preferred to the Czechoslovak scheme, with the Mongolian scheme least preferred.

The second reason to minimize the scope of experiments is that when things go wrong, as they inevitably will, there will be spillovers across sectors. A unique characteristic of the East European transition is the large number of companies that will simultaneously be subject to the stress of change. Declines in performance in one area will be reinforced by the pressures of adversity elsewhere. Whereas moderate amounts of adversity might be salutary, inducing productive reactions, extreme adversity appears to produce highly dysfunctional response, enhancing crisis rather than diminishing it. It is thus important to ensure that a crisis produced by a failed experiment does not affect too many areas of the economy simultaneously. This is one of the lessons from the effects of the decline of the CMEA that should be brought to bear on the present debates over privatization.

Experience Versus Design

The radical reforms are the crystallization of the faith in reason over experience and experiment. An evolutionary approach values the accumulated experimental wisdom of society—the stock of its personal knowledge. That approach therefore views with skepticism reforms that use wholly new schemes derived purely from theory, particularly those that exhibit speed, irreversibility, and large scale. Here the Chinese reform experience is extremely instructive. That reform was initiated with successful experiments in the Chinese countryside, out of the purview of the national leaders. The national leaders put in place at the national level a policy that had already been seen to be successful. Theory had naught to do with the choice; the driving force was the replication of experience.

Market Process Versus Market Product

Even a slow reform will eventually destroy many of the existing economic ties. Much personal information will be lost. The process of reform should therefore generate replacement information as it proceeds. Reformers of all shades believe that the market itself is the most successful means of creating such information. Market processes can destroy and rebuild the ties between organizations and between individuals as reform proceeds. This focus on market process contrasts with the view that reform should strive for a desired end-product, without analyzing the process by which that product would be most effectively reached.

An example of employing market processes is the search for the "natural owners" of firms during the privatization process by using market-type methods to identify buyers (Stark 1990). Natural owners are those who have the appropriate characteristics to run the newly private concerns. Given that such capacities involve personal knowledge, a process is needed to match owners with enterprises. As one can very quickly learn from the von Mises critique of socialism, this matching process is one of the prominent elements of a market economy that synthetic schemes cannot replace, because they do not use the information that already exists in society concerning who has the characteristics of a natural owner. The call for the use of market process, conserving and enhancing society's information stock, is directly counter to the use of the synthetic voucher schemes of privatization that are presently the vogue in Eastern Europe and further afield.

The emphasis on another element of market process follows from asking how market systems accomplish the task of renewal. Such systems do not accomplish change by asking existing organizations to perform completely new functions. Existing entities are often replaced, gradually and haltingly. New entities arise to accomplish the new tasks. If this is a fair characterization of market process, then it is clear that privatization of existing government enterprises can answer few hopes in reforming socialist countries. Rather, policy should encourage a new private sector that is uncommitted to the past and in which a viable process of selection of the best organizations can take place. This policy resonates most strongly with another aspect of the evolutionary approach, the need for policies to directly address the largest problems of the existing system. The renewal process of entry and exit is at the heart of the superiority of market over socialist systems.

A Dual Economy Versus the Unified, Liberalized Market Place

The radical reform approach advocates economy-wide liberalization as an absolute priority for a first step. This priority stems from a focus on the distortions that arise in market economies when distinct parts of the economy face separate rules, a focus reflective of theory centering on resource allocation. In contrast, evolutionary theory, which is information-based, on a crucial feature of an economy at the beginning of the reform—the information held by existing organizations is germane to the old economy, while there is the vital need to create entities that are much more attuned to the new.

This presents two contradictory needs. First, some of the existing institutions must be preserved; change must be slow enough to avoid the collapse of productive organizations. Second, a spurring of the entry-and-exit process is needed in the private sector. It is possible that a dual economy will be required to meet these contradictory needs during the transition. For example, administrative control of the state sector might be required to forestall the draconian stabilizations that will inhibit the growth of the nascent private sector.

By acting upon these information-based concerns, evolutionary reforms violate one of the basic tenets of existing economic-policy doctrine and especially of the radical schemes of reform. There will be a large asymmetry in the way that the various organizations in society are handled. This is simply a product of the fact that reform itself bifurcates history, which has determined the characteristics of society's organizations. One can ignore this fact and pursue economy-wide liberalization, as the radical schemes dictate. But the result will be the destruction of much of the informational basis of economic performance.

Predictions

This chapter itself summarizes analyses contained in a number of other works. Therefore, in place of a summary in this section, I use evolutionary theory to offer some predictions concerning the future of the countries undergoing reforms and the likely course of reforms themselves. First, the evolutionary approach suggests that the most successful reforms will be in those countries that effect change consistently over an extended time period, rather than in those that attempt to use economic strategies to create a sudden divide between the past and the future. For example, Hungary, which was much criticized in 1990 for not implementing the radical model, now appears likely to outpace Poland and Czechoslovakia in economic performance over the next few years. Second, the voucher schemes of privatization, because they are large-scale speculative programs that have never been tested, will encounter severe problems at the implementation stage. These problems have the potential to stall the progress of reform in those countries that have set great store by these schemes.

Third, economic performance will not be positively related to the speed of privatization of the large-scale enterprises. In fact, there might even be an inverse correlation. The basic variable that will most determine the speed of reform is the extent to which resources are freed for the new private sector. Undertaking the formal process of creating free markets is not enough. Resources must be prized free from the large enterprises of the old state sector. Moreover, liberalization with stabilization will not accomplish the freeing of resources, because such measures will require continuing policy-induced recessions that restrain the private sector as much as the state sector. Fourth, significant recentralization of the state sector in the reforming countries will eventually reverse the liberalization that was carried out in the first flush of reforms. This will be necessitated by the continuing lack of attention to market forces by the old enterprises, which were created in the non-market environment. Governments will come to the realization that the small gains in improved resource allocation created by liberalization will be outweighed by the dysfunctional behavior of the old state enterprises in the new market environment. The dual system advocated by the evolutionary approach will thus be created by economic necessity.

Notes

Peter Murrell is in the Department of Economics at the University of Maryland

The Woodrow Wilson Center and the Center for Institutional Reform and the Informal Sector (IRIS) at the University of Maryland are thanked for support in the writing of this paper. Karen Turner is thanked for her excellent editing.

Bibliography

Burke, Edmund, Reflections on the Revolution in France, 1790.

Kornai, Janos, The Road to a Free Economy. New York: Norton, 1990.

Lipton, David, and Sachs, Jeffrey, "Creating a Market Economy in Eastern Europe: The Case of Poland," Brookings Papers on Economic Activity, January, 1990.

McKinnon, Ronald, The Order of Economic Liberalization: Financial Control in the Transition to a Market Economy. Stanford University, mimeo, 1991.

Murrell, Peter, 1990a, The Nature of Socialist Economies: Lessons from Eastern European Foreign Trade, Princeton University Press.

______, 1990b, "Big Bang Versus Evolution: Eastern European Economic Reforms in the Light of Recent Economic History" PlanEcon Report, VI(26), June 29.

______, 1992a, "Evolution in Economics and in the Economic Reform of the Centrally Planned Economies," In Christopher C. Clague and Gordon Rausser eds. Emerging Market Economies in Eastern Europe, Basil Blackwell.

______, 1992b, "Conservate Political Philosophy and the Strategy of Economic Reform"' East European Politics and Societies.

Nelson, Richard and Sidney Winter, An Evolutionary Theory of Economic Change, Cambridge, Mass: Harvard University Press, 1982.

Nelson, Richard, "Capitalism as an Engine of Progress," Research Policy, 19, pp. 193–214, 1990.

Oakeshott, Michael, Rationalism in Politics and Other Essays, New York: Basic Books, 1962.

Polanyi, Michael, Personal Knowledge: Towards a Post-Critical Philosophy, Chicago: University of Chicago Press, 1962.

Popper, Karl, The Open Society and Its Enemies, Princeton: Princeton University Press, 1971.

Schumpeter, Joseph A., Capitalism, Socialism and Democracy, New York: Harper, 1950.

Stark, David, "Privatization in Hungary: From Plan to Market or from Plan to Clan?" East European Politics and Societies, 4(3), 1990: 351–392.

Stiglitz, Joseph E., Whither Socialism? Perspectives from the Economics of Information, Cambridge, Mass.: M.I.T. Press, 1991.

11

Transition to Market in a Comparative Perspective: A Historian's Point of View

Jacek Kochanowicz

The transition from command to market economy should proceed through the following stages: stabilization, privatization, and restructuring: this is the prevailing opinion. It is based on the assumption that state intervention and, in particular, state ownership leads to inefficient allocation of resources, that a market and private ownership will motivate economic agents to more rational behavior, and that the growth of market opportunities will promote entrepreneurship and, sooner or later, lead to economic growth.

Development and modernization of industries are much less discussed than the institutional problems of the market. Apparently, many participants in the debate assume that once the transition (i.e., first of all, privatization) is accomplished, the problem of growth will solve itself. This may be called a "neo-Smithian" view of economic development. It is based on a rather superficial reading of the economic history of the rise in capitalism in Western Europe, and it does not take into account the experience of the latecomers. Theoretically, this view relies mostly on the fashionable neoclassical, neoliberal school of economics, without due consideration to the theories of economic development. I would argue that such a view has serious flaws.

I question, in particular, the assumption that the transition to whatever we call it—market economy, capitalism, or modern economy—can happen without a very active role being played by the state. I do not want to sound like I am against the market. On the contrary, my claim is that the market is indispensable, but, at the same time, it can't "grow out of itself," and it is insufficient as the sole force of transition and modernization, especially in the case of countries that are relatively backward. My argument is mostly of a historical nature. I will start with a few brief remarks on the interrelationship between the market and politics in the early stages of capitalism, then I'll discuss the development of latecomers, and finally I will comment on the relevance of these experiences for the Eastern European countries.

Western Europe: Capitalism and the State

First, I would like to challenge the hidden assumption of the proposed scheme, according to which the market was really an automatic, autonomous, almost natural force in the course of the economic development of what constitutes the most advanced countries of Western Europe. The market, of course, is a historical phenomena, and Friedrich Hayek was right in saying that, like language, it was not the product of design, but of a long historical process.[1] But this does not mean that the state did not play a role in that first "transition to a market economy," or rather transition to capitalism—quite a long process, by the way, in each and every case.

Contrary to Marxist claims about the "natural course of great epochs of human history," or Smithian-type claims about the "natural" character of the market,[2] there is widespread agreement today that the birth of capitalism in Europe was not something automatic or natural. There was nothing inevitable in the rise of capitalism (or modernity) in Western Europe, as it was rather the result of a particular coincidence of ecological, economic, social, and political circumstances—the result of a "European Miracle." The state, in particular, played quite an important role in this process.[3] Other, more ancient and highly sophisticated civilizations did not develop capitalism.[4]

In medieval Italy, the growth of early capitalism was strongly related to the power of city-states. Likewise, the market and capitalism in Northern Europe were related to the growth of the national state. In contrast to Asia, where empires predominated, Europe developed a system of mutually interdependent and competing national states. In order to mobilize resources for armaments, rulers of these states found it more useful to cultivate entrepreneurs than to simply seize their wealth. The national state, therefore, developed and protected the legal structures necessary for private entrepreneurship and enabled currency and credit systems to operate.

These observations of historians have been interpreted theoretically by the school of "property rights"—efficient allocation of resources through the market requires that transaction costs be relatively low, which in turn demands that property rights be clearly defined and contracts enforced.[5] At the same time, the growth of the state—of armies and navies—provided a stimulus for the manufacturing industries. The financial needs of the city-states, and of the national state, and their constant reliance on the public debt, helped to create a capital market.[6] Introducing vagrancy laws, police forces, work houses, and prisons, the state was an enforcer of modern labor and social discipline.[7]

If we look now at the history of European industrialization in the nineteenth century, the only case that happened "spontaneously" was that of Britain. As Alexander Gerschenkron argued, industrialization of other countries was not a repetition of the English model, but rather a series of deviations, with banks substituting individual investors in the case of France, Germany, and Austria, and the state playing a leading role in Russia. In cases of industrialization spurts that failed, such as Austria or Italy, Gerschenkron argued, it was precisely the lack of state policies that lay at the root of the failure.[8]

The market is not "automatic" in yet another sense. Its very operation is usually, if not always, advantageous to some and disadvantageous to others, and bloody wars were fought to enforce legal structures favorable for market activities. Authors as far apart as Karl Polanyi and Joseph Schumpeter argued that development of a market produces forces operating against it. The nascent working classes of the seventeenth, eighteenth, and nineteenth centuries were extremely difficult to harness to factory work discipline and they quickly started to fight against the free market for labor.[9] As a result, the labor market soon became regulated. Similarly, other markets were regulated during the following centuries.

Latecomers

But should we compare Eastern Europe with the most developed countries? The proper object of comparison should rather be those countries that were "latecomers."[10] Their problems are lack of capital, lack of entrepreneurship, and often, a disadvantageous position within the world economy. Sometimes political elites try, therefore, to play the role of agents of modernization.

The aim of political elites is survival and expansion. They are constantly challenged, on the one hand, by other states and, on the other, by various segments of their own societies. In one situation, they might respond by attempting to develop their military capacities, in another by attempting to raise the standard of living of their population, in yet another they might be unable to respond at all. In the modern world, the most frequent response to the challenges to power elites is economic development.

But, if that is so, is the removal of obstacles to the market enough? In other words, is a rational allocation of resources through the market enough to trigger the process of growth in a less developed country? It is not that evident. A backward country must substitute for the missing preconditions of growth, as Gerschenkron observed. Growth depends on accumulation and technological innovation. Savings, however, are determined by incomes, which are low in a poor country. The state in such a country—if it wants development—has to be active in mobilizing capital, either from abroad or through forced savings. Investment funds must be properly allocated, and the debate whether the market is always the best indicator for long term allocative decisions is by no means settled.

Technological innovations are produced in the most advanced, or "core," countries, which have a research infrastructure and high level of investment in human capital. Peripheral regions can only count on the process of diffusion of innovations. There is ample place for state policies in fostering the introduction of foreign innovations, which starts with raising the level of education. One should, however, beware of being too general. It is one thing to be a latecomer in the nineteenth century and another to be one at the end of the twentieth. Technologies, markets, institutions, and patterns of social participation were different during the periods of "early" (up to ca. 1870), "mature," and "late" (after World War II) industrialization.[11] I am leaving the early period aside here.

During the epoch of mature industrialization, technological problems were still manageable within a country's own borders. Technologies were relatively simple, so many in the Third World shared with the Soviet-type countries an idea that if, through a painful but decisive push—a great leap forward—modern heavy industry could be established, then the rest of the problem would somehow solve itself automatically. It was probably as late as the beginning of the 1970s that industrializing countries realized that this idea might not be correct.

During that stage, urbanization brought into being a "mass society," "mass democracy," and popular pressure on real wages. Because of the mass nature of production, the problems of markets initially became far more acute than they had been before. The search for new markets was therefore one of the most pronounced traits of the epoch of modern imperialism. Later, and especially after World War II, it was the rise of real wages in the most developed countries that helped ease this problem. Only then, in the twentieth century, and maybe only after World War II, did the life of working people in the West start to be safe enough, affluent enough, and free enough to be an attractive model for those from less fortunate parts of the world. Still, in the times of relatively primitive mass communication, people from different countries were far apart and the pressure of the demonstration effect was not so strong.

During the epoch of late industrialization, since the 1960s, technologies have become enormously complicated. Simple copying is out of the question and successful operation demands involvement in the world economy because industries are dependent on whole packages of technologies and on a constant supply of scientific knowledge and industrial components. Learning new technologies is a long, costly, and painful process that is difficult to bear by a single, private enterprise. More than before, a given country has to export if it wants to produce because if it wants to produce, it must import. In the contemporary world, the successful are those who are able to mass produce industrial goods for the world market. It is also in that epoch that the world, due to the electronic media, became a "global village," and so the demonstration effect affects not only elites, but whole societies.[12] Translated into economic terms, it means powerful pressure on rising standards of living of wide masses of the population, pressure which is amplified by the development of modern, mass democracy.

Patterns of Response: Mature Industrialization

Since conditions in each epoch are different and since the latecomers might miss some cultural or institutional prerequisites for market-oriented modernization, it is not unlikely that their behavior might differ from that of the leaders. In particular, they might be expected to substitute for conditions that they were missing.[13] I would like to give a few examples for which the economic transformation cannot be interpreted simply as the outcome of "natural" market forces or a repetition of earlier models. My examples for this epoch are Germany, Japan, and Russia.

Germany

Germany, which, according to Voltaire, would be condemned to everlasting poverty,[14] at the eve of World War I became the leading industrial power in Europe, and its science-based industries (chemical, optical, and electrical) became competitive worldwide. One can easily see that, in many respects, Germany's development was different than the "natural" market-stimulated British model. The Prussian state prepared the "preconditions" for modern growth during the eighteenth and first half of the nineteenth centuries; it also developed its state industrial sector. After unification in 1870, the state was still instrumental in providing the infrastructure for industrial development. Bismarck engaged in a policy of nationalization of the railways, mostly motivated by military considerations.[15] "The railways and the post office were described as 'simply the civilian section of the army.'"[16]

Private industry developed specific forms of organization: integrated concerns, diversified combinations, and cartels. These internationally competitive[17] organizations were—contrary to what happened in the United States—encouraged by the state and popular with the public.[18] Industry was financed—and, to a large extent, controlled—by the banks. They developed comprehensive policies toward industrial concerns and accepted risks and losses when necessary. Banks were linked to the public sector. The president of the central bank was nominated by the government, and shareholders had no word in the bank's policy. Savings banks, which controlled more capital than commercial banks, were for the most part municipal.[19] In that way, German entrepreneurs and managers were part of a much more complicated structure, with blurred boundaries between the state and the private sector. Tax policy was favorable for the accumulation of capital and industrialization[20] and, beginning in the early 1870s, the state protected national industries from foreign competition.

The unparalleled role of science, innovation, and education was the result of great stress put by the state on universal public education and on the development of universities. "It was in education that the Germans sought a substitute for the 'spontaneous' technological originality of eighteenth century England."[21] The German labor force was better educated than the British, while universities produced well prepared bureaucrats, managers, and gradually, researchers (in 1890, Technische Hochschulen acquired the full rights of universities). On a practical level, foreigners were important in bringing in new technologies and managerial techniques. German entrepreneurs and managers also traveled extensively abroad to learn. Germany gradually developed a whole sector that produced knowledge and innovations: institutes of the universities and laboratories of private firms, especially in the chemical and electrical industries. Research became a form of long-term investment; heads of laboratories became involved in strategic decisions of enterprises.[22]

Japan

Meiji Japan is an example of a far more radical development from above, where "modernization proceeded with a *dirigisme* and commitment which makes the efforts of Colbert or Frederick the Great pale by comparison."[23] The main agent of this modernization was bureaucracy, which was formed after the Meiji restoration and has played a dominant role until today.[24] In order to counter the threat of Western imperialism, the Meiji reformers emulated Western institutions and technologies.[25] The government improved the infrastructure and also attempted to create the basics of modern industry: It established pilot factories, granted subsidies, imported foreign machinery, and hired foreign experts. Later, most of the state nonmilitary plants were sold (cheaply) into private hands, but after the 1894–95 Sino-Japanese War, the government founded the state steel industry.[26]

There was close cooperation between the state and the private sector.[27] The government was an important provider of capital (especially for the armament and shipbuilding industries), which it mobilized partly through taxation, partly through subscription of foreign loans. The zaibatsu, as was the case with large German industrial organizations, took advantage of economics of scale. They also established their own banks, some of which (e.g., Mitsui) enjoyed state help in the form of government deposits.[28] Investment banks gained a role during the 1920s.[29]

There has been an enormous effort to adapt foreign technologies to the needs of the Japanese economy, and this trend has continued up to the post–World War II "economic miracle." While German economic development was built upon new inventions, the Japanese economy has grown through adaptation of Western innovations. This is reflected in the patterns of economic growth, where "ups" correspond to the speeding up of the process of adaptation.[30] In order to adapt foreign innovations, Japanese students were sent abroad and foreign specialists were invited to Japan.[31] As in Germany, this process was built upon a considerable educational effort, and as in Germany, education was oriented toward nationalistic goals. Secondary and higher education were expanded both by state and private initiatives. These were built upon a strong tradition of the importance of learning.[32] Stress on education changed a status-oriented society into a merit-oriented one.

Russia

In Russia—similarly to Germany and Japan—modernization efforts had much to do with imperial ambitions. At the end of the nineteenth century, the state—with an already powerful sector of the economy in its hands—entered the economy in a direct and indirect way, and "the finance ministry had become something in the nature of a ministry of national development, its competence reaching into every sphere of national life."[33] Government took over the construction and management of railways, organized the telegraph service, introduced a protective tariff policy. The state developed modern banking.[34] Private industry developed due to state contracts. State armament factories were modernized, and the government took over some private enterprises. At the beginning of the century, modern corporations gradually entered the stage. In a way similar to Germany and Japan, there was a very substantial concentration of production and cartelization.

Despite the spectacular development, Russia remained backward and internally differentiated—a "dual society," as Shanin put it after Herzen,[35] with a tremendous economic, social, and cultural gap between its thin urban sector and vast masses of peasantry. Russia had the largest foreign debt and, despite industrialization, exported mostly agricultural products and wood. In the 1890s the state strove to diminish the military gap between Russia and the West, but results were modest;[36] Russia lost the war with Japan and was not able in 1915 to effectively face the German offensive.

The modernization efforts of Russia are difficult to evaluate because of the discontinuity of its history. The basics of these efforts—the activities of the state in creating a physical infrastructure, developing banks, and promoting private entrepreneurship—are similar to those of Germany and even more similar to those of Japan. There was even a considerable educational effort,[37] although it did not spread to the countryside. Russia seems, however, to have been much less successful in developing the more complicated branches of industry, and it has proved unable to start the process of social modernization of the peasant masses, which later became the main force of the revolution.

Patterns of Response: Late Industrialization

In contrast to the German or American process of "catching up" with the leaders during the second industrial revolution, which was based on original innovation, the late industrialists of the second half of this century tried to modernize on the basis of learning and mastering the existing technologies. Their success depended on the ability of mass exports of industrial goods and also on their abilities to keep consumer aspirations of their societies within limits, which were determined by the rate of economic growth. The most successful cases are Japan, South Korea, and Taiwan. Japan, already quite a developed country despite the consequences of the war, is nevertheless an important case, the more so because it served as a model for other latecomers.[38]

Late development to a large degree consisted of state engagement in the economy. Contrary, however, to interwar "statism"—direct ownership of industrial plants by the state (as in Poland or Turkey in the 1930s),[39] policies in Asian countries took the form of close cooperation between the public and private sectors. On the other hand, industrial policy played a much bigger role than before. Chalmers Johnson spoke about a specific, Japanese model of "developmental state": an elite bureaucracy staffed by the best managerial talent available; a political system that, allowed the bureaucracy considerable autonomy; perfection of market-conforming methods of state intervention; and a pilot organization (MITI).[40] Johnson considered the capitalist developmental state—operating not by displacing the market, but by becoming a player in the market—to be Japan's most important invention.[41]

Scholars analyzing Korea and Taiwan stress the similarity of their military-bureaucratic regimes to Latin American modernizing "bureaucratic authoritarianism."[42] Bruce Cumings proposed calling them Bureaucratic-Authoritarian Industrializing Regimes.[43] Authoritarian regimes, having problems with legitimization, try to justify themselves by economic successes.[44] The state helped in the creation of the private sector and large, powerful companies. In Japan, with the reversal of the postwar occupational policies of MacArthur, constraints on former zaibatsu were lifted. In Korea, their counterparts—chaebol—which rose almost from scratch, were vigorously supported by the government, initially with money from U.S. aid.[45] Korean development was largely financed through foreign loans. Resources were channeled through a nationalized banking system (in the early 1960s), while at the same time, there were serious penalties for illegal attempts at capital exports.

The state exercised very strict control over the private sector. Korean big business was subject to price control and products were licensed.[46] As a result, not only labor, but also capital, was disciplined. The state first promoted a strategy of import-substitution and then of export-oriented development. As Alice Amsden argued, these countries—contrary to the assumption of conventional neoclassical economic theory—could not compete in the world market simply on the basis of cheap labor. Therefore, increased productivity through implementation of borrowed technologies was needed.

In Japan, economic and industrial policies had mostly an indicative, not legally enforceable, character.[47] The main institutions have been the MITI, working through formalized "administrative guidance" ("requests," "warnings," "suggestions," and "encouragement"),[48] the Ministry of Finance, and the Bank of Japan. MITI promoted mergers, licensed products, guided investment, and encouraged cartels in periods of recession.[49] In Korea, the crucial element was subsidies to private enterprises.[50] Subsidies were given only in exchange for performance. Recipients were expected to introduce new technologies, to raise output, to increase productivity, and to export; government was merciless to those firms that were unable to meet the set standards, even if they were the most loyal politically.

Companies, working under the combined pressure of the market and state, had to find ways to make their managers and workers efficient. Japanese firms, employing people for life and paying for seniority rather than performance, relied on group identification and traditional codes of honor and shame.[51] Korean companies concentrated on improvements in management and performance on the shop-floor level. Relatively high wages were treated not as the main motivating force but as a starting point for extracting productivity from workers.[52] Quality control circles, computerized process control, material planning, costs accounting, management information systems, motion studies, and so forth were tried in order to raise productivity. There is no doubt that the lack of democracy helped in achieving this high labor discipline, but the raising of real wages helped to keep social peace.

Success in mastering acquired technologies was possible due to the stress on education. Korea has the highest percentage of students among developing countries. The status of education is high, as is teacher pay. The high level of education has allowed Korean businessmen to learn foreign methods of production—partly through "unpacking" bought technologies, partly through reliance on employment of foreign (mostly Japanese) consultants.

Conclusion

Experience of others shows that the transition to capitalism and modernization in Eastern Europe cannot be quick and easy—if it is to be successful. It also clearly shows the inseparability of the state and capitalism, starting from the early modern era up to the most recent cases of Asian countries. When there were economic successes, they usually came about through an interplay of market and nonmarket methods. Similarly, the state in Eastern Europe cannot simply wait for the transition to happen, but must become its active agent.

Analytically, there are two aspects of state intervention: creation of externalities for the private sector and active promotion of industrial production. Because of the relative backwardness of the Eastern European countries, I doubt whether the former is enough. Some arenas of state involvement are not controversial; these are construction of a legal framework for market activities, provision of a physical infrastructure, investment in human capital, and promotion of research and development.

The last two points are closely connected and are of enormous importance. The experience of latecomers shows that their ability to modernize and compete internationally was conditioned on the presence of a supply of skillful managers, engineers, administrators, and workers. The fact that the United States is today lagging behind in the global economic competition is often explained by insufficient educational efforts.[53] If Polish companies are to develop and to compete, they must draw upon a supply of university graduates who can use personal computers, speak English and German, and have enough basic knowledge and work discipline to be able to initiate on-the-job training. It is the state school system that will have to be the main provider for these people.

The state, however—as the experience of the latecomers shows—did more than just provide externalities. It also acted as an agent of accumulation of capital. The level of state intervention in capital markets was generally larger than in the most developed countries, and there are good reasons for following these examples. James Tobin argued that ex-communist countries should "go slowly" in copying the speculative financial markets (stock exchanges) of the United States and the United Kingdom.[54] It seems that what is particularly needed at the present stage, and what played an important role in other late-developing countries, is a modern banking system.

The state also pursued industrial policies aimed at concentration of production and economics of scale, at technological progress, and competitiveness in international markets. There is a need for such a policy in Eastern Europe as well.[55] I do not think that there is a simple, general answer to the question of why state officials should know better than private entrepreneurs how to allocate resources. Some points, however, can easily be made. First, as Tobin put it, "private markets evidently have great difficulties focusing on long horizons."[56] From the developmental point of view, it is good to work out the frameworks of private decisions that would reward long-term modernization rather than short-term profits.

Second, the government can be helpful when private enterprise needs knowledge about foreign technology and foreign markets and access to these markets. Obviously, no historical experience of Japan or Korea will tell Poland what kind of industrial policy it should pursue.[57] What this experience tells, however, is that if some industries are to be promoted, it should be those that are of higher value added and that show an ability to compete abroad. Industrial policy is not something that is arbitrarily decided; rather, it stems from a detailed and often painstaking process of observation and study of world markets and available technologies. The Japanese observed the German and Americans; the Koreans imitated the Japanese. For the countries of Eastern Europe, the most likely teacher is probably Germany—the closest country, and the one that , after all, has already left an enormous imprint on the cultural, intellectual, and technological traditions of this region. Another lesson is that if some sort of industrial policy is worked out, it should be implemented by guidance and consensus, not by command.

The role of the state is to discipline the enterprises by using market measures. The state may provide subsidies but it should not bail out inefficient, bankrupt enterprises or save workplaces at any cost, —only to pay for productivity and efficiency. The Eastern European countries are faced with the separate, but related, problem of having huge state industrial sectors. Although there are good arguments that in the long run they should be privatized, one shouldn't be overly optimistic as far as the short-term possibilities of that are concerned. There is also danger of ideologizing the issue of privatization, which should be treated pragmatically.[58] At the same time, more attention should be focused on how, in the foreseeable future, state enterprises are to be managed. Once again, why not look at the Polish prewar experience, or French, Italian, Japanese, and Korean experiences in running state enterprises?[59]

I make this point about the role of the state not because I think that it is desirable but because it is unavoidable. I am fully aware of the related dangers. One of them is corruption. I do not have in mind the simple bribery of bureaucrats by representatives of domestic or foreign businesses looking for favors, but the more general behavior pattern of peripheral elites who, transforming themselves into a "state bourgeoisie," turn the state into a revenue-raising instrument in order to secure the upper middle class standard of living of the advanced societies.[60]

One of the formidable tasks facing Eastern European countries will be creating a "civil service," and it is worth remembering the literal meaning of the word "service." If one looks at Britain or France, or even Japan, it turns out that it took generations, rather than years, to develop an efficient, competent, and honest public administration. It won't be easy in Poland, with almost a total lack of tradition in this respect. Historically, a rather disrespectful attitude toward the state has developed as a result of the lack of an absolutist state, followed by partitions, Nazi occupation, and finally communism.

Today even the word "bureaucracy" is almost unanimously associated with stupidity and inefficiency, harassment by petty officials, and bribery rather than with a Weberian-type, efficient method of running a modern society. This does not mean that an effort should not be made, and there are patterns to follow: Civil service as an apolitical corps of officials who are recruited on the basis of competitive examinations and paid and promoted according to merit and seniority, with no rights to outside incomes, and with strict rules governing the possibility of joining the private sector.[61]

There is one lesson of the latecomers that would be better not repeated. The success of late industrialization took place usually, if not always, within the context of undemocratic institutions that served to discipline labor. If Eastern Europe is to modernize, it will have to find other, more democratic ways of solving this problem. It is worthwhile to bear in mind, however, that the twin dangers of populism and authoritarianism are looming somewhere in the background and that—taking into consideration the recent communist experience and the proximity of Western Europe—the authoritarian solution is not only undesirable in principle, but it is also unlikely to be economically effective.

Notes

Jacek Kochanowicz is in the Department of Economics at the University of Warsaw.

An earlier version of this paper was discussed during the U.S.-Polish Economic Roundtable on "Economics and Politics of Privatization," University of Washington, Henry M. Jackson School of International Studies, Seattle, June 7–9, 1991. I wish to thank Peter Wagner and Willfried Spohn for their comments and the Institute for Advanced Study, Princeton, for providing excellent conditions for work on this paper.

1. Friedrich Hayek, "The Use of Knowledge in Society," American Economic Review, vol. 35, 1945, September.

2. About the philosophical assumptions of a "natural order" underlying market models, cf. Pierre Rosenvallon, *Le capitalisme utopique: Critique d'idéologie économique* (Paris: Seuil, 1979).

3. Cf. interesting theoretical discussion of this process in anthony Giddens, *The Nation-State and Violence* (Cambridge: Polity Press, 1985), pp. 122–171; the author's point is that the state must not be reduced to a play of economic forces, and neither must the opposite occur. Cf. Fernand Braudel, *Civilization and Capitalism* (New York: Harper & Row, 1981–84), vol. 2, pp. 514–55, and Charles Tilly, *Coercion, Capital and European States* (Cambridge, Mass: Blackwell, 1990), pp. 161–191, where he discusses the European state system.

4. See, for example, E.L. Jones, *The European Miracle: Environments, Economies and Geopolitics in the History of Europe and Asia* (Cambridge: Cambridge University Press, 1981). A similar argument is made on the basis of very rich material by Braudel.

5. For historical reinterpretation, cf. Douglas North, *Structure and Change in Economic History* (New York, 1981).

6. Cf. Braudel, vol. 2, pp. 522ff.

7. It is enough here to recall the powerful account of Michel Foucault, *Discipline and Punish: The Birth of Prisons* (New York: Vintage Books, 1977).

8. Alexander Gerschenkron, *An Economic Spurt that Failed: Four Lectures in Austrian History* (Princeton: Princeton University Press, 1977); Gerschenkron, *Economic Backwardness in Historical Perspective* (Cambridge, Mass: The Belknap Press, 1962), pp. 72–91.

9. Cf. E.P. Thompson, *The Making of an English Working Class* (Haromndsworth: Penguin Books, 1980); Nina Assorodobraj, *Poczatki klasy robotniczej w Polsce (The Origins of the Polish Working Class)* (Warsaw: PWN, 1966).

10. The distinction is that of Gerschenkron.

11. A very interesting typology of "industrial ages," which stresses different technologies, different types of social organization, and different models of behavior at different stages of the industrial era, was developed by Daniel Chirot, *Social Change in the Modern Era* (San Diego: Harcourt Brace Jovanovich, 1986), pp. 223–30. For reasons of brevity, my "mature" and "late" periods of industrialization are more comprehensive than Chirot's "ages."

12. On the role of "international demonstration effect," see Andrew C. Janos, *Politics and Paradigms: Changing Theories of Change in Social Science* (Stanford, California, 1986), pp. 84–95.

13. The idea of the substitution of the preconditions of modern growth was formulated by Gerschenkron.

14. W.O. Henderson, *The Rise of German Industrial Power: 1834–1914* (London: Temple Smith, 1975), p. 240.

15. R.H. Tilly, "Capital Formation in Germany in the Nineteenth Century," in Peter Mathias and M.M. Postan, *Cambridge Economic History of Europe*, vol. VII: "The Industrial Economies: Capital, Labour, and Enterprise, part I: Britain, France, Germany and Scandinavia" (Cambridge: Cambridge University Press, 1978), p. 415; Gustav Stolper et al., *The German Economy to the Present* (New York: Harcourt, Brace & World, Inc., 1967), p. 41.

16. Henderson, p. 212.

17. Hans-Joachim Braun, *The German Economy in the Twentieth Century* (London and New York: Routlege, 1990), p. 21.

18. Jurgen Kocka, "Entrepreneurs and Managers in German Industrialization," in Mathias and Postan, p. 563.

19. Stolper et al., p. 43.

20. D.E. Schremmer, "Taxation and Public Finance: Britain, France, and Germany," in Mathias and Postan, pp. 483 ff.

21. J.J. Lee, "Labour in German Industrialization," in Mathias and Postan, p. 456.

22. Kocka, p. 571.

23. Paul Kennedy, *The Rise and Fall of the Great Powers* (New York: Random House), p. 207.

24. Cf. Masamichi Inoki, "Civil Bureaucracy—Japan," in Robert E. Ward and Dankwart A. Rustow, eds., *Political Modernization in Japan and Turkey* (Princeton: Princeton University Press, 1964); Chalmers Johnson, *MITI and the Japanese Miracle: The Growth of Industrial Policy, 1925–1975* (Stanford: Stanford University Press, 1982), passim.

25. Chalmers Johnson, "The People who Invented the Mechanical Nightingale," *Dedalus*, Summer 1990, p. 72; for the study of Japanese emulation of the West, see D. Eleanor Westney, *Imitation and Innovation: The Transfer of Western Organization Patterns to Meiji Japan* (Cambridge, Mass: Harvard University Press, 1987).

26. The merits of direct state involvement in industry are debated in the more recent literature, as the pilot factories were incurring heavy budgetary losses and their managers were not that keen to open them up to private entrepreneurs to learn. Seymour A. Broadbridge, "Aspects of Economic and Social Policy in Japan, 1868–1945," in Peter Mathias and Sidney Pollard, eds., *The Cambridge Economic History of Europe*, vol. VIII: "The Industrial Economies: The Development of Economic and Social Policies" (Cambridge: Cambridge University Press, 1989), pp. 1111–2.

27. cf. Broadbridge, p. 1114.

28. Kozo Yamamura, "Entrepreneurship, Ownership and Management in Japan," in Mathias and Postan, part II: "The United States, Japan and Russia" (Cambridge: Cambridge University Press, 1978), p. 241.

29. Yamamura, p. 241.

30. Kazushi Ohkawa and Henry Rosovsky, "Capital Formation in Japan," in Mathias and Postan, part II: "The United States, Japan and Russia" (Cambridge: Cambridge University Press, 1978), pp. 136, 156ff.

31. Broadbridge, p. 1118.

32. cf. Herbert Passin, *Society and Education in Japan* (Tokyo: Kodansha International Ltd., 1982), pp. 62–99.

33. Olga Crisp, *Studies in the Russian Economy before 1914* (London: Macmillan, 1976), p. 24.

34. As Olga Crisp notes: "[U]nlike the governments of some contemporary underdeveloped countries, who use the money creating facilities of the banking

sector as an alternative taxation, the government of Russia like that of Japan transferred resources obtained by taxation to the banking system. In effect, they used a combination of tax power of the state and the specialized talents of the bankers to shift resources from consumption to production." Crisp, *Studies*, p. 155.

35. Teodor Shanin, *The Awkward Class* (Oxford: Clarendon Press, 1972).

36. For a comparison of Russia and the Western powers in that matter, cf. Kennedy, pp. 203, 208.

37. Crisp, *Studies*, p. 53.

38. I am, obviously, refraining from any attempt to explain the causes of their success, restricting myself to pointing out the "nonmarket" elements of these cases. I am also not trying to spell out circumstances under which—gradually, not instantly—Korea and Taiwan turned to developmentalism. There is an enormous literature on Japan. For an overall account, see, for example, Kozo Yamamura and Yasukichi Yasuba, eds., *The Political Economy of Japan*, vol. 1: "The Domestic Transformation" (Stanford: Stanford University Press, 1987). For Korea and Taiwan (and other newly industrialized countries), see Stephan Haggard, *Pathways from the Periphery: The Politics of Growth in the New Industrializing Countries* (Ithaca and London: Cornell University Press, 1990); Alice Amsden, "Diffusion of Development: The Late-Industrializing Model and Greater Asia," *American Economic Review*, vol. 81, no. 2, p. 286; Amsden, "The State and Taiwan's Economic Development," in Peter B. Evans et al., eds., *Bringing the State Back In* (Cambridge: Cambridge University Press, 1985); Amsden, *Asia's Next Giant: South Korea and late Industrialization* (New York: Oxford University Press, 1989); Robert Wade, *Governing the Market: Economic Theory and the Role of Government in East Asian Industrialization* (Princeton: Princeton University Press, 1990). Bruce Cumings offers a very convincing, comprehensive economic and political analysis of postwar modernization of Japan, Korea, and Taiwan in terms of their role within the world economy and in terms of their place in American policy: "The Northeast Asian Political Economy under Two Hegemonies," in Edmund Burke, ed., *Global Crises and Social Movements: Artisans, Peasants, Populists, and the World Economy* (Boulder and London: Westview Press, 1988).

39. cf. Jan Kofman, "Economic Nationalism in East-Central Europe in the Interwar Period," in Henryk Szlajfer, ed., *Economic Nationalism in East-Central Europe and South America, 1918–1939* (Genève: Libraire Droz, 1990), pp. 191–249.

40. Chalmers Johnson, *MITI*, pp. 314–20.

41. Johnson, "The People Who Invented the Mechanical Nightingale," p. 74.

42. The concept of Guillermo A. O'Donnell, *Modernization and Bureaucratic-Authoritarianism* (University of California, Berkeley: Institute of International Studies, 1973); and a discussion in David Collier, ed., *The New Authoritarianism in Latin America* (Princeton: Princeton University Press, 1979).

43. Cumings, "The Northeast Asian Political Economy," p. 254.

44. Cumings, "The Abortive Abertura: South Korea in the Light of Latin American Experience," *New Left Review*, 173/1989, p. 7.

45. Cumings, "The Abortive Abertura," p. 14; Richard M. Steers, Yoo Keun

Shin, Gerardo R. Ungson, *The Chaebol: Korea's New Industrial Might* (Grand Rapids: Harper and Row, 1989), pp. 19–32 and passim.

46. In 1986, prices of 110 main commodities were controlled. amsden, "Third World," p. 22.

47. Yasusuke Murakami, "The Japanese Model of Political Economy," in Yamamura and Yasuba, eds., p. 46. There is by no means agreement as to the efficiency, or even desirability, of Japanese industrial policy, which neoclassical economists generally oppose. For a review of the discussion, see George C. Eads and Kozo Yamamura, "The Future of Industrial Policy," in Yamamura and Yasuba, eds.

48. Johnson, *MITI*, p. 302.

49. Murakami, p. 46.

50. As Alice Amsden notes: "If the metaphor of the First Industrial Revolution is 'laissez faire' and that of the Second 'infant industry protection,' then that of late industrialization is a category comprehensive enough to overcome the penalties of lateness—call it 'the subsidy' [. . .] [t]he governments of Korea and Taiwan had to intervene to subsidize the production of even cotton textiles—a relatively labour-intensive good—until either productivity at home or the wages of foreign competitors rose enough to make subsidies redundant." Alice Amsden, "Third World Industrialization: 'Global Fordism' or a New Model?" *New Left Review*, 182/1990, pp. 16, 22. Cf. also Amsden, *Asia's Next Giant*, Ch. 6: "Getting Relative Prices 'Wrong': A Summary."

51. Cf. Eiko Ikegami, "The Logic of Cultural Change: Honor, the Samurai and State Making." A talk presented at the School of Social Sciences, Institute for Advanced Study, Princeton, December 6, 1990.

52. Amsden, "Third World Industrialization," p. 26; Amsden, *Asia's Next Giant*, p. 281.

53. Cf. Martin K. Starr, ed., *Global Competitiveness* (New York-London: W.W. Norton & Co., 1988), pp. 261–63, 308–10. Cf. also the discussion in the American media, which was taking place while this paper was being written.

54. James Tobin, "One or Two Cheers for the 'Invisible Hand,'" *Dissent*, Spring 1990, pp. 233–34.

55. The previous Polish government of Jan Bielecki started, in the face of recession, to change its approach in this respect. The nomination of Ms. Henryka Bochniarz as a Minister of Industry and Commerce marked the beginning of interest in industrial policies. See interviews with Ms. Bochniarz in *Polityka*, August 10, 1991; and *Zycie Gospodarcze*, August 25, 1991. However, the change of government after the election discontinued these efforts and the present administration—the product of a shaky parliamentary coalition—does not seem able to formulate any clear industrial policy.

56. Tobin, p. 234.

57. Despite the prevailing neoliberal climate of Polish economic thinking, there is the beginning of interest in Asia's experience. See, for example, Adam Lipowski and Jan Kulig, *Panstwo czy rynek? Wokól zródel "cudu gospodarczego" w Korei Poludniowej* [*State or Market? Origins of the "Economic Miracle" of South Korea*] (Warsaw: Poltex, 1992).

58. Empirical research on the behavior of state-owned firms under the new market rules shows that many of them do behave in quite an efficient way. Cf. Janusz M. Dabrowski et al., "Stabilization and State Enterprise Adjustment: The Political Economy of State Firms after Five Months of Fiscal Discipline, Poland 1990," Program on Central and Eastern Europe Working Paper Series, #6 (Cambridge, Mass: Minda de Ginzburg Center for European Studies, 1990).

59. Cf. interesting study of the Italian IRI, stressing that while its role was to serve government strategic ends, it fulfilled it through managerial autonomy and conforming to the market rules. Stuart Holland, ed., *The State as Entrepreneur* (London: Weidenfeld and Nicolson, 1972). Quite recently—in early 1992—the Polish Ministry of Privatization, apparently more and more conscious that privatization was not as smooth as they might have wished, organized a conference on the experiences of Polish prewar state enterprises. On the whole, however, this experience is fairly well forgotten and the conference papers exist only in mimeographed form.

60. Andrew C. Janos, *Politics and Paradigms: Changing Theories of Change in Social Science* (Stanford: California, 1986), p. 91.

61. Once again, there are positive signs—the school of civil service (modeled on French ENA) was recently established in Poland, and the government is considering a bill on civil service and another barring civil servants from private business activities.

12

Is There a J-Curve for the Economic Transition from Socialism to Capitalism?

Josef C. Brada and Arthur E. King

Much economic thinking about current developments in Eastern Europe, where the transition from plan to market and from socialism to capitalism is underway, seems to show, once again, that economics is, indeed, the dismal science. Specifically, both western observers and policymakers in these countries appear to believe that there is some sort of large and negative supply-side shock that this transition imparts to the reforming economies. For lack of a more pejorative term, we will call this J-curve pessimism. Such J-curve pessimism does not appear to dominate other aspects of life. People who undertake diets or begin to exercise, for example, can correctly expect that this course of action will lead them to lose weight or become fitter in a way that is directly related to the rigor of their diet or exercise regime. It is only the dismal science of economics that would have them believe that their efforts would first lead to gains in weight or worsened fitness, and only in the distant future to an improved state of health.

Perhaps the most graphic example of this economic pessimism is the so-called theory of the J-curve effect of the devaluation of a country's currency. Countries in deficit are generally advised to devalue their currency so as to improve the trade balance by making their exports cheaper and imports dearer. Dismally, the short term effect of the devaluation is to worsen the trade balance since, with quantities unable to respond to prices in the short run, the main consequence of devaluation is that foreigners need to spend less of their currency for the country's exports. Only in the long run, when quantities adjust, will the trade balance improve. Traced out over time, the balance of trade post-devaluation thus describes a J, first worsening and then gradually improving.[1]

Similarly it is argued that the introduction of economic reforms associated with the transition must reduce the productive capacity of the economy. Gomulka (1991) argues that changes in prices, combined with rigidities in resource allocation, will "reduce the (maximum) potential output" (p. 77) of the economy. This inward shift of the production possibilities frontier, or worsening of the economic situation, will later be compensated by the fact that such a decline "represents Schumpeterian creative destruction, designed to release resources locked in unproductive or insufficiently productive uses, for their future use elsewhere" (p.72). Clearly, the worse the misallocation of resources, the greater the destruction that will be wrought and the more pronounced the J-curve effect.

Murrell (1990, 1991a), on the other hand, allows for the mobility of resources but, following some rather misleading and wrongheaded analysis of statistical evidence conducted by Whitesell (1990), concludes that planned economies are so efficient at allocation that marketizing reforms can do little to improve the existing allocation of resources. Indeed, reforms, by destroying existing economic institutions and mechanisms, must cause a temporary inward shift of the production possibilities, and new sources of information will evolve to replace the old mechanism only very slowly. In the interim, lack of coordination and thus a fall in the potential, and actual, output of the economy is inevitable.

On virtually all counts, the introduction of economic reforms in Eastern Europe has, indeed, coincided with a worsening of economic performance. As Table 1 shows, production has fallen sharply; unemployment, previously unheard of in these countries, has risen to levels that may soon surpass what is tolerable in market economies: inflation is reaching levels where the prefix hyper is no longer merely political hyperbole; and the trade balance appears to be worsening for many of the countries of the region. Moreover, this deterioration of economic performance is not perceived as a short-term phenomenon. Polish architects of the "big bang" had hoped that by the end of 1990 industrial production would be recovering from the shock-induced decline of the first half of the year, but this rebound has not materialized as yet.

In Hungary, the imposition of tight monetary policy by the Antal government was supposed to weed out the inefficient and uncompetitive firms, leaving the field to the strong and able, who would then lead

TABLE 1 Macroeconomic Indicators for Eastern Europe

	1986	*1987*	*1988*	*1989*	*1990*[d]
Industrial output (% Δ)[a]					
Bulgaria	4.0	4.2	5.1	2.2	-15.0
Czechoslovakia	3.2	2.5	2.1	1.0	-4.5
Hungary	1.9	3.5	-0.3	-2.5	-9.5
Poland	4.7	3.4	5.3	-0.6	-24.0
Romania	6.2	3.6	3.0	-2.1	-22.0
Unemployment (% labor force)[b]					
Bulgaria					
Czechoslovakia					1.3
Hungary					—
Poland					6.9
Romania					1.5
Inflation (% Δ)[c]					
Bulgaria	0.1	0.2	3.8	0.8	40.0
Czechoslovakia	-0.4	-0.1	1.5	1.0	9.2
Hungary	3.8	8.2	15.0	21.2	28.9
Poland	19.1	28.2	68.0	315.0	535.0
Romania	—	—	—	—	—
Balance of trade with West (billion $)[a]					
Bulgaria	-1.5	-1.6	-1.7	-1.6	-0.9
Czechoslovakia	0.4	0.1	0.1	0.4	-0.1
Hungary	-0.6	-0.3	0.1	-0.2	—
Poland	0.7	0.8	0.7	-0.1	1.7
Romania	1.9	2.7	2.8	2.4	-0.6

[a]1990 represents estimates from the ECE, statistical offices and PlanEcon.

[b]1990 data are end of September, 1990, with the exception of Czechoslovakia, which is year end.

[c]1990 data are January–September 1990 except Czechoslovakia, which is January–December.

[d]1990 growth rates covering periods less than a year are calculated relative to the corresponding period in 1989.

Sources: United Nations Economic Commission for Europe, *Economic Bulletin for Europe* 42:90. New York: United Nations, 1991; Brada (1991) and *PlanEcon Report*, Dec. 21, 1990.

an industrial resurgence. Here too, there has been a sharp fall in production coupled with accelerating inflation, with the Minister of International Economic Relations, Bela Kadar, complaining that austerity measures were choking off the possibilities for the expansion of even the most export-competitive firms in Hungary. Finally, the Czechoslovak Federal Statistical Office has compiled a set of projections of the economy to 1995.[2] It foresees a decline in output that will bottom out in 1991–92 for some indicators, and somewhat later for others, and then improve in classical J-curve fashion.

The belief in this J-curve of economic reform has given rise to a considerable discussion regarding the timing and sequencing of reforms.[3] Two themes permeate this debate. The first is that there is some form of trade-off between the speed of reform and the shape of the J-curve. Specifically, it is often argued that a "big-bang" reform will yield a sharp J-curve, with a severe deterioration of economic performance as extensive reforms are introduced, followed by an equally rapid and sustained improvement as the suddenly freed market forces make themselves felt within a broad range of economic activities.

Skeptics argue that such big bangs may lead to a sharp decline fol?lowed by so great a dislocation of the economy that there may be only a very slow and painful recovery at best, yielding something that looks more like an L than a J. The natural implication of such a scenario is that reforms should be introduced slowly, yielding a more shallow J-curve, where the decline in economic conditions is held to tolerable levels, while, correspondingly, improvements in economic performance will also be stretched out over a longer period of time. In such a scenario, where the reform package is not introduced all at once, the sequencing of economic reforms becomes important as well.[4]

The second theme is that there are political constraints on the implementation of reforms. Lipton and Sachs (1990) argue for a fast reform program in part because they believe it to be consistent with the political realities of the Polish situation. On the other hand, gradualists point to the fact that there is a floor below which economic performance may not fall without political repercussions. Lech Walesa's electoral victory is seen as proof that the Polish reform program had pushed the economy to levels that were intolerable to the electorate. In Czechoslovakia knowledgeable observers argue that

> . . . unemployment higher than 5 or 6 percent could—as a first reaction—provoke social unrest and negative response of such an extent that it could slow down further reform steps. (Janacek et al. 1990, p. 11).

The result is, as Murrell (1991b) has observed, that

> the transition process in Eastern Europe and the Soviet union . . . (reflects) . . . the primacy of politics . . . Normative arguments based on narrowly

economic considerations now take a back-seat role. Thus in privatization debates, distributional considerations command center stage; nationalist struggles and fears of foreign domination exert excessive influence on property laws; and in discussions of the speed of price decontrol, the stability of governments becomes paramount.

Does a Macroeconomic J-Curve Exist?

The fundamental conceptual obstacle to identifying a supply-side J-curve for economic reforms is the need to distinguish between the effects of reforms and those of other, exogenous, factors that have had a negative impact on economic performance in the region. The issue is further complicated by the difficulty in reaching agreement on which factors should be viewed as exogenous and which should be seen as reform-related. In addition to these conceptual issues, the quantification of these effects is hampered by the relative brevity of the reform experience, by data difficulties and by the great changes in system parameters wrought by the reforms.

Exogenous Shocks: Foreign Trade

By any account, the largest shock to the Eastern European economies has come from the foreign trade sector. Trade between the Soviet Union and Eastern Europe fell by around 10 percent and intra–East European trade by almost twice as much in 1990. As Table 2 indicates, only Poland was able to increase exports to Eastern Europe and the Soviet Union; all other countries experienced sharp declines, accompanies by somewhat smaller decreases in imports.

TABLE 2 Changes in East European Trade in 1990 (% Δ)

	Exports			Imports		
	Other East Europe[a]	USSR[a]	West[b]	Other East Europe[a]	USSR[a]	West[b]
Bulgaria	–22.7	–21.2	14	–7.7	–11.7	–27
Czechoslovakia	–33.7	–20.3	14	–9.9	–25.0	27
Hungary	–15.4	–16.8	21	–17.9	–10.7	14
Poland	18.2	17.9	30	–42.9	–14.6	–1
Romania	–57.8	–36.2	–26	–0.8	–19.0	141

[a]First 6 months of 1989 vs. first 6 months of 1990.
[b]First 6 months of 1990.

Although both price adjustments and changes in the national valuations of the transferable ruble (TR) have some impact on these trends, there are numerous forces at work reducing these trade flows. In the case of exports to the USSR, the economic and political collapse of that country, including the decline in production, particularly of oil, and the disruption of the supply system, have reduced the ability to pay for Eastern European goods, as well as the ability to distribute and utilize them. The reform of the Soviet foreign trade mechanism, the chaos surrounding the Soviet Union's attempts to increase economic contacts with the West and the attendant payments problems have exacerbated the decline in demand. The Eastern European countries have, at the same time, been forced to limit exports to the USSR, some, such as Hungary, by means of export licensing schemes, others, such as Poland, by revaluing their currencies against the TR, thus making exports to the USSR less profitable.

This was done to eliminate large TR surpluses vis a vis the USSR, in part because the debts resulting from these surpluses would not be repaid at the official TR/$ exchange rate and in part because there may have been considerable uncertainty about the ability of the Soviet Union to settle such debts expeditiously.[5] Finally, exports of specific products, many related to the Soviet defense sector, simply ceased. Imports from the USSR slowed as well, the most problematic aspect of this decline being the sharp reduction in Soviet deliveries of crude oil. For the first half of 1990, these deliveries were about 20 percent below the volume of the corresponding period in 1989, and they are believed to have been even more severely curtailed in the second half of the year.

Intra–Eastern European trade decreased as precipitously as did trade between the region and the USSR, in many cases for the same reasons, a decline in economic activity in many countries, and a desire to redirect economic relations toward the West. In Czechoslovakia and Hungary there was also a certain amount of financially induced import substitution as firms turned from foreign suppliers who had to be paid promptly to domestic suppliers who would be willing to face payment delays in an environment of steadily increasing recourse to inter-enterprise debt. The main factor in the collapse of intra–Eastern European trade was, of course, the reunification of Germany. Enterprises in the GDR canceled contracts for the importation of equipment and components as their sales fell and their ability to pay for imports dwindled. At the same time, GDR exports to Eastern Europe declined because the postunification DM/TR exchange rate made such exports less profitable. A number of Eastern European countries retaliated by limiting imports from the GDR to avoid large TR deficits with that country, which would have to be repaid in hard currencies. Finally, the collapse of the CMEA trading mechanism played some role in reducing the volume of trade as well.

The near-term outlook for trade among the former members of the CMEA offers few prospects of improvement for the reforming countries. The turn to world market prices and hard currency clearing has imposed terms of trade losses on the East European countries, and the transactions demand for hard currency will also act as a brake on intraregional trade. Moreover, the demise of CMEA as an integrating force has quite naturally led to a decline in this trade.

Table 2 also shows that trade with the West increased quite rapidly, but this was not sufficient to offset the decline in intraregional trade, in part because East-West trade volumes are not as great as are intraregional ones and in part because goods cannot be easily diverted from intra-CMEA trade to East-West trade.[6] In extraregional trade most of the countries were affected negatively by the Gulf crisis, some because they had contracted for oil deliveries from Iraq, others because the embargo prevented them from fulfilling export contracts in the region. On the positive side, the Gulf crisis did not raise world petroleum prices by the amount initially expected, and thus the most dire expectations about the terms of trade and hard currency trade balances of the East European Countries have failed to materialize.

Although the external shocks to the reforming economies are easy to catalog, determining what their effect on economic activity has been is more problematic. The decline in the total volume of foreign trade and its redirection from East to West is generally seen as having a negative impact on output in the reforming countries. In some cases, such as the production of weapons for the USSR, lost exports represent lost production, since output can be neither consumed domestically nor diverted to world markets, and the short-run opportunities for reconversion to civilian production are nonexistent. Other exportables, however, can be diverted to other markets or used domestically, so that the net effect of lost exports on production due to lack of substitutability in production, consumption or trade remains an open question. Similarly, difficult to quantify is the effect of lost imports of industrial inputs and particularly of petroleum and other energy carriers, which may create production bottlenecks, idling other resources and resulting in lost production.[7]

A second effect of external shocks is through the trade balance. If one assumes that the economy is characterized by shortages and repressed inflation then an increase in the trade deficit should have a multiplier effect on output. The so-called supply multiplier results from the fact that households who withhold labor due to rationing on the goods market will respond to increased supplies of consumer goods by increasing their labor supply, thus leading to additional increases in output. On the other hand, if the economy is demand-driven, then a worsening of the trade balance represents a decline in autonomous demand, and the result is a multiplier effect leading to a decline in aggregate output.

Exogenous Shock: Domestic Economy

All the economies of Eastern Europe have undergone major upheavals in the domestic economy, some induced by price changes, others by macroeconomic policy. Some of these, such as the large shifts in relative prices due to the elimination of subsidies, can be legitimately viewed as the consequence of economic reform and thus as potentially contributing to the supply-side J-curve effect. others, for example the effort to balance government budgets, may be viewed as policy measures that are independent of reform efforts and thus ought not be counted among the causes of the J-curve effect.[8] In this section we briefly examine the effect that domestic policy has had on aggregate supply and on the components of aggregate demand in the three countries where reforms have progressed the furthest, Czechoslovakia, Hungary and Poland.

Perhaps the domestic shock most independent of economic reforms per se has been the effort by all three countries to follow conservative fiscal and monetary policy. Czechoslovakia and Poland both set goals of a government budget surplus for 1990, Czechoslovakia at 1–1.5 percent of NMP and Poland at 2 percent. Hungary hoped to reduce its budget deficit during the year. Within a macroeconomic context, then, an increase in the budgetary surplus should be deflationary if aggregate output is demand-determined.

While we have argued that fiscal policy may be seen as being independent of the reform of the economy, it is worth noting that an important component of all reforms has been the effort to eliminate the extensive government subsidies on food and other consumer goods. Thus, in fact, an essential element of the reform measures has to a large extent driven the dynamics of the government budget. At the same time, the vast differences between the pre- and postreform structure of taxes and government outlays makes it difficult to judge the consequences of the budget for aggregate economic activity.

All three countries have also attempted to follow a restrictive monetary policy. These efforts have yielded the appearance of success, with M1 in 1990 falling slightly in Czechoslovakia and rising modestly in Poland, although from a level about one-half of that of the previous year. At the same time, inter-enterprise credit has increased sharply in all three countries. Thus monetary policy has tended to limit investment, and hence to have a generally deflationary effect on aggregate demand.

Whether this restrictive monetary policy can be viewed as being independent of economic reform is unclear. Monetization of the economy, and the limitation of the expansion of credit are surely critical aspects of creating markets and imposing financial discipline on firms. Thus, whatever success the resort to orthodox monetarism may have had in these economies, it may be argued that the transformation requires such a policy as a vital component. On the other hand, the easing of orthodox monetarist policies in Hungary at the beginning of 1991 and in Poland even earlier in order to stimulate economic growth suggests that the transformation may be attempted under less austere monetary regimes than those imposed in these countries in 1990.

The final macroeconomic shock faced by these economies is one that acts on consumption, and specifically on what may be viewed as the autonomous component of consumption. Since consumption depends in part on wealth, it is reasonable to assume that the inflation that has accompanied all the transformation efforts has reduced real wealth by sharply reducing the value of cash holdings, an important component of wealth in these countries. The long-run effect of this reduction in wealth is a downward shift in the consumption function as households attempt to bring wealth and income levels back into equilibrium. In the short-run, at the beginning of the transition, there may, however, be the opposite effect, as households realize that price increases are imminent and attempt to reduce their cash holdings and to purchase goods whose prices are expected to increase in the future. Such behavior was amply evident in Poland before the "big bang" and in Czechoslovakia during the last months of 1990.

Measuring the Demand-Side Shocks

If there is some effect of the transition process that acts to reduce output beyond what it would otherwise be based on the level of aggregate demand, then we ought to be able to detect its presence and magnitude by accounting for the effects on aggregate demand and output of the exogenous shocks faced by these economies. Any changes in aggregate output beyond those accounted for by exogenous shocks can then be attributed to the effects of transition on aggregate supply, through a diminution of the production possibilities frontier. While such a procedure is easy to propose, its implementation requires some heroic leaps of faith, both with respect to modeling and with respect to the treatment of the data.

The Model and Parameter Estimates

We begin by assuming that in 1990 the economies of Czechoslovakia, Hungary and Poland could be better described as demand-determined economies characterized by some measure of Keynesian unemployment than as classical planned economies where output was supply-determined. This assumption is perhaps most apt for Poland and least so for Czechoslovakia, which undertook its first steps toward the transition only in the Summer of 1990.[9] If we accept that output was demand-determined, then, particularly in the absence functioning credit and capital markets in any of these countries, aggregate output can be explained by the simple multiplier model

Equation 1

$$Y = (1/1 - MPC)(A + I + (X - M))$$

where Y = aggregate output; MPC = marginal propensity to consume; A = autonomous consumption; I = investment; and $X - M$ = exports − imports or the trade balance.

Implicitly we assume that the level of consumption, C, is given by

Equation 2

$$C = A + MPC \cdot Y$$

We omit the government sector and taxes primarily because of the large changes in the nature of taxes and government reforms and the rather more gradual change in the budget surplus or deficit in these countries. By doing so we fail to consider in our analysis one of the deflationary impacts on these economies, although the effects of the tax increase may be captured by changes in autonomous consumption. Given the absence of a functioning financial sector and the continuation of both formal and informal price controls in all these countries in 1990, the use of a simple multiplier model rather than a more complex IS-LM model appears warranted.

To implement the model, we estimated the parameters for Equation 2 utilizing data from 1980 to 1990. The independent variable was Gross National Income Produced for Czechoslovakia and Gross Domestic Product for Hungary and Poland.

For Czechoslovakia we obtained,[10]

Equation 3

$$C = -99.29 + 0.8697 \cdot Y \quad \overline{R}\,\overline{R}^2 = .9390$$
$$(42.81) \quad (0.0699) \qquad DW = .5395$$

for Hungary,

Equation 4

$$C = 126.93 + 0.4491 \cdot Y \quad \overline{R}^2 = .6240$$
$$(87.55)\ (0.1071) \qquad DW = .7007$$

and for Poland,

Equation 5

$$C = 317.92 + 0.4892 \cdot Y \quad \overline{R}^2 = .7047$$
$$(878.92)\ (0.0981) \qquad DW = 1.061$$

In all three cases the estimate of *MPC* is significantly different from zero, and the magnitude of the standard errors suggests that the *MPC* was relatively stable over the sample period. There is a marked difference between the results for Czechoslovakia and those for Poland and Hungary with respect to the constant. In the case of Czechoslovakia, the constant is significant suggesting that the consumption schedule was not subject to very great shifts over the sample period. This is consistent with the Czechoslovak experience of price stability and expectations of future price stability until 1990. On the other hand, the constant in the regressions for Hungary and Poland is not significant, reflecting greater shifts in autonomous expenditure over the period as the result of either inflation-induced changes in household wealth or changes in expectations regarding future price changes.[11] This sort of result is, as in the case of Czechoslovakia, consistent with the actual developments in these countries.

The Effect of External Shocks

Data on investment, the balance of trade and consumption in 1989 and 1990 are presented for Czechoslovakia, Hungary and Poland in

Tables 3–5. The only aspect of this data requiring some explanation is the construction of the trade balances. The practice of these countries is to report a TR balance for their intra-CMEA trade and a dollar balance for trade with the West. Each country employs its own TR/$ cross rate. In 1989 Czechoslovakia's was 1.51 TR/$, Hungary's 2.09 TR/$, and Poland's 2.96 TR/$. Rather than employing these national rates, we employ the average of all national rates of CMEA countries, 2TR/$ for converting each country's TR balance into dollars.[12] The dollar balances then need to be converted into domestic currencies at some exchange rate, a task fraught with even more uncertainty than the conversion of TR balances to dollars, both because equilibrium rates do not exist and because the equilibrium rate is a moving target in countries undergoing both inflation and a major reorientation of trade.

TABLE 3 Determinants of Aggregate Output in Czechoslovakia 1989 and 1990 (in billion 1984 koruny)

	1989	*1990*	*Change*
Gross Investment*	187.6	192.0	4.4
Balance of Trade			
(a) at 7 kčs/$	1.5	–6.4	–7.9
(b) at 28 kčs/$	5.9	–25.6	–31.5
Consumption			
Actual	490.0	502.4	12.4
Predicted	484.0	481.7	–2.3
Difference			14.7
Gross National Income Produced			
Actual	670.8	668.1	–2.7
Predicted Change Due to Change in:			
Gross Investment			33.7
Balance of Trade			
(a) at 7 kčs/$			–60.4
(b) at 28 kčs/$			–217.8
Autonomous Consumption			114.1
Net Explained Change			–100.0 to 91.4

*Undeflated.

Source: PlanEcon Report and author's calculations.

TABLE 4 Determinants of Aggregate Output in Hungary 1989 and 1990 (in billion 1981 forints)

	1989	*1990*	*Change*
Gross Investment	200.9	173.7	–27.2
Balance of Trade*			
(a) at 68 ft/$	55.2	70.1	14.9
(b) at 100 ft/$	81.2	105.0	23.8
Consumption			
Actual	506.2	456.8	–49.4
Predicted	514.5	487.8	–26.7
Difference			–22.7
Gross Domestic Product			
Actual	863.0	803.0	–60.0
Predicted Change Due to Change in:			
Gross Investment			–49.5
Balance of Trade*			
(a) at 68 ft/$			27.1
(b) at 100 ft/$			43.3
Autonomous Consumption			–41.3
Net Explained Change			–47.5 to –63.7

*Undeflated.
Source: PlanEcon Report and author's calculations.

For Czechoslovakia we converted the dollar trade balance into koruny at 7 kcs/$, the approximate purchasing power parity rate, and at 28 kcs/$, the official rate of 1990. For Hungary the conversion was at 68 ft/$, the official rate in late 1990, and at 100 ft/$, an approximation of the black market rate. For these two countries no adjustment for inflation of the domestic-currency-denominated balance of trade was made; especially in the case of Czechoslovakia such as adjustment would be superfluous. For Poland both exchange rate changes and inflation required greater care in the conversion of dollar balances to zloty. For 1990, the official rate of 9,500 zl/$ comes close to the equilibrium rate, and the zloty balance obtained through this rate was deflated to 1984 prices using the consumer price index. For 1989, when the zloty depreciated precipitously, we employed two rates, 1,000 and 7,000 zl/$, and then converted the zloty balance to 1984 prices. This double

TABLE 5 Determinants of Aggregate Output in Poland 1989 and 1990 (in billion 1984 zloty)

	1989	*1990*	*Change*
Net Investment	1594	1172	–422
Balance of Trade*			
(a) at 1000 zl/$	194	—	766
(b) at 7000 zl/$	1359	—	–398
(c) at 9500 zl/$	—	961	—
Consumption			
Actual	5225	3866	-1359
Predicted	5221	4314	–907
Difference			–452
Gross Domestic Product			
Actual	10025	8170	-1855
Predicted Change Due to Change in:			
Net Investment			–827
Balance of Trade			
(a) at 1000 zl/$			1501
(b) at 7000 zl/$			–780
Autonomous Consumption			–886
Net Explained Change			–2493 to –212

*Deflated to 1984 zloty.
Source: PlanEcon Report and author's calculations.

deflation of the dollar trade balance, first by the exchange rate and then by the CPI is excessive to the extent that the depreciation of the zloty reflected the difference between Polish and world inflation. However, not deflating by the CPI led to extremely large changes in the zloty trade balance.

Data for consumption include both the actual levels and the levels predicted by means of Equations 3–5. In keeping with the spirit of the exercise, we assume that the difference between the actual change in consumption between 1989 and 1990 and the change predicted by the estimated consumption function represents a change in autonomous consumption. Thus, for Czechoslovakia, the actual increase in consumption from 1989 to 1990 was 12.4 billion kcs, while the consumption function predicted a decline of 2.3 billion kcs. This increase in consumption was largely due to panic buying in the second half of 1990 in anticipation of the freeing of prices in 1991. Thus we conclude that, with the MPC stable, autonomous consumption in Czechoslovakia increased by 14.7 billion kcs. The situation in Hungary and Poland was quite the opposite of the Czechoslovak experience. In both cases, consumption decreased by more than the consumption-function-based estimates predicted, reflecting a decline in autonomous consumption partly due to decreased wealth and partly to the rebound from anticipatory purchases in 1989 in the case of Poland.

The second part of Tables 3–5 provides data on the change in aggregate output between 1989 and 1990. In all three countries, output declined. The estimates of demand shocks discussed above are used to derive predicted changes in aggregate output by means of Equation 1. In our discussion of the demand shocks, we argued that those emanating from the foreign trade sector could be seen as unrelated to the transformation process and thus as the most exogenous factors influencing economic activity. In the case of Czechoslovakia, the impact on aggregate output of the deterioration of the trade balance clearly accounts for more than the slight decline in GNIP that Czechoslovakia experienced. In the case of Hungary, the balance of trade improved, and thus the decline in GDP experienced by Hungary cannot be attributed to changes in the trade balance.[13] In the case of Poland, the estimated effects of the trade sector range from an increase of 1501 billion zloty to a decline of 780 billion. Thus, the actual decline in GDP of 1855 billion zloty cannot be accounted for entirely by the shocks from the foreign trade sector.

In sum, with the exception of Czechoslovakia, where reforms in 1990 were extremely mild, in Hungary and Poland the decline in aggregate output in 1990 exceeded that predicted by changes in the balance of trade. Thus to argue that the foreign sector alone was responsible for these declines in output one would have to posit that there were large efficiency and output losses associated with the reduction in the volume of trade. It is noteworthy that in Czechoslovakia, where similar declines in the volume of trade occurred, there seems to have been no such output losses.

Restrictive monetary and fiscal policies and the imposition of hard budget constraints on enterprises may also be viewed as only partly the consequence of economic reform. As Table 3 indicates, in Czechoslovakia investment increased, thus helping to increase aggregate output. In Hungary and Poland, where austerity was more severe and enterprise balance sheets in worse condition, investment declines clearly played a significant role in causing aggregate output to fall. In Hungary the output decline due to investment decreases was almost equal to the observed decrease in output while in Poland it accounted for about one-half of the observed decline.

In Czechoslovakia, autonomous consumption increased in 1990 as consumers sought to stock up on goods in anticipation of the price increases introduced in January, 1991. Thus, consumption and investment shocks both were positive, increasing aggregate demand 19.1 billion koruny, and, via the multiplier effect, aggregate output by 147.8 billion koruny. This was offset by the negative effects of the foreign trade sector on aggregate demand and output, whose magnitude, due to the broad range of exchange rates employed, ranges from –60.4 to –247.8 billion koruny. The net effect of these shocks yields a range that brackets the actual decline in aggregate output, and thus it is entirely conceivable that the aggregate level of output in Czechoslovakia was determined by demand-side elements and that no large supply-side collapse is needed to explain the level of GNP in that country.

In Hungary, the level of consumer demand declined by more than predicted, and this fall in autonomous consumption is translated in Table 4 into a decline in aggregate output of 41.3 billion forints. Summing the negative consumption and investment shocks with the positive effects of an improvement in the trade balance yields a predicted change of GDP of –47.5 to –63.7 billion forints, which brackets the actual decline of 60 billion forints. Thus, as in Czechoslovakia, the change in aggregate output predicted on the basis of exogenous shocks to aggregate demand explains the decline in aggregate output, and no recourse to supply-side shocks as an explanation is necessary.

The story for Poland is the same. The pre–big bang buying spree, as well as the decline in consumer wealth and expectations of hard times, caused a large fall in consumer demand. The net effect of domestic and shocks on GDP also brackets the actual decline in GDP, obviating the need to resort to a supply-side induced collapse. Indeed, in Poland, 1990 produced the most graphic evidence of the demand-induced nature of the decline in output. Large state-owned enterprises continued to produce consumer manufactures, even though there was no demand for their goods. This production collapsed in the end not because of supply uncoordination but because producers could not finance the prodigious level of inventory accumulation that maintaining production levels implied.

Conclusion

In this paper we have shown, using a simple model of aggregate output determination, that the decline in aggregate output in Czechoslovakia, Hungary, and Poland can easily be explained by shocks to aggregate demand. From this, two conclusions follow. The first is that the process of transformation need not entail a great worsening of economic performance due to the effects of the transition process on aggregate supply. The second then follows from the first; macroeconomic policy in these three countries may well have been excessively deflationary and hopes for an economic recovery will require governments to adopt a more expansionary stance than they have been willing to countenance to date. To the extent that policymakers accept the belief that economic performance is subject to some form of a supply-side J-curve phenomenon, they will continue to retain rigidly deflationary policies that will leave their economies subject to further exogenous shocks and that will make the J-curve phenomenon a self fulfilling prophecy.

Notes

Josef C. Brada is in the Department of Economics at Arizona State University. Arthur E. King is in the Department of Economics at Lehigh University

This paper benefited from comments following presentations at Princeton University, the University of Washington and the Catholic University of Leuven. Brada also wishes to acknowledge the hospitality of the Bundesinstitut fur internationale und ostwissenschaftliche Studien and the financial support of their fellowship program, sponsored by the Volkswagen Foundation, hospitality and support of the RFE/RL Research Foundation and the financial support of the American Council of Learned Societies.

1. For some discussion of the phenomenon, see Magee (1973).

2. These projections are generated by a large econometric model of the economy and utilize a variety of assumptions about exogenous variables. An explicit assumption is that the reform will at first reduce, but subsequently increase, productivity.

3. The debate on the sequencing of reforms is related to, but also somewhat different from, the one among development economists on the sequencing of liberalization in developing countries. For a concise survey of the issues germane for developing countries, see Edwards (1990).

4. For a somewhat different argument for gradual reform, see Murrell (1990).

5. Lavigne (1990) provides a useful analysis of the issues.

6. Of course, the true relative volumes are obscured by varying TR/$ exchange rates. For some of the structural issues involved, see Brada (forthcoming).

7. This is indeed a supply-side shock but one that is not caused to be the transition process in the importing country, and thus should not be seen as part of the cost of transition.

8. This effect is independent of the reform-induced J-curve phenomenon for

two reasons. The first is that stabilization may be a prerequisite for reform but could clearly be carried out without a reform. Second, stabilization operates, as Gomulka (1991) rightly argues, on the demand side.

9. On the other hand, the Czechoslovak economy is alleged not to have suffered from excessive repressed inflation according to most observers. See Dlouhy (1989), Dyba and Svejnar (1991), Brada (1991).

10. Standard errors in parentheses.

11. The poor Durbin-Watson statistics suggest either serially correlated errors or, more likely, a misspecification of a constant value of A. Examination of the residuals shows that expectations and changes in wealth well account for the serial correlation of the residuals.

12. This exchange rate would be seen by most observers as overvaluing the TR. In the agreements to settle Soviet TR debts with Eastern Europe, the Soviets are offering a rate of less than one TR per dollar.

13. We hasten to point out that we do not wish to deny that Hungary suffered severely from the decline in the volume of its intra-regional trade, but the model employed here does not take this into account.

Bibliography

Brada, Josef C., "The Economic Transition of Czechoslovakia From Plan to Market." *Journal of Economic Perspectives*, 5:4, 1991.

Brada, Josef C., "Integrating Eastern Europe and the Soviet Union into the World Economy." In Richard E. Baldwin and J. David Richardson (eds.) *The Uruguay Round and Beyond: Problems and Prospects*. Cambridge: NBER (forthcoming).

Dlouhy, Vladimir, "Disequilibrium Models of Czechoslovak Economy." In C. Davis and W. Charemza (eds.), *Models of Disequilibrium and Shortage in Centrally Planned Economies*. London: Chapman and Hall, 1989.

Dyba, Karel and Svejnar, Jan, "Czechoslovakia: Recent Economic Prospects and Developments." *American Economic Review*, May, 1991.

Edwards, Sabastian, "The Sequencing of Economic Reform: Analytical Issues and Lessons from Latin American Experiences." *World Economy* 1–14, 1990.

Gomulka, Stanislaw, "The Causes of Recession Following Stabilization." *Comparative Economic Studies*, 33, 2:71–89 (Summer 1991).

Janacek, Kamil, et al. Social Feasibility of Czechoslovakia's *Economic Reform*. Prague: Ekonomicky Ustav Ceskoslovenske Akademie Ved, 1990.

Lavigne, Marie. "CMEA: The Transition from the Transferable Rouble to Payments in Hard Currency and at World Prices." manuscript, September, 1990.

Lipton, David and Sachs, Jeffrey, "Creating a Market Economy in Eastern Europe." *Brookings Papers on Economic Activity* 75–147, 1990.

Magee, Stephen P., "Currency Contracts, Pass Through, and Devaluation." *Brookings Papers on Economic Activity* 1:303–325, 1973.

Murrell, Peter, "'Big Bang' versus Evolution: East European Economic Reforms in the Light of Recent Economic History." *PlanEcon Report*, VI:26, June 26, 1990.

______, "to be added in proof—" *Journal of Economic Perspectives*, 5,4: Fall, 1991a.

______, "Public Choice and Socialism." *Journal of Comparative Economics*, 14, 2, June, 1991b.

Whitesell, Robert, "Why Does the Soviet Economy Appear to be Allocatively Efficient?" *Soviet Studies*, 42, 2:259–268, (April, 1990).

International Studies in Economics and Econometrics

1. T. Harder: *Introduction to Mathematical Models in Market and Opinion Research.* With Practical Applications, Computing Procedures, and Estimates of Computing Requirements. Translated from German. 1969 ISBN 90-277-0096-6
2. A.R.G. Heesterman: *Forecasting Models for National Economic Planning.* 2nd rev. and ext. ed. 1972 ISBN 90-277-0224-1
3. A.R.G. Heesterman: *Allocation Models and Their Use in Economic Planning.* 1971 ISBN 90-277-0182-2
4. M. Durdağ: *Some Problems of Development Financing.* A Case Study of the Turkish First Five-Year Plan (1963-1967). 1973 ISBN 90-277-0267-5
5. J.M. Blin: *Patterns and Configurations in Economic Science.* 1973 ISBN 90-277-0203-7
6. A.H.Q.M. Merkies: *Selection of Models by Forecasting Intervals.* Translated from Dutch. 1973 ISBN 90-277-0342-6
7. H.C. Bos, M. Sanders and C. Secchi: *Private Foreign Investment in Developing Countries.* A Quantitative Study on the Evaluation of the Macro-Economic Effects. 1974 ISBN Hb 90-277-0410-4; Pb 90-277-0439-2
8. R. Frisch: *Economic Planning Studies.* A Collection of Essays. Selected, introduced and edited by Frank Long, with a Preface by Jan Tinbergen. 1976 ISBN Hb 90-277-0245-4; Pb 90-277-1194-1
9. K.L. Gupta and M. A. Islam: *Foreign Capital, Savings and Growth.* An International Cross-Section Study. 1983 ISBN 90-277-1449-5
10. C.A. van Bochove: *Imports and Economic Growth.* 1982 ISBN 90-247-3052-X
11. O. Bjerkholt and E. Offerdal (eds.): *Macroeconomic Prospects for a Small Oil Exporting Country.* 1985 ISBN 90-247-3183-6
12. D. Weiserbs (ed.): *Industrial Investment in Europe.* Economic Theory and Measurement. 1985 ISBN 90-247-3270-0
13. J.-M. Graf von der Schulenburg and G. Skogh (eds.): *Law and Economics & The Economics of Legal Regulation.* 1986 ISBN 90-247-3377-4
14. S. Pejovich (ed.): *Socialism: Institutional, Philosophical and Economic Issues.* 1987 ISBN 90-247-3487-8
15. R. Heijmans and H. Neudecker (eds.): *The Practice of Econometrics.* Studies on Demand, Forecasting, Money and Income. In Honor of Jan Salomon Cramer. 1987 ISBN 90-247-3502-5
16. A. Steinherr and D. Weiserbs (eds.): *Employment and Growth.* Issues for the 1980s. In Honor of Albert Kervyn de Lettenhove. 1987 ISBN 90-247-3514-9
17. M.J. Holler (ed.): *The Logic of Multiparty Systems.* 1987 ISBN 90-247-3515-7

18. J.M. van Brabant: *Regional Price Formation in Eastern Europe.* Theory and Practice of Trade Pricing. 1987 ISBN 90-247-3540-8
See also below under Volume 23
19. A.M. Wesselman: *The Population-Sample Decomposition Method.* A Distribution-Free Estimation Technique for Minimum Distance Parameters. 1987 ISBN 90-247-3603-X
20. P. Coffey (ed.): *Main Economic Policy Areas of the EEC - Toward 1992.* The Challenge to the Community's Economic Policies when the 'Real' Common Market is Created by the End of 1992. 3rd rev.ed., 1990 ISBN 0-7923-0810-7
21. A. Breton, G. Galeotti, P. Salmon and R. Wintrobe (eds.): *The Competitive State.* Villa Colombella Papers on Competitive Politics. 1991 ISBN 0-7923-0835-2
22. S. Pejovich: *The Economics of Property Rights.* Towards a Theory of Comparative Systems. 1990 ISBN 0-7923-0878-6
23. J.M. van Brabant: *Remaking Eastern Europe.* On the Political Economy of Transition. 1990 ISBN 0-7923-0955-3
24. J.M. van Brabant: *Privatizing Eastern Europe.* The Role of Markets and Ownership in the Transition. 1992 ISBN 0-7923-1861-7
25. J.M. van Brabant: *Integrating Eastern Europe into the Global Economy.* Convertibility through a Payments Union. 1991 ISBN 0-7923-1352-6
26. G.W. Kołodko, D. Gotz-Kozierkiewicz and E. Skrzeszewska-Paczek: *Hyperinflation and Stabilization in Postsocialist Economies.* 1992 ISBN 0-7923-9179-9
27. P. Mihályi: *Socialist Investment Cycles.* Analysis in Retrospect. 1992 ISBN 0-7923-1973-7
28. A. Breton, G. Galeotti, P. Salmon and R. Wintrobe (eds.): *Preferences and Democracy.* Villa Colombella Papers. 1993 ISBN 0-7923-9321-X

KLUWER ACADEMIC PUBLISHERS – DORDRECHT / BOSTON / LONDON

FSC
www.fsc.org
MIX
Papier | Fördert
gute Waldnutzung
FSC® C083411

Kolibri 360 GmbH
Ferdinand-Jühlke-Straße 7
99095 Erfurt, Deutschland
produktsicherheit@kolibri360.de